SKI & SNOWSHOE ROUTES:

COLORADO'S FRONT RANGE

Skier on the Zimmerman Lake Trail enjoys her powder day.

COLORADO
MOUNTAIN CLUB
GUIDEBOOK

SKI & SNOWSHOE ROUTES:
COLORADO'S FRONT RANGE

ALAN R. APT

The Colorado Mountain Club Press
Golden, Colorado

Ski & Snowshoe Routes: Colorado's Front Range
© 2017 Alan Apt

PUBLISHED BY

The Colorado Mountain Club Press
710 10th Street, Suite 200, Golden, Colorado 80401
303-996-2743   I   e-mail: cmcpress@cmc.org   I   website: http://www.cmc.org

Founded in 1912, The Colorado Mountain Club is the largest outdoor recreation, education, and conservation organization in the Rocky Mountains. Look for our books at your local bookstore or outdoor retailer or at www.cmc.org/books.

CONTACTING THE PUBLISHER

We would appreciate it if readers would alert us to any errors or outdated information by contacting us at the address above.

Alan Apt: photographer unless noted otherwise
Erika Arroyo: design, composition, and production
Mira Perrizo: copyeditor
Clyde Soles: publisher

Cover photo: Skiers enjoying the Sawmill Creek Trail with a Commanche Peak backdrop.

DISTRIBUTED TO THE BOOK TRADE BY

Mountaineers Books
1001 SW Klickitat Way, Suite 201, Seattle, WA 98134, 800-553-4453
www.mountaineersbooks.org

We gratefully acknowledge the financial support of the people of Colorado through the Scientific and Cultural Facilities District of greater metropolitan Denver for our publishing activities.

TOPOGRAPHIC MAPS are copyright 2017 and were created using National Geographic TOPO! software

ISBN 978-1-935052-51-5

ACKNOWLEDGMENTS

I especially want to thank my family, Amy, Kate, Laura and Ryan, Jeremiah, and Lylah for their continued support and enthusiasm.

I also appreciate the following people who accompanied me on my field research, and/or gave me advice and information: Gina Apt, Kate Apt-Bannasch, Bill Black, Dan Bowers, David Bye, Larry and Margie Caswell, Joel Claypool, Jeff and Catherine Eighmy, Lars and Becky Eisen, Lenny and Susan Epstein, Phil Freidman, John Gascoyne, Bill Jacobi, Amy Johnston, Rodney Ley, Ward Luthi, John Mattson, Jim and Shereen Miller, Ellen Montague, Joseph Piesman, Sharon Roggy, Jay Stagnone, Dian Sparling, Alan Stark, Jim Welch, members of the Colorado Mountain Club, and members of the Bryan Mountain and Diamond Peaks Ski Patrols.

I especially want to thank Nancy Olsen, who accompanied me on countless excursions.

Betsy Armstrong's expert advice on the avalanche material was greatly appreciated. Thanks to John Anderson for his material on the snowshoe trails and maps at Eldora Mountain Resort. In addition, Joe Grim provided a detailed review of trails that was invaluable, and Rodney Ley also provided valuable suggestions. John Gascoyne made marvelous suggestions. My daughter, Kate, also read parts of the manuscript and made valuable suggestions.

I thank John Bartholow, Eric Erslev, Joe Grim, Eva Light, and Ward Whicker, and especially Dave Cooper, for providing excellent photos for the book. And Kevin Philbin for taking the superb product photos. I also thank the anonymous people who appear in some of the photos, and Bill Jacobi and Joe Piesman for appearing in the cover photo.

Thanks to the Colorado State Forest, US Forest Service, and Rocky Mountain National Park employees who answered countless questions and provided excellent information, including: Maribeth Higgins, Vicki McClure, Diana Barney, Becky Kelly, Patti Turecek, Dick Putney, and Jeff Maugans, to mention just a few. I especially thank Kristi Wumkres of the Canyon Lakes Ranger District for the Poudre Canyon Nordic Ranger photos she provided for the first edition.

I want to thank the staff at Colorado Mountain Club Press, especially Publisher Clyde Soles, and Mira Perrizo: who copyedited the manuscript, and Rachel Vermeal and her staff for marketing, Mountaineers and Robin for sales.

I thank the CMC, the Sierra Club, Jax, the Boulder Book Store, Barnes & Noble, Firehouse Books, and especially REI for hosting snowshoeing presentations and stocking my books.

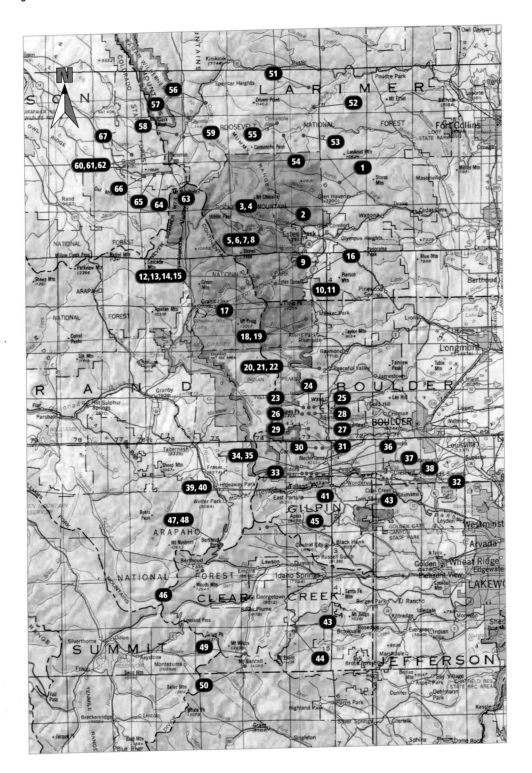

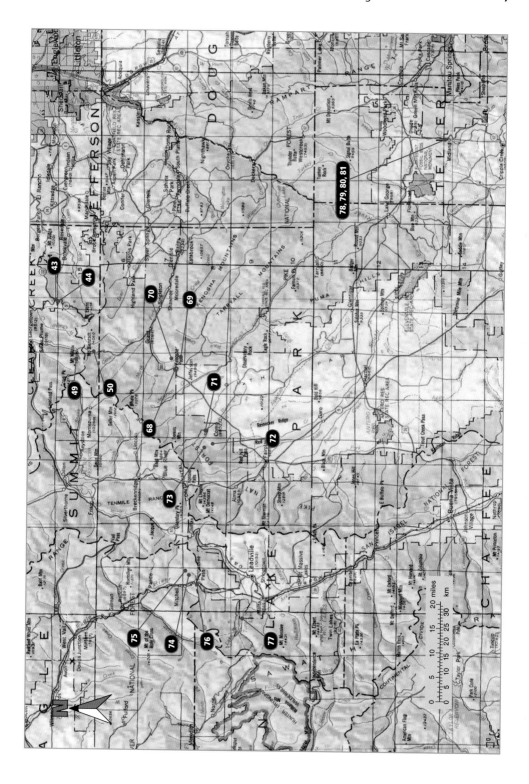

Contents

Introduction **13**

SECTION 1: ROCKY MOUNTAIN NATIONAL PARK

Chapter 1. **Rocky Mountain National Park—Northeast**............ 34
  1. North Fork Trail 36
  2. Deer Mountain 40
  3. Hidden Valley 43
  4. Trail Ridge Road 46
  5. Cub Lake 49
  6. Fern Lake and Odessa Lake 52
  7. Hollowell Park and Mill Creek Basin 54
  8. Sprague Lake Trails 57
  9. Alberta Falls and The Loch 60
  10. Mills Lake, Jewel Lake, and Black Lake 63
  11. North Longs Peak Trail 66
  12. Bear Lake Loop 69
  13. Nymph Lake, Dream Lake, and Emerald Lake 72
  14. Flattop Mountain 75
  15. Lake Helene 79

Chapter 2. **Rocky Mountain National Park—Southeast**........... 82
  16. Estes Cone 84
  17. Chasm Lake 87
  18. Copeland Falls, Calypso Cascades, and Ouzel Falls 90
  19. Allenspark Trail and Finch Lake 94

SECTION 2: INDIAN PEAKS AREA

Chapter 3. **Peaceful Valley Area** 97
  20. Buchanan Pass Trail and Middle Saint Vrain Creek 99
  21. Beaver Reservoir-Coney Flats Trail 102
  22. North Sourdough Trail 105

Chapter 4. Brainard Lake Recreation Area 108

23. South Sourdough Trail 110
24. Niwot Mountain and Ridge 114
25. Red Rock Lake and Brainard Lake 116
26. Mitchell and Blue Lakes and Mount Toll 121
27. Mount Audubon 124
28. Long Lake and Lake Isabelle 126
29. Rainbow Lakes and Arapaho Glacier Overlook Trail 128

SECTION 3: NEDERLAND AREA

Chapter 5. Nederland Foothills 131

30. Caribou Ranch 133
31. Mud Lake Open Space 136
32. West Magnolia Trails 138

Chapter 6. Eldora Mountain Resort and Hessie 141

33. Jenny Creek Trail 143
34. Fourth of July Trail/Road 146
35. Lost Lake Trail 149
36. Woodland Lake Trail 152
37. Lakes Loop Trail 155
38. Twisted Trail 158
39. Lonestar Loop Trail 160
40. Rising Sun and Setting Sun Trails 162

Chapter 7. Rollinsville Area 165

41. Rogers Pass Lake and Heart Lake 167
42. Forest Lakes 170
43. Arapaho Lakes Trail 173
44. Mammoth Gulch Road 176
45. Raccoon Loop Trail 179

SECTION 4: CENTRAL COLORADO

Chapter 8. Mount Evans Area 182

46. Echo Lake, and Chicago Lakes Trails 184

SECTION 4: CENTRAL COLORADO *(continued)*

47. Mount Evans Byway 187

48. Saint Mary's Glacier and James Peak 189

49. Beaver Brook Watershed 192

50. Chief Mountain 195

51. Jones Pass Trail-Butler Gulch Trail 198

Chapter 9. Berthoud Pass-Winter Park Area 201

52. Eastside Trail-Continental Divide Trail-Colorado Mines Peak 203

53. Westside Trail 206

Chapter 10. Devil's Thumb Ranch 208

54. Lactic Grande 209

55. Ranch Walk and Basin Trails 212

56. Moosestomp 214

Chapter 11. Guanella Pass Area 217

57. Silver Dollar Lake 219

58. Mount Bierstadt 222

SECTION 5: NORTHERN COLORADO

Chapter 12. Poudre Canyon 225

59. Crown Point Road 227

60. Signal Mountain Trail 230

61. Stormy Peaks Trail 233

62. Cirque Meadows and Emmaline Lake 236

63. Big South Trail 239

64. Blue Lake Trail 242

65. Sawmill Creek Trail 245

66. Trap Lake and Park, Iron Mountain 248

67. Zimmerman Lake and Meadows Trail 251

68. Montgomery Pass Trail 255

69. Cameron Connection Trail 258

Chapter 13. Colorado State Forest 260

70. Michigan Ditch, American Lakes, and Thunder Pass Trails 262

71. Lake Agnes 266

72. Seven Utes Mountain and Mount Mahler 269

73. Ranger Lakes and Silver Creek 273

74. Grass Creek Yurt Trails 276

SECTION 6: SOUTHERN COLORADO

Chapter 14. Como Area 279

75. Kenosha Pass—Colorado Trail West 281

76. Kenosha Pass—Colorado Trail East 284

77. North Twin Cone Peak 287

78. Boreas Pass Road and Halfway Gulch 290

79. Gold Dust Trail South 293

80. Gold Dust Trail North 296

Chapter 15. Leadville Area 299

81. Vance's Cabin 301

82. Taylor Hil 304

83. Mitchell Creek Loop 306

84. Twin Lakes 309

Chapter 16. Colorado Springs Area 312

85. School Pond and Preachers Hollow Loops 314

86. Peak View, Elk, Livery, and Revenuer's Trails 315

87. Homestead and Black Bear Loop 318

88. The Craggs 320

Appendix 323

About the Author 327

Checklist 328

Snowshoers approaching Shoshoni Peak in the Indian Peaks. PHOTO BY CHRIS CASE

INTRODUCTION

Let's start with a bit of truth-telling: no one book can answer all of your questions about winter gear or tell you every place where you can have fun in the snow.

This, my third winter-oriented guidebook, will, nevertheless, provide a great deal of information about exciting places to enjoy and the equipment you'll want when you get there. Whether you're a seasoned Colorado resident, or just arrived here from the flatlands, you're certain to benefit from this updated and more comprehensive information. If you have just moved to Colorado you might not know if you want to be a skier or snowshoer or savor both sports. This book provides the information you need to have fun skiing or snowshoeing in our glorious state

Topics

Trails, both those you may be familiar with from my earlier books and some new ones to offer new adventures, most within easy driving distance from Front Range cities and towns. This edition offers:

- Skiing information for every skiable trail (most of them are skiable) and all can be snowshoed
- Family-oriented, easy outings for beginners or youngsters
- Challenging mountain summits for experienced mountaineers and those who aspire to be
- A great number of available experiences between these poles

Gear and more gear. I'll talk about the ups and downs of both snowshoes and cross-country skis. (Hint—I'll advocate your trying some of each before buying. This book is intended to help you make informed equipment choices, but the final decisions must be your own.)

Safety. Outdoor winter adventures need to be safe and we'll talk about how that can be achieved.

I moved to Colorado in 1973 and fell in love with mountain adventures almost immediately. I've since skied and snowshoed many, many hundreds of miles, and of course, all the trails in this book, most multiple times. I've also hiked and biked—and written about—hundreds of our best off-season trails. "Off season" for me means when there's little snow on the ground. (Okay, I have my preferences.)

When I first arrived in Colorado, I fell in love with cross-country skiing. I didn't understand the joys of snowshoeing until the late '90s, when my daughter Kate introduced our family to emerging snowshoe technology that provided easier-to-use, better-designed equipment. For me, this allowed winter adventuring with less downhill and uphill angst than could come with the skinny skis of that era. The traction provided by the shorter, lighter-weight snowshoes was wonderful, and the learning curve for using them was short. Still, though, there's no denying the pleasures of zooming downhill on cross-country or telemark skis, carving your way across fresh powder snow. You can simulate that feeling descending through powder on snowshoes too.

So, which is the better choice for you?

Skis versus snowshoes—red wine versus white; dark beer versus pilsner. This guidebook is about both snowshoeing and cross-country skiing, and I continue to enjoy both. Advancements in technology have made both methods of playing in the snow far more efficient over the past several decades. Rather than referring to skiing and snowshoeing equipment as evolutionary, let's call the phenomenon revolutionary—innovations following one after another at a rapid-fire pace.

Snowshoes of the '70s were long, unwieldy, and required a good deal of energy. Design and materials are quite different now, and you can move with a good deal more ease and speed.

So, why choose them over skis? When traveling downhill on snowshoes, you'll trade the speed of skis for complete control of your destiny and your destination. You can still run and float through deep powder, as on skis, but you won't have to endure the embarrassment of face plants or grabbing at trees to arrest your downhill plummet. Snowshoeing requires only minimal equipment and is quite easy to learn. If you can walk, you can snowshoe. You simply strap the snowshoes on your boots and explore the closest snow-covered terrain.

Cross-country skis had their own problems in the old days: single-ply leather boots were too flexible, and three-pin bindings meant "skinny" skis were difficult to maneuver, especially on a downhill run. Telemark skis were beefier, wider alternatives, but they required skilled bent-knee turning, and were heavy to drag back uphill.

Today, you can rent or buy skis offering some of the same uphill and downhill advantages that come with snowshoes. Modern Alpine Touring (AT) and telemark skis are lighter in weight and wider as well. "Skins" allow you to climb with excellent traction, and metal edges and high-tech boots and bindings allow good control on descents. There are even Nordic skis with built in skins to allow you to climb without wax or patterns. They also glide downhill very well.

THE BOTTOM LINE

This book is about enjoyment and achievement. It's also about where to go and what to use when you get there. However you choose to make your way, say a little prayer for snow.

The Eldora Mountain Resort and the Snow Mountain Ranch-YMCA both have new Alpine Touring pilot programs as this book goes to press. I will have information about both programs on my website and/or Facebook pages for next season, as well as any other new programs.

I will be posting more photos and timely information at my Facebook page: Ski and Snowshoe Routes, Colorado's Front Range and website.

Ski Buyers Guide

CROSS COUNTRY SKIING

This is a more interesting, and challenging, task than buying snowshoes due to the wider variety of skis now available. The type of ski you will want to try and possibly buy depends on the type of backcountry or cross-country skiing you want to do. Most skis require wax for grip on flat terrain and moderate uphills but many now have climbing patterns on the bottoms so you don't have to wax for grip (they still need glide wax on the tips and tails for easy sliding). If the terrain is very steep, then you will want to rent or buy climbing skins that fit your skis and make uphill travel much easier.

GROOMED NORDIC AREAS

If you want to ski in groomed ski areas, then traditional, narrower skis (skinny skis) would be a good choice, with or without metal edges. Metal edges make it easier to turn on steep or icy runs, but do add weight to the ski. Modern skis without metal edges actually turn more easily. Many have climbing patterns that vary in effectiveness, and waxable skis are usually not available for rent. Waxable skis climb better than pattern skis if the right wax is chosen for the temperature. They become challenging when the temperature changes while you are skiing, that is why many MORE people ski on pattern skis. There are different widths available as well. The narrower skis are generally more appropriate for experienced skiers who want more glide in their kick and glide, a bit more speed, and can negotiate downhills without edges. Wider skis with edges are better for beginners. Patterns skis are sometimes a bit slower than waxable skis, but offer more slowing on downhills, which is good for beginners. You won't want to use Alpine Touring (AT) or telemark skis on easy, relatively flat backcountry trails, or in Nordic areas. They are awkward and heavier than you need for mellow, groomed trails.

EASY BACKCOUNTRY TRAILS

If you want to try un-groomed forest trails that are not challenging you can use mid-width Nordic skis with metal edges, and climbing patterns, or wax. They are usually still called cross-country skis rather than AT or telemark skis.

MODERATE TO CHALLENGING BACKCOUNTRY TRAILS

The general rule to apply is the more challenging the trail, the deeper the powder, the wider the ski. You can choose from wider AT or telemark skis with metal edges. Alpine Touring and telemark skis can also be used in ski areas, so you can potentially get twice as much usage. If you are a downhill skier who is just starting to go "off piste," the European term for un-groomed snow skiing, then take advantage of your parallel turning skills with AT skis. If you have never skied before, I suggest that you take either a downhill or telemark lesson at your local ski area, and then decide which style of skiing you want to learn. Telemark skiing is a bit more challenging if you have already tried traditional downhill because you have to unlearn parallel techniques. Both styles work equally well in the backcountry on moderate to steep trails.

Some highly skilled teleskiers still use traditional three-pin bindings. Most modern AT and telemark bindings now resemble downhill bindings but are much lighter.

The boots are almost all plastic or synthetic and are generally stiffer and much lighter than downhill boots and even leather boots. The stiffness gives you much more control of the skis. They are generally warmer and often more comfortable than the leather boots I still have in my closet.

HELMETS

Though you don't need a helmet for snowshoeing unless you are on technical terrain, it is wise to use one on steep downhill terrain when backcountry skiing, where you will be dodging trees. It doesn't take long to determine that even skinny little tree branches don't give way and can do damage to your noggin.

Snowshoe Buyer's Guide

Before you purchase snowshoes, you will probably benefit by renting a few different types, brands, and sizes. It's a good idea to rent snowshoes from a local snowshoe store that also sells them. The staff will be more knowledgeable, so the salesperson will get the snowshoe that is right for you.

Most models of snowshoes are much alike, but there are also some significant differences. They feature underfoot claws, webbing or a solid piece of plastic to walk on, and straps to hold your boots in place. Some snowshoe manufacturers have buyer's guidelines on their websites for the different models they sell. Pick the shoes that are the easiest to get in and out of, that are not too big for your needs, and that are comfortable to walk in.

TIP: Ask the salesperson whether your snowshoes have a right and left foot, and if so, to show you how to determine one from the other if they are not clearly marked.

DESIGN AND FUNCTION

Snowshoe designs vary according to the type of use anticipated. Some snowshoes are better than others for climbing steep slopes and maneuvering on tricky traverses. Others are designed for running or racing on packed trails but their asymmetric shape makes them terrible for the backcountry. Some snowshoes are solid rather than made of webbed material. These can perform well in the outback, be easier to maneuver, and cost less than webbed models. Some of the solid snowshoes have extra cleats along the sides that make climbing steep slopes easier. If you plan to do some winter mountaineering you will want as many cleats as possible for climbing steep slopes. Check and compare the number of cleats.

A longer backcountry snowshoe is suitable when you carry a heavy backpack, which can increase your weight significantly; a shorter, lighter model is suitable for day trips. If you are planning to be out in the light, fluffy powder of December and

January, you will find that flotation is not as good as it is on more consolidated or heavier, wetter, late-season snow. Some snowshoes come with extensions, or tails, that can be added on or removed depending on snow conditions.

SIZE

The appropriate size of a snowshoe is determined by the size and weight of the snowshoer, as well as the type of snow expected. What you are looking for is the ability to stay on top of, or float on, the snow. While more length still tends to mean more flotation, there are now other considerations. With advances in technology and snowshoe design, shorter snowshoes can provide good flotation, which varies from model to model. With the right snowshoes on, even larger, heavier people can use somewhat smaller shoes and not sink deeply into the snow.

A larger, taller person can better handle a larger, wider snowshoe. A shorter, smaller person is more comfortable propelling a shorter, narrower, lighter-weight snowshoe. When you try on snowshoes, walk in them to see if the width widens your stride too much or if the length makes them too awkward to propel and control.

Here are some general guidelines: If you are at the heavier end of the range, then opt for the longer or wider snowshoe, especially if you are expecting deep powder as the norm. If the snowshoes are primarily going to be used for day trips and you are likely to be on heavily used and firmly packed trails, the low end or middle of the size range is a good choice. If you will be carrying a backpack, add its weight to your own when figuring which weight range is appropriate for you.

Shorties (for carrying 100–140 pounds): The smallest, shortest snowshoes are those used for running, racing, or fast-paced fitness outings on firm snow. They are usually 21 inches in length and no more than 8 inches in width. A length of 21 to 25 inches and width of 8 inches will work for a variety of uses. For someone at the lower end of the weight range, a snowshoe this size can work even in deeper, less firm snow. You might sink down as much as 6 inches, but in powder that is not unusual with snowshoes of any length.

Midsize (for carrying 140–250 pounds): Midsized snowshoes are good on firm snow, or for lighter people in deep powder. They measure from 27 to 33 inches in length and are 8 to 9 inches in width. They could be used with a backpack. If you are at the top end of this weight range, the longer, wider snowshoes are advisable.

Large (for carrying 160–270 pounds): Larger snowshoes should be used for deep powder and rolling terrain, especially if the snowshoer is a larger individual. Larger snowshoes are 8 to 10 inches wide and measure 30 to 36 inches long. If you are very tall, or have short legs, you might not want to use the longest snowshoes in this range, even for carrying heavier weight. The wider snowshoes might make your gait very uncomfortable, and powering long, wide shoes might be more difficult than sinking in a bit more with shorter shoes.

Jumbo (for carrying more than 200 pounds): If you weigh more than 200 pounds and will be carrying a heavy backpack and traveling in deep, unconsolidated snow, then opting for the longer, wider snowshoe is the safer choice. These shoes are 10 to 11 inches wide and 37 to 42 inches long. Here again, you won't want the longest snowshoes unless you are planning a serious backcountry expedition in deep snow, and you are tall and strong enough to power them up significant grade changes.

STRAP SYSTEMS/BINDINGS

The fastening devices for snowshoes have become much easier to use. Ask the outdoor-store staff to show you how they compare. The strap system used to hold your foot to the snowshoe can be crucial, especially in cold, icy conditions. A simpler system is better. Be certain that you know how to tighten and loosen the straps. You want to be darn sure you know how to make them fit comfortably and can get them on and off, especially in deep snow, or in freezing temperatures with ice coating the straps. This is especially desirable if your party will include children of any age.

Try renting to get a feel for what you want. If you are relatively new to the activity but want to own rather than rent for your first season, look for one style, make, and size that fits most of your anticipated needs.

CARE AND USE OF SNOWSHOES

Snowshoes are tough, but they aren't indestructible. Snowshoes perform best in soft, powdery snow for running or jumping. In fact they relish nice, big bites of the soft stuff without any chewy stumps or dirt. Walking or running on hard surfaces such as rocks, trees, or really thin snow over a hard, icy surface can bend or break the claws on your snowshoes. I have seen the claws on a friend's quality snowshoe bend when he ran on late-season, hard-packed snow.

What to Take

BOOTS AND GAITERS

Snowshoers will need waterproof boots or over boots. If you have lightweight, high-top summer hiking boots that can be thoroughly waterproofed and you are planning a very short, close-to-the-car trek you can probably avoid freezing feet and frostbite wearing them. It is highly recommended, however, that you use heavier, insulated, waterproof boots with thin synthetic liners and thick wool socks. You can sometimes rent snowboarding boots along with your snowshoes if you don't have adequate winter footgear. Felt-lined rubber boots, insulated hunting boots, or even snowmobiling boots should also work.

TIP: Do not use low-top boots or you will risk freezing feet and frostbite. You can wrap your low-top boots or non-waterproof boots in heavy-duty yard waste bags for short excursions.

Keep in mind that every pound on your foot is equivalent to two pounds on your back, so avoid heavy snowshoe or ski boots if you can. You also want to avoid getting blisters. Bring moleskin in case your rental boots create hot spots on your heels, soles, or ankles. If you are wearing rental boots or new boots, you can apply moleskin or duct tape to your heels before you get on the trail in order to prevent blistering. If you have the opportunity, wear your new boots around a bit before wearing them to snowshoe or ski. This will allow them to mold to your feet some-what, and you can tell where hot spots might develop out on the trail.

Snowshoes usually spray snow on your feet and the backs of your legs as you walk—the deeper the snow, the heavier the spray. A pair of gaiters works well to keep the snow out of your boots and off your lower legs. If your boots are completely waterproof and calf-high, you may get by without gaiters; but if you are wearing ankle-high boots without this protection you will likely have some snow in your boots and possibly very wet, cold feet in a short time. Some rental shops also rent gaiters, so rent them or invest in a pair.

Tip: If you do end up snowshoeing without gaiters and get snow in your boots, you can try to modify your gait so that you spray less snow onto and into your boots. Try sliding your foot more across the snow rather than lifting your feet high with each step.

POLES

Poles are optional equipment and many avid snowshoers do not use them, but they can be very useful. Most rental shops offer poles at a slight or no additional cost. If you have cross-country ski poles, they work fine for snowshoeing if they are not too long. A good length allows your elbow and arm to assume a 90-degree position. The poles must have large baskets that will prevent them from sinking into the snow.

Poles are very useful off the trail in deep snow or on a steep slope. They are especially helpful when you are traversing downhill or crossing uneven hillocks of snow. When you are descending through deep powder you can almost simulate skiing with jump turns and feel like you are floating downhill. Poles take thousands of pounds of pressure off your knees—a major asset if you are prone to knee problems. Poles also add extra stability and power to your effort. If weight loss is a goal, using poles also gets more of your body involved in the activity and provides an upper-body workout.

PACKS

On day trips, carry a day pack—you will want it for carrying the clothing layers you peel off so you don't overheat. You'll need a pack large enough for bulky winter clothing. You might also have to carry your snowshoes or skis over bare spots and strapping them on a pack is very handy rather than carrying them in your arms. Some packs include loops for carrying skis.

ALWAYS CARRY THE TEN ESSENTIALS:
   1. Extra fleece or wool clothing.
   2. Extra food and water for one additional day in case of emergency.
   3. Sunglasses and goggles for strong winds and subzero windchill, and SPF 30 sunscreen
   4. Knife
   5. First-aid kit

6. Fire starter (especially important in snowy terrain)
7. Waterproof matches or lighter
8. Flashlight with spare batteries, or a headlamp
9. Map
10. Compass

Other safety gear to consider includes a whistle, a space blanket and/or tarp, and two black garbage bags for emergency shelter. Good additions for steep or avalanche-prone areas include a shovel (one per person), an avalanche beacon/locator (one per person), a snow probe (one per person), and an ice axe or ski poles. A GPS locating device is a worthwhile item (smartphones often do not work in remote areas).

There is some controversy about the use of cellular phones as a safety device because they are often not usable in high mountain valleys and cold weather can sap the batteries unless carried next to your body.

Pack your clothing around your water bottle to prevent your water from freezing. Start with warm water so it is less likely to freeze solid.
Be prepared! Bring hand and foot warmers (packets) if you tend to get cold easily. Bring a pair of prescription glasses if you wear contacts.

CLOTHING

Fortunately, the high fashion standards of downhill skiing have not made an impact in the world of snowshoeing or backcountry skiing. You can dress yourself for snowshoeing with warmth in mind, rather than fashion, because you won't encounter fashion police on the trails. As with most active outdoor backcountry winter sports, dress in layers. When you pack, imagine warm and sunny followed by driving snow and subzero wind. In other words, pack for all conceivable conditions using water-repellent or waterproofed gear and moisture-wicking clothing such as nylon, synthetics, or wool.

Begin your excursion dressed a bit lightly for the given day's conditions. You may be somewhat cold at first, but as you walk, you will warm up nicely. If you are dealing with extreme conditions, pay particular attention to what your body is telling you. Don't go too long before putting on warmer layers if needed, and you will warm up quicker as you travel uphill. Rest often rather an overheating or, especially, breaking into a sweat and creating a potential chill situation later when you stop. When you break for lunch, you will cool off quickly, and you will want to put some layers back on. It is warmer to have a pad to sit on.

Cotton is not recommended, including jeans. When cotton gets wet or damp, it does not dry out easily nor will it insulate you against the cold. On your average winter day, a pair of synthetic or merino wool long underwear is highly recommended. Avoid cotton completely if you can. For the next layer, a wool sweater, fleece, or a lightweight down- or synthetic-insulated jacket will work. Fleece is more effective than wool when wet—it dries out more easily. Your outer layer should be breathable and waterproof.

Headgear is especially important because you lose much of your body heat through your head and neck. Keep it covered with a good wool or synthetic hat that covers your ears. A ski mask or balaclava is also a good idea in case it gets windy or starts to snow. Goggles are important for an enjoyable experience in wind or snow. Mittens are generally warmer than gloves, but either should be waterproof, and at least double-layered with insulating material. If you don't have waterproof mittens or gloves, you will want more than one pair of non-waterproof gloves. For snowshoeing and skiing in comfort, refer to the following list before you head out:

- Long underwear tops and bottoms
- Turtleneck shirt or wool scarf to protect your neck
- Fleece or wool sweater
- Wind- and waterproof outer coat or shell
- Wool or very warm synthetic socks
- Warm mittens or gloves
- Warm cap
- Face or ski mask

FOOD AND WATER

Take the same sorts of food and drink when you go snowshoeing or backcountry skiing that you would when hiking. Be practical, however, and consider what the cold will do to your hands if you are trying to peel an orange, for instance.

Bring easy-access snacks such as energy bars or trail mix. You will burn lots of energy and calories snowshoeing, perhaps up to one thousand calories per hour. Exercising in the cold burns far more calories than summer mountain activities, so plan accordingly. Eating something with a bit of fat in it will also help to keep you warm. Arctic explorers ate large quantities of butter, lard, or blubber; you might prefer something more palatable such as chocolate. Bring extra high-calorie food in case of an emergency, and ask your compatriots to bring enough so you won't have to feed them, too.

Much has been made of the new high-protein diets and foods designed as an adjunct to exercise. Although eating something that contains protein along with carbohydrates works well, carbohydrates are still the key ingredient for energy production. Exercising aerobically for longer than forty minutes will cause your body to use fat stores as energy. If you don't want to deplete your glycogen supply (the fuel your muscles use) and want to stay as fresh as possible, stop for a small snack about once an hour. Try to exercise at an aerobic pace without being constantly out of breath.

Also carry water, at least one quart or liter if you plan an all-day trek, and carry it in something that will prevent it from freezing. Don't wait until you feel thirsty to drink some water; drink regularly as you go. Eating snow as a substitute for drinking water is a poor idea at best—it will chill you to the bone. This is especially true when you are cold, and you could be increasing the likelihood of hypothermia.

You can add a sports drink or fruit-juice mixture to your water. Alcohol lowers your metabolic rate and can make you feel colder. A thermos of tea or hot chocolate is highly recommended.

Safe Winter Recreation

PICKING YOUR FIRST ADVENTURE

Be conservative your first time out. Pick a short, easy round trip that will be an enjoyable half-day jaunt. That will give you a chance to see how your body reacts to snowshoes or skis and how you react to dealing with the equipment in the cold and snow, plus the altitude.

Snow conditions can vary drastically and unpredictably at any time of the season. Snow trails that are normally relatively easy to negotiate can become very challenging in deep powder or on a crust that breaks under your feet. Deep, fluffy powder is typical in mid-winter, which means you could sink in a foot deep or more with every step, regardless of the length or style of snowshoe. Spring conditions can vary greatly and can make even a short jaunt exhausting due to poor flotation.

SAFE SNOWSHOEING AND SKIING TECHNIQUES

Establishing a steady, consistent rhythm is much more enjoyable and easier on the body than lots of sprints, stops, starts, and high stepping. Sliding the back of your snowshoe across the snow rather than lifting your feet high with each step is a technique that is easier to maintain on a long trek, simulating the kick and glide of skiing. Sometimes snow conditions don't allow this because you will sink in too much to slide effectively.

When you are climbing steep hills off-trail it is usually more effective to create your own switchbacks. Traversing is easier than taking on steep snow slopes head-on. There are times however, when traversing at an angle with your snowshoes or skis sideways to the slope is more difficult due to the slope of the terrain and deep, loose snow. Then it makes sense to face your snowshoes or skis straight uphill and step or slide diagonally in a crablike traverse.

Jogging downhill on snowshoes in deep powder can be fun, especially with poles. You can do jump turns similar to what you would do on skis. Be careful to not point your snowshoes straight downhill, and keep your weight back, or you will do a face-plant. Traversing is the best way to jog downhill safely. Make sure the snow is deep enough to cover stumps and rocks before attempting it.

You will generally find the snow to be more powdery in or under the trees. *Watch out for tree wells that are hidden by drifted snow: don't get too close to tree trunks because sometimes a well of air or loose snow can form, and if you fall in, it is almost impossible to get out without assistance. They can collapse suddenly, and throw people into the tree causing injury and suffocation.*

MANAGING RISK IN AVALANCHE COUNTRY

Colorado has the highest number of reported avalanches in the United States—there were 275 deaths from 1950 to 2016.The number of avalanche deaths has skyrocketed, roughly proportionate to the number of backcountry recreationists. This section cannot take the place of an avalanche safety course or in-depth avalanche guidebooks. If you haven't taken a course or attended a lecture, use the tutorial on avalanche.org, and also check out the videos. The Colorado Avalanche Information Center website—caic.org—also has excellent information, which I use daily in the winter

The climate in Colorado's Front Range tends to produce light, dry, fluffy powder snow that skiers love, but it tends to evolve into a highly unstable and dangerous snow underlayer that propagates avalanches. When such snow first falls, it is known as *surface hoar*. When these layers of powder snow are buried beneath subsequent layers of heavier snow, they are called *depth hoar*. The water content of this hoar snow is often only one-half that of snow in other regions; even Utah has much wetter snow.

The first question you need to ask yourself about avalanche danger is if you really want to risk traveling in avalanche terrain. If your answer is no, then pick a trail from the book that has low or no avalanche danger. In addition, you should know how to recognize avalanche terrain and practice good route-finding techniques to avoid it.

When you are planning a backcountry snowshoe or ski trip that might venture into avalanche terrain, start thinking about your trip well in advance. Most of the routes in this book are low-hazard routes. There is an avalanche rating for every trail option. You can avoid avalanche terrain completely if you plan your trip to do so. Check the rating of the trail, and then check conditions in the area you plan to visit at least a few days before. You can begin by calling or logging on to your local avalanche advisory website, the Colorado Avalanche Information Center (CAIC), to get the mountain weather forecast and the avalanche forecast with snow stability information. You don't want to be surprised by local conditions upon arrival. Recent major snowfall or changing temperatures can enhance avalanche danger on steep slopes. On the morning of your trip, check the CAIC website again so you will know current and predicted conditions, since forecasts can change, often overnight. CAIC usually posts their forecasts everyday by 7:00 a.m. This information will help you get started in your decision-making process.

Most avalanches run on slopes that are 30-45 degrees. These are steep slopes, and you don't want to determine their steepness when you are already on one. Avoid slopes that are above 20 degrees, and you will avoid most avalanches. To educate yourself about slope steepness, first learn how to read a topographic map so you can identify steep slopes on the map and for your potential route. Find a very short but steep little slope and measure slope angle with an inclinometer or slope meter. If you don't have a slope meter, put two ski poles together to form a 90-degree angle. Look through your poles at 45 degrees in the center at the slope you are measuring to estimate the angle. Test slope angle on slopes of different steepness. Expert slopes in ski areas are rarely steeper than 30 degrees.

Learn about the parts of an avalanche path: the starting zone, the track, and the runout zone. If you are walking below a steep slope, rather than on it, you might still be in the runout zone, meaning that the snow above you on a steep slope could slide down on to you. If you are above a steep slope, you might be in the starting zone. That means stay as high as possible on steep slopes, and avoid crossing them if you can. If you must cross one, do so single-file and spread out so some self-rescue is possible if it does slide. Plan your route carefully before you start so you will know you are avoiding potentially hazardous areas. Take a compass and a good topographical map with you and know how to use them. If you are planning winter mountaineering, rather than casual outings below tree line on safe trails, take an avalanche course so you will be prepared since you will probably be traveling through potential avalanche terrain.

Terrain, weather, and the condition of the snowpack determine the likelihood of avalanches. Inform yourself as to the most current weather and snow conditions and then pick the safest terrain possible. Call the Colorado Avalanche Information Center (see Appendix) for avalanche hazard ratings (defined later in this section) before entering the backcountry so you know the risky areas and can plan accordingly. The reports tell which aspects of the hills are most dangerous at a given time. Call your local forest service office or weather bureau (see Appendix) and ask about the safety of the trail you plan to explore. Take avalanche warnings seriously. Those steep, powdery slopes can be inviting, but they can also be deadly, especially to the unwary.

Don't snowshoe or ski alone when avalanche danger is high. I stay away from steep terrain whenever avalanche danger is high. Even a small slide 10 feet across and 5 feet deep can bury and smother a person. Carry a shovel and avalanche beacon and know how to use them. If you have any question about the safety of a proposed route, turn around and follow your own route back to a known safe destination.

You need to make sure you have both considerable knowledge and experience in identifying avalanche terrain and evaluating the stability of the snowpack in all its aspects and at all the elevations you plan to visit if you will be winter mountaineering. If you choose to travel in avalanche terrain, you are not going to learn enough here to guarantee safe travel. Take an avalanche course that takes you into the snow, read books and rent videos that show you how to understand the interaction between the terrain, the snowpack, and the weather. Only when you understand all three will you have the knowledge and the confidence to make good decisions, including the occasional decision to change your plans and stay safe.

AVALANCHE HAZARD RATINGS

Low: On steep, snow-covered gullies and open slopes, avalanches are unlikely and snow is mostly stable except in isolated pockets. Natural and human-triggered avalanches are unlikely. Backcountry travel is generally safe.

Moderate: Areas of unstable snow and slabs make avalanches very possible on steep, snow-covered gullies and open slopes. Human-triggered avalanches are possible. Backcountry travelers should use caution.

Considerable: Unstable slabs make human-triggered avalanches probable. Naturally triggered avalanches are possible. Backcountry travelers should use extreme caution.

High: Mostly unstable snow on a variety of aspects and slopes makes natural and human-triggered avalanches likely. Avalanches are likely on steep, snow-covered gullies and open slopes. Backcountry travel is not recommended.

Extreme: Widespread areas of unstable snow on a variety of aspects and slopes make natural and human-triggered avalanches a certainty on steep, snow-covered gullies and open slopes. Large, destructive avalanches are possible. Backcountry travel should be avoided.

AVOIDING AVALANCHES

Stay on marked trails when danger is high. A marked trail reduces but does not eliminate risk. Check your route with the forest service if it is not familiar to you. Avoid walking on, or below, steep slopes. Most avalanches occur on slopes of 30 to 45 degrees but also occur on slopes of 25 to 55 degrees. North-facing, leeward slopes

View from Forest Lake Trail.

are usually most dangerous in the winter months. They stabilize more slowly and are likely to have wind-drift snow. Avoid north-facing, shaded slopes in the winter, especially after recent snow- and windstorms. South-facing slopes are most dangerous in the spring because of dramatic solar heating and melting. Open slopes are more likely to slide than those with tree cover or rocks that can anchor snow. However, avalanches can occur on tree-covered slopes as well: The sparser the cover, the more likely the avalanche.

Stay high, on ridge lines if possible, but away from cornices. Cornices are masses of overhanging snow, blown by wind, which typically form along ridges. Don't ski or walk on or under cornices.

Go straight up or down the edge of the slope if you have to descend or ascend a possible avalanche slope, and avoid the middle portion.

Move across dangerous slopes one person at a time and as high as possible. Generally stay far apart. This provides for less weight stress on the underlying snow and enhances the opportunity for at least one person to be available to assist in a rescue effort.

Avoid old avalanche chutes or slide zones. Don't walk below steep slopes that might be avalanche- starting zones. These could catch you in a run-out area.

If you hear a whumping sound, alert your companions and make your way to trees or the edge of the slope. If ever it sounds as though the snow is collapsing beneath you, you are in a dangerous position and should take immediate precautions.

Avoid areas with fracture lines in the snow. This indicates that a slab avalanche, the largest and most destructive kind, is likely to activate in the area.

Beware of cold temperatures, high winds, and snowstorms with accumulations of more than 6 inches of snow or a rate of snowfall of 1 inch per hour or greater. Keep in mind that 90 percent of avalanches occur during or after snowstorms. Dry, powdery snow is more likely to avalanche than wet, heavy snow, unless the heavy snow is on top of the weak, powdery layer known as depth hoar.

Never assume that an area is safe simply because others have safely used it.

Avoid holes and gullies, not just steep slopes.

CROSSING A POTENTIAL AVALANCHE SITE

Wear an avalanche beacon. Ensure that your companions are wearing similar models and know how to use them. When crossing a hazardous area one at a time, the person crossing sets his or her the beacon to "transmit," and everyone else sets theirs to "receive."

Equip everyone in the party with shovels and probes. When crossing a hazardous one at a time, everyone waiting to cross should have his or her probe at the ready.

Slip your hands out of the pole straps if you are using poles.

Study the area and ask yourself, "If I am caught, where will I end up?" Discuss this with your companions.

Loosen pack straps. Unfasten belt and chest straps and be prepared to shed the pack.

There are back country packs available that inflate, or balloon, when you pull a rip cord to float you on top of the snow. They are very expensive (hundreds of dollars), but are considered to be the safest option if you will always be skiing, snowshoeing, or even snowboarding into avalanche terrain.

SURVIVING AN AVALANCHE

Shed as much of your gear as possible if you are caught in an avalanche. Shed large packs but retain small ones for protection when caught. Small packs can protect from debris while large packs can trap you.

Swim to stay on top, grab a rock or tree if possible and try to stay on top or as close to the top as possible.

Make an air space for breathing with your arm or hand.

Hold one hand up so rescuers can find you more easily.

Remain calm; focus on breathing fully and slowly.

FINDING AN AVALANCHE VICTIM

Don't leave to go for help; rescue by companions is a victim's best chance for survival. After a half hour beneath the snow, the victim's chances for survival are less than 50 percent. Time is critical.

Mark the spot where you last saw the victim.

Search downhill from where you last saw the person; use beacons or probe with ski poles.

Try to excavate the victim immediately; the longer a person is buried, the less likely it is he or she will survive.

The appendix lists a number of good books but you can also go to the CAIC website for lists of courses, videos, and publications to help you become a safe backcountry traveler.

ALTITUDE

The best snow in Colorado is usually found in the mountains rather than the foothills, at higher elevations. The primary way to determine reliable snow cover is by the altitude of the trail. Generally, the higher the trail, the better the snow cover will be. Most of the trails I have included are at an elevation of 8,000 feet and above. Early in the season (November through January), trails around 8,000 feet can still have thin, or no snow cover. This can vary of course by location and the number and intensity of early season snowstorms. Snowfall can be very localized, so checking the latest forecasts and calling the local US Forest Service, national park, or state park office is a good idea in order to assess trail conditions before leaving home. A major Front Range upslope storm can often offer good early-season, low-altitude cover. February, March, and April are usually Colorado's snowiest months. Trails that are 9,000 to 10,000 feet high are more reliable before February. Above 8,000 feet it can snow into May, but snow cover will likely be marginal or last only until the sun appears. You can often still ski or snowshoe above 10,000 feet into June. Tree-sheltered trails feature much more snow than trails exposed to sun and wind, regardless of elevation. Snow cover can vary greatly on the same trail, so be prepared to carry your snowshoes over thin or windswept sections. Rocks are not good for snowshoes.

Since most of the ski and snowshoe routes in this book are at relatively high elevations, if you are accustomed to exerting yourself in the high country, you have little reason for concern. If you rarely venture above 5,000 feet, recognize your and your party's potential limitations at higher elevations. Keep in mind the effects of altitude are unpredictable, especially for those who are visiting from sea level.

If you or visitors have just arrived from a lower elevation, take at least one or two days to acclimate before venturing above 5,000 feet. If you live at or above 5,000 feet, less time is needed to adjust.

Drinking a lot of water before and during high-altitude exercise is a good, though not foolproof, preventive measure against altitude illness. Have at least one quart or liter of water with you for an all-day excursion. Take along some headache medication (aspirin substitute, because aspirin can upset the stomach) and nausea medication (some feel that antacids have ingredients that can prevent the effects of altitude), just in case.

Altitude and elevation gain can certainly slow you down. Assume that you will travel one mile per hour or 1,000 feet of elevation gain per hour, at most, even if you are well conditioned. Physical conditioning helps, but it doesn't prevent altitude illness.

ALTITUDE ILLNESS

Mild altitude illness is the most common manifestation of the high-elevation phenomenon called mountain sickness. Symptoms of altitude illness are severe headache, nausea, loss of appetite, a warm flushed face, lethargy, and insomnia or poor sleep with strange dreams. Altitude illness, also called Acute Mountain Sickness (AMS), can last a couple of days. Resting, snowshoeing at lower elevations, eating lightly, and drinking more non-alcoholic liquids can help. Avoid taking barbiturates as sleeping pills because they can aggravate the illness. Some people, most often women, experience swelling of the face, hands, and feet.

Nosebleeds are more common at higher elevations because of the very dry air. Staying hydrated and avoiding catching a cold are the best ways to avoid them. The most effective way to stop a nosebleed is to gently pinch the nose shut for five minutes.

High Altitude Pulmonary Edema (HAPE) is a more severe form of mountain sickness and is a condition caused by fluid filling the lungs. Symptoms include difficulty breathing, a severe headache with incoherence, staggering, and a persistent, hacking cough. This is a serious illness caused by altitude.

High Altitude Cerebral Edema (HACE) is a critical condition caused by swelling of the brain. Symptoms include persistent vomiting, severe and persistent headache, extreme fatigue, delirium or confusion, staggering, and/or coma. This is the most serious illness caused by altitude and can be fatal.

Though extremely rare in Colorado, if you or anyone in your party experiences the symptoms of either HAPE or HACE, go to a lower altitude immediately and get to a physician as soon as possible.

If you always suffer at altitude, ask our doctor about Diamox, a prescription drug used to prevent altitude sickness.

HYPOTHERMIA

Hypothermia is deadly. It is an acute traumatic event that occurs when your body's core temperature drops below 95 degrees. It does not take extremely low temperatures to get into trouble—people have died from hypothermia with air temperatures in the 40s and 50s Fahrenheit. Core temperature loss can easily happen if someone falls into a lake or stream and is not able to get warm and dry right away. It can also happen if you are simply not dressed adequately when temperatures drop, the wind picks up, or it snows or rains on you.

You can avoid hypothermia by taking along the right kinds of clothing. Preventing hypothermia is much wiser than waiting until the situation becomes life threatening. Some symptoms of hypothermia are uncontrollable shivering, slurred or slow speech, fuzzy thinking, poor memory, incoherence, lack of coordination causing stumbling or vertigo, and extreme fatigue or sleepiness.

If you observe any of these symptoms in yourself or another person, take immediate action to warm the individual experiencing the problem. Stop and use your emergency supplies to make a fire and provide warm liquids, or wrap the individual in additional warm clothing and urge him or her to move around enough to warm up. A backpacking stove is ideal for heating up liquids or providing warmth.

Weather in the mountains can change dramatically in a matter of minutes. Early fall or late spring blizzards are especially sneaky. Pay attention to weather forecasts: pack extra gear, and when the weather is in doubt, head back out! Zero-visibility snow conditions, known as whiteouts, have been deadly for more than one winter recreationist. If you study the histories of winter disasters you will find that most of them could have been prevented by better preparation and by knowing when to retreat from difficult conditions.

SUN PROTECTION

The sun's rays are much stronger at higher elevations. With the added effect of reflection off the snow, even on a cloudy day you can end up with a severe burn. The harmful effects of the sun are magnified at high altitudes, so covering up and avoiding direct sunlight is the best strategy, especially between the hours of 10:00 a.m. and 2:00 p.m.

Sunscreen is essential at high altitude. Use one that is SPF 30 to avoid sun damage and reapply during the day. Excess sun also adversely affects the immune system. Your dermatologist will tell you that there is no such thing as a healthy tan.

Sunglasses or goggles are also essential to avoid sun damage to the eyes. If you do not protect your eyes you might become temporarily snow-blind, which is very painful and makes travel difficult.

MOUNTAIN WATER—A CAUTION

You need to drink plenty of water, but don't drink from mountain streams and lakes. Though they look crystal clear and inviting, they are not creature-free. Cold does not purify mountain water and a nasty parasite called *Giardia lamblia* actually thrives in cold water and can cause giardiasis, or diarrheal disease, if you drink untreated water. If you want to drink from streams and lakes, take along water-purifying tablets. Mountain water can also be boiled to kill *Giardia* without tablets or a filtering system. Take along plenty of water from home or the right purifying equipment and know how to use it. Filtering water in the winter can be a challenge.

TRAVELING SAFELY

Do not ski or snowshoe alone; go with a companion. Let others know where you are going and when you will be coming back. Sign in on trail registries.

Watch for trail markers and be very aware of your surroundings. Route finding, even on marked trails, is more challenging in winter.

Prevent frostbite by keeping your hands, feet, and face well protected. Tingling and numbing sensations are the early warning signs of frostbite. Beware of frostnip on your ears and tip of your nose.

Use extreme caution whenever you are crossing what appear to be frozen streams and lakes. They are often not frozen solid, especially around inlets and outlets, and falling through the ice far from your car or tent can be fatal.

A Note About Safety

Safety is an important concern in all outdoor activities. No guidebook can alert you to every hazard or anticipate the limitations of every reader. Therefore, the descriptions of roads, trails, routes, and natural features in this book are not guarantees that a particular place or excursion will be safe for your party. When you follow any of the routes described in this book, you assume responsibility for your own safety. Under normal conditions, such excursions require the usual attention to traffic, road and trail conditions, weather, terrain, the capabilities of your party, and other factors. Keeping informed on current conditions and exercising common sense are the keys to a safe, enjoyable outing.

Winter Lodging

RENTAL YURTS, CABINS, AND HUTS

The Tenth Mountain Division Huts Association: During World War II, Camp Hale near Tennessee Pass north of Leadville was the training center for the elite Tenth

Mountain Division troops who fought courageously in the Alps. After the war, many of the veterans returned to Colorado to found the Aspen, Breckenridge, Vail, Steamboat, Loveland, Arapaho Basin, and Winter Park Ski Areas. They also converted the training huts they used during the war so they could be used as European-style climbing huts by snowshoers and backcountry skiers. Staying in these huts is a terrific way to explore the high country around Leadville in winter. There are more than sixteen Tenth Mountain Division huts stretching from Vail Pass on Interstate 70 north of Leadville to Aspen in the west on Highway 82. Getting to some of the huts is a challenging long-distance trek, but others are close to civilization and can be reached by the reasonably fit winter snowshoer. I have included an easy-access hut, Vance's Cabin, in the route guides. You can find out more information by visiting the Tenth Mountain Division Hut Association website (see Appendix).

The Never Summer Nordic Yurt System and Colorado State Parks Cabins at State Forest: These yurts and cabins are two good, inexpensive, less-demanding alternatives to camping on snow for winter overnights in the high mountain winter paradise of the Colorado State Forest north of Highway 14. Never Summer Nordic rents circular, tent-like canvas and wood yurts built on a wood deck. The Colorado State Parks/State Forest rents several rustic cabins in the Gould area on North Michigan Reservoir. The settings for these yurts and cabins are dramatic, with the Rawah Range in the Medicine Bow Mountains forming an enormous and majestic backdrop to the east and north.

The yurts vary in size and sleep 6 to 10 people. They are heated with wood-burning stoves and have a variety of bunks and beds. Dancing Moose Yurt and Grass Creek Yurt are 0.25 and 0.6 mile from the road respectively; the others are farther. The website includes complete descriptions, pictures, and prices (see Appendix A).

The latest addition to the Never Summer Nordic yurt system, the Nokhu Hut on Lake Agnes Road, is a delightful, low-stress way to spend the night in the Cameron Pass area. Plan well in advance to use this hut because reservations with Never Summer Nordic are necessary and it is a popular hut that is often booked up for weekends. It is inexpensive, but prices can change, so check the website for the latest price. The hut includes a wood-burning cook stove that is also used for heat. Wood is included in the rental fee. Though there are beds, bring sleeping pads and warm bags because it gets quite cool when the stove goes out overnight. There are nice, easy trails in and around the hut with views in every direction. To get to the Nokhu Hut, go west over Cameron Pass on Highway 14 and watch for the turnout in about 2 miles on the left side of the road. The road to the cabin and summer parking area is closed in the winter; walk the closed road to reach the hut.

The North Michigan Reservoir cabins are heated either by wood-burning stoves or propane. Water is available nearby. There are vault toilets within walking distance of the cabins. Each cabin sleeps 6 to 10 people on bunk beds. They are between 100 and 400 feet from parking places.

SKI AND SNOWSHOEING TRIPS

The following organizations host snowshoeing outings that you may enjoy: the Colorado Mountain Club, Rocky Mountain Sierra Club, Rocky Mountain National Park Nature Association, and the staff of Rocky Mountain National Park. I have listed contact information in the Appendix. Check their websites for detailed information.

VOLUNTEERING

If you want even more enjoyment in the outdoors, please consider volunteering to lead or support outings and activities. You can take advantage of these rewarding opportunities with the following organizations: Ignite Adaptive Sports at Eldora Mountain Resort, Colorado Special Olympics, the National Sports Center for the Disabled at Winter Park, Rocky Mountain Sierra Club, Colorado Mountain Club, and any local, state, or national parks.

WILDERNESS ETHICS

We aren't inheriting the Earth from our fathers, we are stealing it from our children.
— David Brower, *Let the Mountains Talk, Let the Rivers Run* (2007)

Public land is not "government land." It is land that we, the public, own. Our national forests are valuable land that is protected and maintained for us by government employees. This ownership comes not only with the opportunity for recreation—for re-creation of the body and soul—but also with the responsibility to care for and respect our land. Many of the areas described in this book are wilderness areas that require extra precautions and work to prevent deterioration of the wilderness experience and wildlife for present and future generations. We should all try to apply the Leave No Trace philosophy to the use of public lands. The things that move us to go into the wilderness are what make it one of our most cherished national treasures.

PLAN AHEAD

Know the risks and regulations of the area you are visiting.

To minimize your impact on the land, visit the backcountry in small groups and carpool or take public transportation if possible. Try to avoid popular areas in times of high use.

To minimize your visual impact on others, use naturally hued clothing and equipment. Although, note that some winter recreationists will wear bright-colored clothing as a safety measure—in the event of avalanche or rescue, bright colors are easier to spot.

To minimize garbage, repackage food into reusable containers that won't leak.

LEAVE NO TRACE

- Camp at least 200 feet from trails, water sources and muddy areas, and wildlife forage or watering areas. Animals are stressed in winter and your activities could reduce their chance of survival.

- Avoid building a fire: bring a lightweight stove and extra clothing for cooking and warmth. Open fires are illegal in wilderness areas. On overnight stays, enjoy a candle instead of a fire. Where fires are permitted, use them only for emergencies and do not scar large rocks, overhangs, or trees with the flame from your fire. Use only downed or dead wood and do not snap branches off of live trees. If you burn garbage, burn only paper; remove all unburnable and unburned trash and bury ashes.
- Pack out whatever you pack in.
- Dismantle snow structures and cover snow pits.
- Use backcountry toilets whenever they are available. Get as far off the trail as possible when you have to answer nature's call—at least 50 feet for a urination stop—and camouflage soiled snow. Use bare ground for burial or pack out human waste; don't bury it in the snow. Dispose of solid waste at least 200 feet from trails or water sources.
- Pets are allowed in most national forests and state parks, but not on trails in national parks. If possible, leave your pets at home; they will love you for it. Snow and ice often cause painful paw injuries, and dog booties rarely work properly. If you do bring a pet, control it at all times. They sometimes run off of steep slopes and are unable to get back up because of very deep snow. Beware that dogs have been seriously injured by the sharp edges of skis; skiers can't always turn or stop when descending narrow trails. Camouflage soiled snow from your dog's urination. Bury dog feces off of the trail.
- Leave what you find. Do not remove trees, plants, rocks, or historical artifacts—they belong to everyone.

Rocky Mountain National Park

Chapter 1

ROCKY MOUNTAIN NATIONAL PARK— NORTHEAST

"Beyond the wall of the unreal city, beyond the asphalt belting of superhighways, there is another world waiting for you. It is the old true world of the deserts, the mountains, the forests, the islands, the shores, the open plains. Go there. Be there. Walk gently and quietly deep within it."

—Edward Abbey, *Beyond the Wall: Essays from the Outside* (1984)

One of the gems of the national park system, perhaps even the crown jewel, Rocky Mountain National Park features some of North America's most spectacular scen-

Another world awaits you above the clouds.

ery. Its winter landscape casts an almost mystical spell. Rocky Mountain National Park is truly "beyond the wall." There are few places that encompass so much natural beauty in such limited geography. From the craggy peaks of the Continental Divide to the gentle beauty of the glacial moraines and meadows or the cascading frozen streams, it is a captivating environment that makes you want to stay. Moraine Park's ever-changing mountain weather and light make it a magical place where elk roam freely and birds of prey hover. This stunning setting features one of the most scenically impressive glacial moraines in the Rockies. Glacier Gorge is an entry point to massive rock, frozen waterfalls of hanging ice, Black Lake, and the Loch. The majestic cliffs of Mount Lady Washington and Longs Peak soar to the south with views of the Mummy Range gracing the horizon to the north. The spectacular beauty of the Bear Lake and Hallet's Peak area with its easy accessibility, wide variety of trails, and reliable snow conditions make it one of the most popular areas in the park year-round. The majestic backdrops of frozen Bear, Bierstadt, Dream, Emerald and Jewell lakes are almost mystical, as spin drift and filtered winter light float down from the summits. You can also explore the shoulders and summits of Flattop and Hallet's Peak or, if you are very ambitious, attempt their summits.

To get to Rocky Mountain National Park from Denver, take I-25 north 40 miles and exit at Loveland/US 34. Take US 34 west through Big Thompson Canyon 40 miles to Estes Park. Allow at least one hour and 30 minutes. Other routes from Denver include US 36 northwest through Boulder and Lyons for 60 miles to Estes Park; and I-25 north for 30 miles to Highway 66, west on Highway 66 for 15 miles to Lyons, and northwest on US 36 for 20 miles to Estes Park. Once in Estes Park, follow the signs to the park entrance.

Montgomery Pass.

1. North Fork Trail

ROUND TRIP	13 miles to Lost Falls; 16.2 miles to Lost Lake
DIFFICULTY	Easy to challenging
SKILL LEVEL	Novice snowshoers and skiers
HIGH POINT	9,900 feet
ELEVATION GAIN	2,000 feet
AVALANCHE DANGER	None to low
MAP	Trails Illustrated #200, Rocky Mountain National Park
CONTACT	Rocky Mountain National Park Canyon Lakes Ranger District

COMMENT: This lesser-known trail (also known as the Dunraven Trail and Lost Lake Trail), featuring varied topography in a beautiful riparian area, winds its way through the short-forested canyon of the North Fork of the Big Thompson River, with its striking rock outcrops and meadows. The trail goes through a narrow portion of the Comanche Peak Wilderness before entering Rocky Mountain National Park. It then climbs through a backcountry campground in the Comanche Wilderness, more broad meadows, and eventually ventures above tree line and to Lost Lake. Because of the low elevation at the start, this trail is only reliable if there has been a major Front Range snowstorm. However, if you are willing to unstrap your snowshoes and possibly hike for a mile or two, it can still be a great way to spend a day in a beautiful pine-forested valley. After the initial descent, the trail is very level for a considerable distance, making it a good choice for family excursions or mellow outings. Nordic skinny skis are the best choice for this route. The initial descent is the only major hill.

GETTING THERE: From Denver, take I-25 north 40 miles and exit at Loveland/US 34. Take US 34 west through Big Thompson Canyon to Drake. In Drake, turn right onto CR 43 toward Glen Haven and drive northwest 6 miles. Turn right on Dunraven Glade Road/CR 51B. Drive northwest for 2.4 miles on the well-maintained dirt or snow-packed road to its end, where you will find the Dunraven trailhead.

THE ROUTE: From the parking lot you can see the well-marked trailhead. Proceed to the right of the privy and up a slight hill. The trail then descends about 0.5 mile down to the North Fork of the Big Thompson River, losing 200 feet of elevation. At the bottom is a wonder world of pretty brook-side winter settings with tall pines and

View to the south from the North Fork (also called Dunraven or Lost Lake) trailhead.

a meandering, babbling or frozen brook. There are a few very narrow, potentially icy or wet spots in the first mile. The snow conditions can vary widely depending on sun exposure and the first mile is likely to be snow-free.

After 0.5 mile you will pass next to the private Cheley Camp. Though you are in a thick forest, the trees are tall so there are good views all the way. You go through open areas and a large meadow in the first 2 miles. There is a good bridge for a stream crossing. At this point the snow might be questionable for a while until you enter the trees again, but you are steadily gaining elevation so odds of better snow are good as you proceed.

The trail to the first Comanche Peak Wilderness backcountry campsite is 2.1 miles from the trailhead and other campsite trails are between 2.7 and 3.4 miles from the trailhead. The trail then climbs significantly before you enter Rocky Mountain National Park just before 4 miles, but then levels again. Reach park campsites about 4.25 miles from the trailhead.

At about 4.5 miles there is a trail junction. To the left is the North Boundary Trail. Stay straight/right. As you travel the next 2 miles along the river, there are meadows and more backcountry campsites as the trees thin and the trail opens up. You reach Lost Falls at about 6.5 miles where there is another trail junction. To the right is Stormy Peaks Trail, Route 8; stay straight/left.

WARNING: Going all the way to Lost Lake means traveling below a high ridge just beyond Lost Falls. If you plan to go that far, check with the National Park Service or the Arapaho-Roosevelt National Forest office to see if there is avalanche danger, and proceed accordingly. Up to that point, about 7 miles from the trailhead, there are no avalanche hazards.

The last mile to the lake goes through Lost Meadow, finally reaching the stark beauty of the glacial cirque at 8.1 miles. You can decide to turn around at any point depending on the conditions and your ambitions.

Looking west from the North Fork (Dunraven or Lost Lake) trailhead.

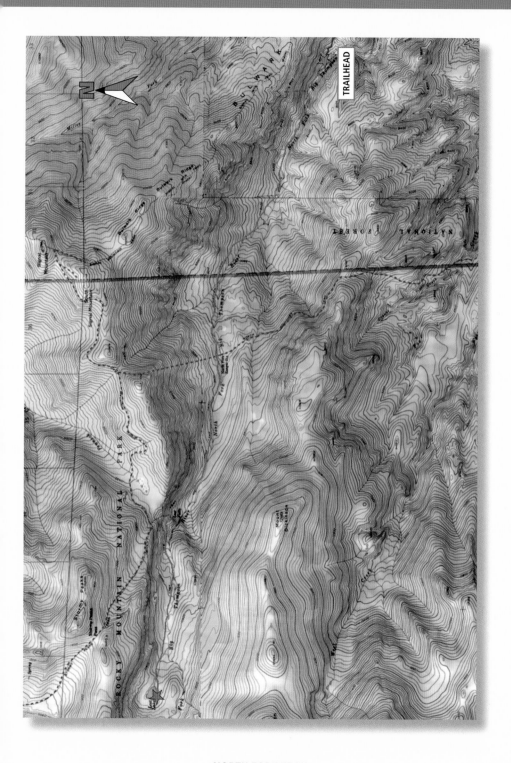

TRAILHEAD

NORTH FORK TRAIL

2. Deer Mountain

ROUND TRIP	6 miles
DIFFICULTY	Easy to moderate
SKILL LEVEL	Novice
HIGH POINT	10,013 feet
ELEVATION GAIN	1,075 feet
AVALANCHE DANGER	None
MAP	Trails Illustrated #200, Rocky Mountain National Park
CONTACT	Rocky Mountain National Park

COMMENT: This trail offers some of the best views of the Continental Divide and Longs Peak for the least amount of effort. The lower end of the trail is often snow-free early or late in the season because of its elevation and exposure to the sun. You are likely to have enough snow after the first mile. There are nonstop views from the beginning and throughout the route. It offers good, short excursions for young families and beginners, or a nice moderate climb for more experienced snowshoers. Its elevation and terrain make it most suitable for snowshoeing.

GETTING THERE: From Denver, take I-25 north 40 miles and exit at Loveland/US 34. Take US 34 west through Big Thompson Canyon 40 miles to Estes Park. Allow at least one hour and 30 minutes. Other routes from Denver include US 36 northwest through Boulder and Lyons for 60 miles to Estes Park; and I-25 north for 30 miles to Highway 66, west on Highway 66 for 15 miles to Lyons, and northwest on US 36 for 20 miles to Estes Park. When you reach Estes Park, continue west to the third traffic light, where you will see a sign for the park. Turn left at the sign and go up a hill, bear right at the stop sign, and then bear right at the intersection 0.5 mile after the next traffic light. You will see signs for the Beaver Meadows Visitors Center. From the Beaver Meadows entrance, at the Bear Lake Road turnoff on the left, stay straight/right and drive 4 miles northwest to Deer Ridge Junction. There is parking on both sides of the road.

THE ROUTE: The trail begins in an impressive grove of tall, mature ponderosa pines, starting off on some stone steps. Look to your left as you begin the trek and you will see a small hill with some rock outcrops on top. If you want a terrific view of the Mount Chapin, Mount Chiquita, and Ypsilon Mountain massif to the northwest, then detour to the top of the rocks. This is a great photo opportunity at the start of the trek.

The trail rolls a bit at the start, goes slightly downhill, and then turns east and begins to climb more steeply. The panoramic views of Longs Peak to the south and west are superb until the trail enters the trees. There are numerous opportunities for photos on both sides of the trail for the first 0.75 mile. This trail is graced by a pleasing mixture of aspen, lodgepole pine, and limber pine trees. The snow depth on the trail can vary widely because of its sunny aspect, but it deepens with every switchback. There are lots of switchbacks, but they make the climb a gradual one. With almost every switchback there is a somewhat different view. If you have children along, it is unlikely you will want to go for the summit. Pick the end of a switchback and take a snack or water break, declare victory, and turn around. The summit is fun to reach, but it isn't a major viewpoint in comparison to what you'll see along the way. In fact, at a little under the 2-mile mark, you will reach a broad ridge with views comparable to the summit. If the snow conditions are challenging, or the weather is changing, this is a good place to claim your "summit." If you do choose to go to the very top, you will see the summit trail in another 0.8 mile. It is a spur that goes off to the right. The summit might be wind-swept with less snow, or it might be much deeper as you ascend. Mother Nature is not predictable, and she often demands respect, with elements like cold winds blowing down from the Continental Divide.

Ypsilon Mountain from the Deer Mountain Trail.

DEER MOUNTAIN

3. Hidden Valley

ROUND TRIP	2 miles to Trail Ridge Road; 3 miles to top Tombstone Ridge
DIFFICULTY	Moderate to challenging
SKILL LEVEL	Novice snowshoers; intermediate skiers
HIGH POINT	11,500 at top of Tombstone Ridge; 10,500 at Trail Ridge Road
ELEVATION GAIN	1,200 feet to Trail Ridge Road; 2,200 feet to top of Tombstone Ridge
AVALANCHE DANGER	Low to moderate
MAP	Trails Illustrated #200, Rocky Mountain National Park
CONTACT	Rocky Mountain National Park

COMMENT: This winter playground is a former small alpine ski area that is now great for snowshoeing, tubing, and cross-country and telemark skiing. The park has installed a warming hut and heated restrooms and expanded the parking lot. The ski runs are still well defined, making it impossible to get lost. Go out as far as you like, and turn around when you have gained enough elevation to enjoy the views of the Mummy Range. If you continue on for an additional trek on Trail Ridge Road you will have even better views of the Mummies. AT or tele skis are the best choice for this area.

GETTING THERE: From Estes Park, continue west to the third traffic light, where you will see a sign for the park. Turn left at the sign and go up a hill, bear right at the stop sign, and then bear right at the intersection 0.5 mile after the next traffic light. You will see signs for the Beaver Meadows Visitors Center. From the Beaver Meadows entrance, at the Bear Lake Road turnoff on the left, stay straight/right and drive 4 miles northwest to Deer Ridge Junction. Continue straight through the intersection toward Trail Ridge Road. After 2.25 miles, you will round a sharp hairpin turn and the Hidden Valley parking lot will be on the left/west side of the road

THE ROUTE: The area offers an initially uphill, out-and-back option, as well as a potential car shuttle. From the warming hut, travel uphill past the tubing area on the left/south side. You will see two potential uphill routes that are former ski runs. They are unmarked and unnamed. They will appear on the northwest/right side of the trail. You can take either run uphill. You can snowshoe along the edge of the

Hidden Valley from Trail Ridge Road.

trees, and occasionally meander into the trees that line both sides of the very wide ski runs. The trails get gradually steeper as you climb, so go as far as you like before turning around. If you continue for 1 mile, you will climb more steeply to intersect Trail Ridge Road, which is closed in the winter from October through May. If you turn around at the road, you will have a 2-mile round trip and around a 1,000-foot gain. If you want more exertion, and even more impressive views, you can cross the road and climb much more steeply up near the top of Tombstone Ridge, the top of the old ski area. That is another 1,000 feet of climbing in just over 0.5 mile, a very vertical stretch. This section is steep enough to avalanche, so don't climb it unless you know the snow is very stable, or can dig a snow pit to check it. If you don't want steeper climbing, but do want a longer trek, take Trail Ridge Road east or west. You can of course still do this as an out-and-back trip, and return to the base area. If you turn west, you will go uphill. Another easier option is a car shuttle, though you would need two cars. Leave a car at the road closure and then drive back to the base area and climb up and across Trail Ridge Road and back to the car at the closure. After ascending to Trail Ridge Road, turn left/east on the road. It is 2.75 miles to the road closure and your vehicle. The road descends gradually downhill to the closure, losing around 600 feet. Your one-way trip will be around 4 miles. You can, of course, do it the other way around.

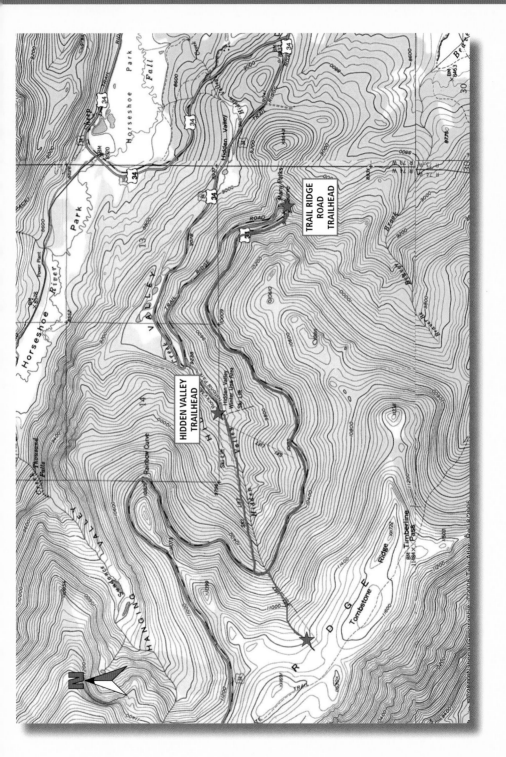

HIDDEN VALLEY

4. Trail Ridge Road

ROUND TRIP	5.5 miles
DIFFICULTY	Easy to moderate
SKILL LEVEL	Novice snowshoers; intermediate-advanced skiers
HIGH POINT	10,484 feet
ELEVATION GAIN	700 feet from road closure; 1,000 feet from base area
AVALANCHE DANGER	Low to considerable
MAP	Trails Illustrated #200, Rocky Mountain National Park
CONTACT	Rocky Mountain National Park

COMMENT: This road goes all the way over the Continental Divide to Grand Lake. In the summer, Trail Ridge Road is jammed with traffic. In the winter, it is a quiet, windswept route to spectacular scenery, especially views of the Mummy Range—Chapin, Chiquita, Ypsilon, and Mummy, to name a few.

Experienced skiers can use any style of ski on this route if you aren't skiing the steep routes.

If you have a car shuttle set up you can ski the road to the top of the former ski area and descend a trail to Hidden Valley. Or ski down and skin back up to the road. For that kind of adventure you will need AT or tele skis and advanced skills.

GETTING THERE: From Denver, take I-25 north 40 miles and exit at Loveland/US 34. Take US 34 west through Big Thompson Canyon 40 miles to Estes Park. Allow at least one hour and 30 minutes. Other routes from Denver include US 36 northwest through Boulder and Lyons for 60 miles to Estes Park; and I-25 north for 30 miles to Highway 66, west on Highway 66 for 15 miles to Lyons, and northwest on US 36 for 20 miles to Estes Park. When you reach Estes Park, continue west to the third traffic light, where you will see a sign for the park. Turn left at the sign and go up a hill, bear right at the stop sign, and then bear right at the intersection 0.5 mile after the next traffic light. You will see signs for the Beaver Meadows Visitors Center.

From the Beaver Meadows entrance it is 8.3 miles to the Trail Ridge Road closure. At the Bear Lake Road turnoff on the left, stay straight/right and drive 4 miles northwest to Deer Ridge Junction. Continue straight through the intersection up Trail Ridge Road. You will round a sharp hairpin turn and pass the Hidden Valley parking lot on the right/west side of the road. Continue about 2 miles to the road

Alan Stark on Trail Ridge Road.

closure, unless you plan a loop with a car shuttle. There is a plowed parking area at the closure.

THE ROUTE: This is another option in Rocky Mountain National Park where the route is easy to follow and you can't get lost. The only downside is that the wind can be fierce at times and blow snow from sections of the road. You will have to be prepared to take off and put on your snowshoes or skis because of the wind scouring. The views are non-stop and there is a sense of adventure as you wind your way up the road, which tops out at 12,000 feet. It is much more peaceful to enjoy the route without the vehicles.

There are several adventure options: you can snowshoe or ski out and back from the road closure or from the warming hut; you can do a loop route with a car shuttle if you want to start from the road closure and then descend via the former Hidden

Valley ski runs down to the Hidden Valley recreation area warming hut, You can climb up from the warming hut to Trail Ridge Road and back, or continue to the road closure after you have climbed up. You should allow an entire day for this most challenging option.

One other option is less safe: starting at the warming hut and going straight up to the top of Tombstone Ridge from Trail Ridge Road. The top of the former ski area offers spectacular views, but also avalanche danger and a very steep additional 1,000-foot climb. Check with the rangers about avalanche danger before climbing or skinning to the top. It is fairly safe in late spring when the snow has consolidated and is not known to frequently avalanche.

If you start from the road closure you will get the best sustained views although probably the least consistent snow. As you travel northwest on Trail Ridge Road you will be looking at the Mummy Range across the valley. After less than a mile, you will see the former ski area and the route from the bottom to Trail Ridge Road. You will be climbing steadily but gradually as you follow the road toward the top of the ski area, where shuttle buses used to drop off skiers. You can turn around at any time after you have had your fill of the sweeping mountaintop scenery, or ski down if you have solid intermediate to advanced skills.

If you wait until spring and the opening of Trail Ridge Road, you can drive to a turnout 0.5 mile east of the Ute trailhead. You can traverse over to the top of the former Hidden Valley ski runs but be prepared to hike snow-free areas.

SEE MAP ON PAGE 45.

5. Cub Lake

ROUND TRIP	4 miles
DIFFICULTY	Easy to moderate
SKILL LEVEL	Novice snowshoers and skiers
HIGH POINT	8,600 feet
ELEVATION GAIN	500 feet
AVALANCHE DANGER	None
MAP	Trails Illustrated #200, Rocky Mountain National Park
CONTACT	Rocky Mountain National Park

COMMENT: On this pleasant out-and-back it is not unusual to encounter elk along the way. It is a popular trail for elk viewing in late September and early October before there is enough snow for snowshoeing. Because the trail starts and ends at relatively low elevations and includes several sections of rock, wait until a good snow year or until there is good snow cover. Even then, you might have to take off your skis or snowshoes to get over the rocky sections and pick your way carefully around and over the rocks. You can do the route as a loop and return on the Fern Lake Trail but you will have almost a mile (.7 mile) of road walking back to the Cub Lake trailhead and another 0.2 mile to the winter parking area. This trail can be skied with skinny cross-country skis because of its gentle gradient.

GETTING THERE: From Denver, take I-25 north 40 miles and exit at Loveland/ US 34. Take US 34 west through Big Thompson Canyon 40 miles to Estes Park. Allow at least one hour and 30 minutes. Other routes from Denver include US 36 northwest through Boulder and Lyons for 60 miles to Estes Park; and I-25 north for 30 miles to Highway 66, west on Highway 66 for 15 miles to Lyons, and north-west on US 36 for 20 miles to Estes Park. When you reach Estes Park, continue west to the third traffic light, where you will see a sign for the park. Turn left at the sign and go up a hill, bear right at the stop sign, and then bear right at the intersection 0.5 mile after the next traffic light. You will see signs for the Beaver Meadows Visitors Center.

From the Beaver Meadows entrance, take the first left at 0.25 mile, onto Bear Lake Road. After 0.5 mile there is a hairpin S-turn and a sign for Moraine Park. Take the next right, and then, at the next junction, bear left and continue 1 mile

Cub Lake trailhead looking west.

to the Cub Lake trailhead. (If you continue straight, you go into the Moraine Park Campground, which remains open in the winter.)

THE ROUTE: At the start, the Cub Lake Trail goes south to cross two streams over wooden bridges. It might be advisable to wait until you cross before putting on your skis or snowshoes. You encounter the first rock crossing in about 0.5 mile; go to the left around the rocks. The trail turns west and climbs slowly, encountering another rocky section after another 0.25 mile or so. It then parallels a marshy area as the tree cover thickens and it starts its gentle climb. The first mile or so borders the open expanses of Moraine Park and offers nice views back to the east and south. You will have views of the ridge line that separates you from the Sprague Lake and Bear Lake area.
Eventually you enter a beautiful tree tunnel and then, as you get within 0.5 mile of the lake, at 1.5 miles, the trail opens up and climbs steeply to the edge of the lake. This is the steepest section of the trail, but it isn't a very long climb.

To intersect the Fern Lake Trail, Route 34, walk west past the west end of Cub Lake to a trail junction in 0.5 mile. The trail to the left goes to Bear Lake; stay straight/right. The trail climbs the ridge line to the north about 200 feet to meet the Fern Lake Trail in another 0.75 mile.

SIDEBAR: DAYPACK

Taking along a daypack is always a good idea. It allows you more flexibility in what you wear so you can adjust to changing weather. Choose a pack that has straps and can be used to carry your snowshoes when necessary. Snow conditions are always unpredictable, especially early and late in the season, and for sections of many trails you won't need your snowshoes or skis all of the time.

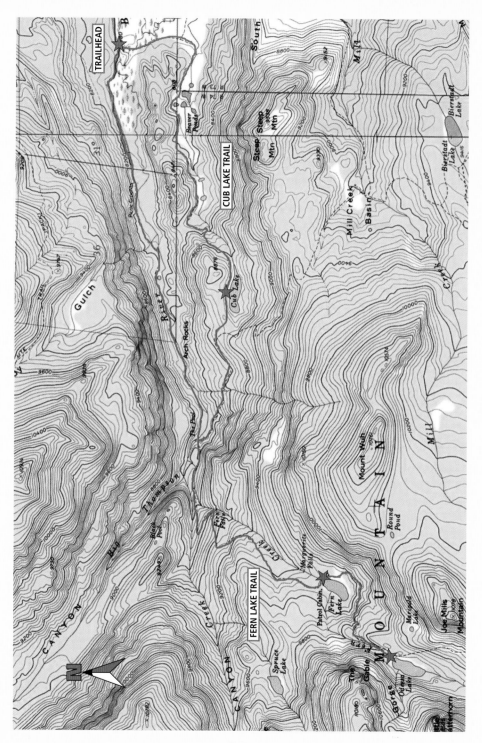

CUB LAKE

6. Fern Lake and Odessa Lake

ROUND TRIP	Up to 8.7 miles
DIFFICULTY	Moderate to challenging
SKILL LEVEL	Novice snowshoers; intermediate skiers
HIGH POINT	Fern Lake 9,543; Odessa Lake 10,023 feet
ELEVATION GAIN	Fern Lake 1,393 feet; Odessa Lake 1,873 feet
AVALANCHE DANGER	None (Fern Lake) to considerable (Odessa Lake)
MAP	Trails Illustrated #200, Rocky Mountain National Park
CONTACT	Rocky Mountain National Park

COMMENT: This is a nice climb and a very striking trail as an out-and-back to Fern Lake, or a longer adventure to Odessa Lake. Fern Lake has charms enough of its own: Windy Gulch Cascades, Fern Falls, and Marguerite Falls to name a few. If that isn't enough fun, you can climb another 500 feet and 0.7 mile up to Odessa Lake. That part of the trail is steep and includes avalanche danger. For a major adventure you can also use the Fern Lake Trail by starting at Moraine Park and finishing at Bear Lake. That would require a car shuttle and an early start, especially in mid-winter when the days are short. The Bear Lake trek is strenuous, and should only be attempted by the very fit with solid skiing, snowshoeing, and winter route finding experience. The steep sections would be more comfortable with wider skis. Wait for excellent snow cover to ski it.

GETTING THERE: From Denver, take I-25 north 40 miles and exit at Loveland/US 34. Take US 34 west through Big Thompson Canyon 40 miles to Estes Park. Allow at least one hour and 30 minutes. Other routes from Denver include US 36 northwest through Boulder and Lyons for 60 miles to Estes Park; and I-25 north for 30 miles to Highway 66, west on Highway 66 for 15 miles to Lyons, and northwest on US 36 for 20 miles to Estes Park. From Estes Park, continue west to the third traffic light, where you will see a sign for the park. Turn left at the sign and go up a hill, bear right at the stop sign, and then bear right at the intersection 0.5 mile after the next traffic light. You will see signs for the Beaver Meadows Visitors Center.

From the Beaver Meadows entrance, take the first left at 0.25 mile onto Bear Lake Road. After 0.5 mile there is a hairpin S-turn and a sign for Moraine Park. Take the next right, and then at the next junction bear left at the sign for the Cub Lake and Fern Lake trailheads. (If you continue straight you go into the Moraine

Cub Lake trailhead looking west.

Park Campground, which remains open in the winter.) The Cub Lake trailhead is on the left in a mile and the Fern Lake trailhead is approximately a mile farther, with some parking at the end of the road. In the winter the road is closed 0.2 mile from the Cub Lake trailhead, so you will have an additional 0.9 mile to reach the Fern Lake trailhead.

GETTING THERE: The trail starts as a very gradual climb, covering terrain that is similar to the Cub Lake Trail. The major difference is that you climb out of the Moraine Park lowlands more quickly. In 0.5 mile you encounter Windy Gulch Cascades to the right, and then at around 1.5 miles the trail steepens considerably. At 1.6 miles you will reach a trail junction (the trail to the left goes to Cub Lake) where you continue straight/right.

After crossing Fern Creek, the trail begins to switchback at about 2.25 miles, rising for about a mile to surmount a higher plateau. At about 3.6 miles there is a trail junction (the trail to the right goes up to Spruce Lake) with Marguerite Falls on the left; continue straight/left to the larger Fern Lake at 3.5 miles.

If avalanche danger is low, you can continue around the lake and up Fern Creek a steep 0.7 mile to Odessa Lake, then switchback high onto the ridge and gain spectacular views of the entire Moraine Park valley. If you have the time, ambition, and a car shuttle you can even climb up and over into the Glacier Gorge–Bear Lake drainage another 4.5 miles or so to Bear Lake. It is one of the more spectacular jaunts in the park without going up to the very highest reaches

SEE MAP ON PAGE 51.

7. Hollowell Park and Mill Creek Basin

ROUND TRIP	5 miles to overlook
DIFFICULTY	Easy to moderate
SKILL LEVEL	Novice snowshoers; intermediate skiers
HIGH POINT	9,200 feet
ELEVATION GAIN	800 feet
AVALANCHE DANGER	None
MAP	Trails Illustrated #200, Rocky Mountain National Park
CONTACT	Rocky Mountain National Park

COMMENT: Hollowell Park is an expansive, classic high-mountain meadow rimmed by stately pine trees interspersed with aspen. As you head south on Bear Lake Road, this is the first trailhead after Moraine Park. It is a fairly gradual climb. The snow might not be very good in the meadow, but it improves dramatically as you gain elevation. The trail can be turned into an out-and-back of any length and also offers a very nice view of Cub Lake from above. This trail can be used for a steeper one-mile trek up to Bierstadt Lake from Mill Creek Basin or as the beginning of a 6.4-mile loop back to the Cub Lake trailhead. Check for excellent snow conditions before skiing. Skinny or mid-width Nordic skis are appropriate.

GETTING THERE: From Denver, take I-25 north 40 miles and exit at Loveland/ US 34. Take US 34 west through Big Thompson Canyon 40 miles to Estes Park. Allow at least one hour and 30 minutes. Other routes from Denver include US 36 northwest through Boulder and Lyons for 60 miles to Estes Park; and I-25 north for 30 miles to Highway 66, west on Highway 66 for 15 miles to Lyons, and northwest on US 36 for 20 miles to Estes Park. When you reach Estes Park, continue west to the third traffic light, where you will see a sign for the park. Turn left at the sign and go up a hill, bear right at the stop sign, and then bear right at the intersection 0.5 mile after the next traffic light. You will see signs for the Beaver Meadows Visitors Center.

From the Beaver Meadows entrance, take the first left onto Bear Lake Road. After a hairpin S-turn, the road travels downhill past the Moraine Park campground and museum and then goes uphill through a pine forest that is adjacent to the YMCA camp. When you emerge from the trees, you are looking at Hollowell Park straight ahead. Just as the road reaches the turnoff approximately 3.5 miles

Longs Peak view from Hollowell Park.

from the Beaver Meadows entrance it makes a hairpin turn to the left; bear right into the parking area.

THE ROUTE: Start by walking west about 100 yards to cross Academy Boulevard. Take the trail west across the meadow and bear left at the first intersection in 0.25 mile. Go up a gradual hill into the trees. You will soon be next to pretty, frozen—or babbling—Mill Creek, lined with pine and aspen trees. At the next intersection, at 1.25 miles, the trail to the left climbs steeply up to Bierstadt Lake; go straight (west) for the overview of Cub Lake. If this sign is completely covered by snow, just bear right or go straight. Don't take the first stream crossing to the left (southwest), and you will know you are on the Cub Lake branch of the trail.

The trail climbs gradually through the trees; at 1.7 miles reach another junction where you stay right (the trail to the left goes to Bear Lake). Soon the trail opens up to a couple of nice small meadows in Mill Creek Basin. It then winds back into the trees, alternating with steeper and flatter sections until it opens up into a great view back up the moraine onto Cub Lake at about 2.5 miles. This is a good place to turn around because the trail descends steeply to Cub Lake.

Retrace your steps—with caution—for the return to the trailhead.

SIDEBAR: SNOW CONDITIONS

Snow conditions can vary widely, from easy hard pack to deep powder, to collapsing crust or ice. It isn't unusual for post-holing, even on snowshoes or skis, on steep slopes or lightly used trails. If the snow conditions are especially challenging, it can be wise to revise your goals and only trek as far as is enjoyable. Using poles can help with varying snow conditions because they give you much more stability and climbing power.

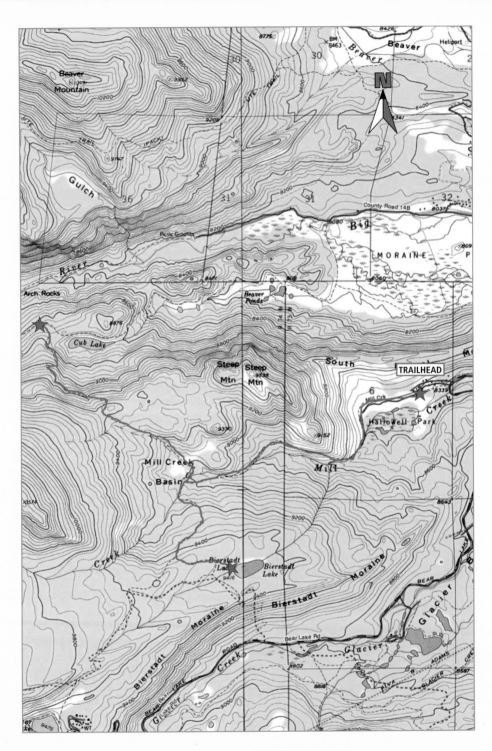

HOLLOWELL PARK and MILL CREEK BASIN

8. Sprague Lake Trails

ROUND TRIP	3.3 miles
DIFFICULTY	Easy to moderate
SKILL LEVEL	Novice snowshoers and skiers
HIGH POINT	8,900 feet
ELEVATION GAIN	200 feet
AVALANCHE DANGER	None
MAP	Trails Illustrated #200, Rocky Mountain National Park
CONTACT	Rocky Mountain National Park

COMMENT: The Sprague Lake area offers a couple of nice, easy loops for beginners or intermediate snowshoers as well as trailheads for more ambitious adventures such as the Boulder Brook and Storm Pass Trails. The easiest trip is simply around the lake itself, which is only 0.5 mile with no elevation gain. The easy longer loop can actually be started at either Glacier Basin Campground (closed during winter) or Sprague Lake. The best views are at Sprague Lake or at the campground, with some nice views through the heavy tree cover along the way. This has been a popular network of easy to moderate trails for skinny skis. Experienced skiers can use any style of ski on this route.

GETTING THERE: From Estes Park, continue west to the third traffic light, where you will see a sign for the park. Turn left at the sign and go up a hill, bear right at the stop sign, and then bear right at the intersection 0.5 mile after the next traffic light. You will see signs for the Beaver Meadows Visitors Center.

From the Beaver Meadows entrance, take the first left at 0.25 mile onto Bear Lake Road. In 5.25 miles, approximately 1 mile after Hollowell Park, the Glacier Basin Campground is on the left. Parking is on the right/north side of road and the trailhead is on the south side of the campground. Approximately 0.5 mile from the Glacier Basin Campground parking lot is the turnoff for the Sprague Lake picnic area and parking lot on the left/south side of the road. When you enter the Sprague Lake parking area, you follow a one-way road to the right; at around 10 o'clock on the road loop you will see the small picnic area and the trailhead.

THE ROUTE: As of this writing, the Petrified Forest Loop starts at the parking The longer 3-mile loop can be planned to end on either a long downhill or a grad-

Hallett Peak–Flattop Mountain ridge from Sprague Lake.

ual uphill. To start and end your trek on uphill sections, start at the Sprague Lake picnic area and follow the route counterclockwise. After ascending a 200-yard, somewhat steep hill you level out to an easy climb and enter the lodgepole pine forest. The trail is marked with orange markers on tree limbs. After about 0.5 mile you reach a trail junction (the trail to the right goes out to Bear Lake Road). The trail entering from the left has a sign that says "Glacier Gorge/Bear Lake." Turn left onto this trail and continue to climb a short distance to another trail intersection. This is where the trail intersects the Boulder Brook Trail (straight ahead) and Glacier Gorge Trail (to the right). Follow the sign to the left to the Glacier Basin Campground.

The trail now goes downhill and over Boulder Brook twice, rolling somewhat before beginning another short climb. At the crest of the hill you intersect the Storm Pass Trail on the right at about 1 mile. Stay to the left and continue downhill toward the campground. You enjoy some views across to the Beirstadt Lake ridge and Mount Wuh and into some glades of aspen and pine. At about 2.25 miles the trail breaks out of the trees for the best view of the route, with the Mummy Range in the distance to the north and Flattop Mountain and Hallet Peak to the west. If the wind isn't blowing, this is a nice sunny spot for a snack or photo break.

At the end of the switchback in about 0.25 mile there is a junction. The trail to the right returns to the picnic area along the creek: go to the left to reach the lake. Once you reach Sprague Lake at about 3 miles, there is another spectacular view to the west, and another trail junction. Either option is a short hop around the lake back to the picnic area. To the left is a trail to a picnic area for the handicapped. The picnic tables are in the shade, but the nice glade below is a windbreak. To complete the loop, take the trail to the right.

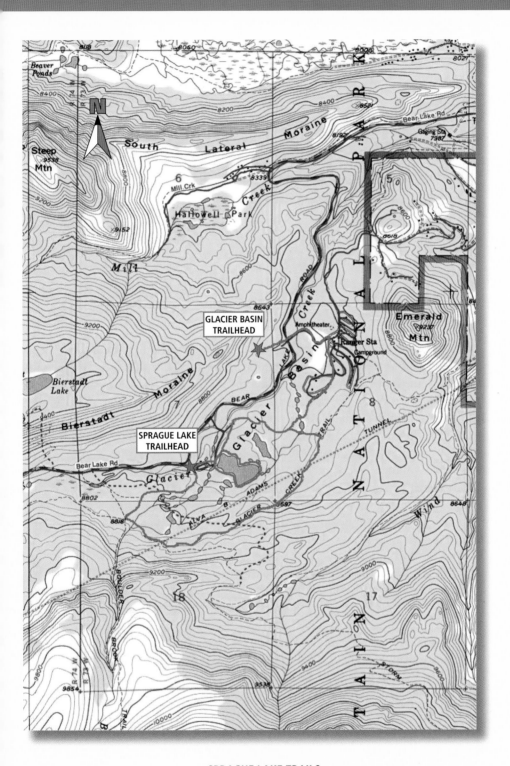

SPRAGUE LAKE TRAILS

9. Alberta Falls and The Loch

ROUND TRIP	1.2 miles to Alberta Falls; 5.4 miles to The Loch
DIFFICULTY	Easy to moderate
SKILL LEVEL	Novice snowshoers; intermediate skiers
HIGH POINT	9,400 feet at falls; 10,180 feet at lake
ELEVATION GAIN	160 feet to falls; 940 feet to lake
AVALANCHE DANGER	None
MAP	Trails Illustrated #200, Rocky Mountain National Park
CONTACT	Rocky Mountain National Park

COMMENT: The trip to Alberta Falls is a beginner family excursion if you have small children or people very reluctant to participate. The trail is usually quite safe because of the hard snowpack. You'll have to take off your snowshoes or skis if you want to walk on the rock, which is not a good idea with small children because it can be slick and ice-coated. Alberta Falls is a short, easy round-trip that can be extended. The trail continues on up to The Loch on one of the prettiest treks in the park. As you climb away from Alberta Falls and Prospect Canyon, you enjoy ever better views of the canyon and the Mummy Range behind you. There is rarely snow good enough for skiing to the falls, but it improves dramatically beyond that point. Check for excellent snow before skiing since the trail can be rocky with thin cover. Experienced skiers can use any style of ski on this route, though AT or tele skis are probably overkill.

GETTING THERE: From Estes Park, continue west to the third traffic light, where you will see a sign for the park. Turn left at the sign and go up a hill, bear right at the stop sign, and then bear right at the intersection 0.5 mile after the next traffic light. You will see signs for the Beaver Meadows Visitors Center.

From the Beaver Meadows entrance, take the first left at 0.25 mile onto Bear Lake Road. Drive 8.2 miles (.8 mile short of the Bear Lake parking lot) to the Glacier Gorge parking lot. Bear Lake Road makes a major curve around the parking lot, which fills up early, summer or winter. If it is full, park in the Bear Lake lot and walk back on the road or, preferably, on the trail connecting the two, which is a pleasant, short jaunt of about 0.4 mile. The new Glacier Gorge lot is impossible to miss, and is 1.2 miles before you reach the Bear Lake lot.

Lovely Loch in spectacular Glacier Gorge.

THE ROUTE: The trail travels west from the parking lot above the small gorge, and then descends and crosses a bridge and begins a steady but not very steep climb. It eventually climbs next to a small gorge carved out by a small stream that can boil for a short time during the spring runoff. In the winter its rock shoulders are snow-covered, and the color contrasts among the rock, trees, snow, and ice can be striking. In 0.6 mile you reach the frozen Alberta Falls, which can take on a wide variety of shapes and makes for some interesting photography.

After you reach the falls, if all is well, try venturing farther up the trail, because with every step the views get better. If you go high enough, you have a spectacular view of the Mummy Range in the distance and the cliffs of the Bierstadt Moraine across Prospect Canyon.

The trail climbs steadily through loose switchbacks to the intersection with the North Longs Peak Trail (Route 38) to the left at 1.1 miles; go right. The trail then climbs around one of the Glacier Knobs on the north side of the Icy Brook drainage, which is icy and rocky. At 1.5 miles you will reach an intersection with the Black Lake Trail to the left (up this way about 0.25 mile is Glacier Falls) and the Dream Lake trail to the right; continue straight ahead.

The scenery gets even more interesting as you near the entrance of the Loch Vale (valley). After about 0.5 mile the switchbacks level out and you enter between steep, canyon-like walls. Then, after winding your way 0.5 mile through the canyon, you will reach The Loch. The Loch, Scottish for "lake," is in a magnificent setting surrounded by Otis, Taylor, and Powell Peaks, offering great photographic opportunities.

Beyond The Loch the trail climbs again with switchbacks to Timberline Falls, Glass Lake, and Sky Pond in another mile.

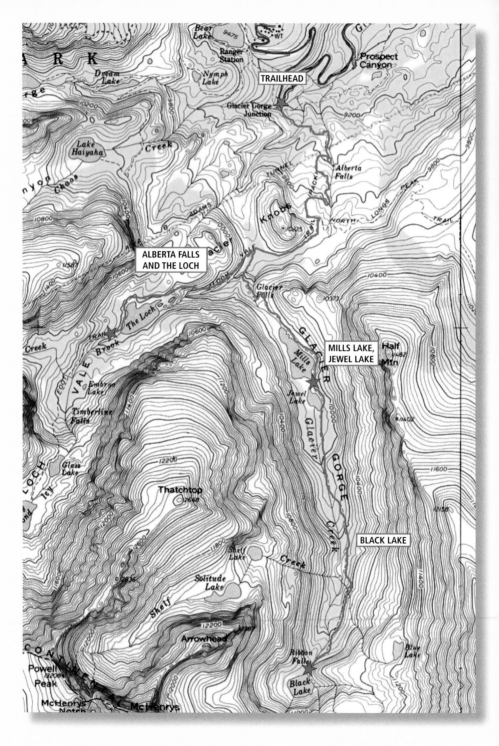

ALBERTA FALLS and THE LOCH | MILLS LAKE, JEWEL LAKE, and BLACK LAKE

10. Mills Lake, Jewel Lake, and Black Lake

ROUND TRIP	4 miles to Mills Lake; 5 miles to Jewel lake; 8 miles to Black Lake
DIFFICULTY	Moderate to challenging
SKILL LEVEL	Novice to expert
HIGH POINT	9,940 feet at Mills Lake; 9,950 feet at Jewel Lake; 10,620 feet at Black Lake
ELEVATION GAIN	700 feet to Mills Lake; 710 feet to Jewel Lake; 1,380 feet to Black Lake
AVALANCHE DANGER	None to low; last hill moderate to high
MAP	Trails Illustrated #200, Rocky Mountain National Park
CONTACT	Rocky Mountain National Park

COMMENT: If you want a superb winter adventure, Black Lake Trail is one of the park's better offerings short of climbing a peak. As with many of these destinations, it takes on an almost mystical quality in the winter that is not quite as profound on a nice summer's day. The trail visits three spectacular frozen lakes. The journey to the first two can be nice day trips in themselves. Venturing all the way to Black Lake in the winter can make for a very satisfying day for the experienced and very fit. It can be challenging for anyone, depending on conditions that often vary between bare rock and deep powder. You can usually expect to take your snowshoes off and on at different points during the trip, even if snow conditions are generally good, so be adept at doing so. Do not attempt this route unless snow conditions in the park are very good, because after about 3 miles it is usually necessary to cross rocky, windswept stretches of trail that are only snow-covered after mid-January (if at all). Check with the park's backcountry office. There are some rocky wind-swept sections that could make skiing more challenging. Good trail for skinny or mid-width skis. Unless there is a major snow dump, it is better to use snowshoes.

GETTING THERE: From Estes Park, continue west to the third traffic light, where you will see a sign for the park. Turn left at the sign and go up a hill, bear right at the stop sign, and then bear right at the intersection 0.5 mile after the next traffic light. You will see signs for the Beaver Meadows Visitors Center.

Early snowshoe season view of Black Lake.

From the Beaver Meadows entrance, take the first left at 0.25 mile onto Bear Lake Road. Drive approximately 8 miles to the new Glacier Gorge parking lot. If it is full, park in the Bear Lake lot and walk back on the trail connecting the two, which is a pleasant, short jaunt of about 0.4 mile.

THE ROUTE: The trail travels west along the small gorge for 0.25 mile and then crosses the creek on a footbridge to the south. The next 1.5 miles of this route follows the Alberta Falls Trail. Once you get beyond Alberta Falls, you continue winding back and forth over Glacier Creek next to the small gorge that gives you more than one photo opportunity. Eventually the gorge opens up, with cliffs soaring above.

At 1.1 miles you come to the North Longs Peak Trail on the left, which goes toward Granite Pass. Take the right branch toward Mills Lake and Loch Vale. The trail steepens here but there are views of The Arrowhead and Chiefs Head Peak in the distance straight ahead with Glacier Gorge on your left.

The trail then goes downhill for a short distance and eventually goes back into the trees. At 1.5 miles you reach the next trail intersection. To the right is the trail to Dream Lake; straight ahead is the trail to The Loch. Take the left branch, the Black Lake Trail, and you soon encounter a stream crossing that uses a log as a bridge. You will have to decide whether you want to cross without snowshoes on. There is a second stream crossing in a relatively short distance that features wooden steps and rocks, which should be snow-covered. Exposed rocks and cairns as well as bare wooden steps might make it necessary to take off your snowshoes temporarily. At 1.75 miles you reach Glacier Falls.

There are at least two good routes to Mills Lake. Pick your way through the best snow or take off your snowshoes and scramble over the large rock formations. You are 0.25 mile from the lake at this point, so it is well worth the trouble of surmounting the rocks and taking a circuitous route through the trees to stay in the snow. Once you reach the north shore of Mills Lake at 2 miles you can see the Keyboard of the Winds on Longs Peak. This is a great place for photos or a snack break. Mills Lake is a good place to turn around if you find the mixture of snow and rocks annoying. One of the interesting aspects of more challenging and remote trails is that they require more flexibility and creativity.

From the north end of Mills Lake you are 1 mile from the Glacier Gorge backcountry campsite and 2 miles from Black Lake. The varied trail continues with lots of interesting options over, under, and around large outcroppings and trees. Don't fret too much about staying on the trail. Don't wander too far upslope to the left (east), stay relatively close to the shores of Mills Lake and Jewel Lake, and you will be safe. Jewel Lake, whose south end is 0.5 mile beyond the north end of Mills Lake, is barely distinguishable as a separate body of water. It can be a very long 0.5 mile under windy conditions. If the lakes are solidly frozen you can use the surface to avoid obstacles, however, walk lightly or you'll damage your snowshoes.

At 3 miles you reach the backcountry campsite. In another 0.5 mile the main trail wanders away from the shore of Glacier Creek, reaching an open meadow with great views of Stone Man Pass, The Arrowhead and Chiefs Head Peak, and McHenrys Peak. You are 200 yards from the very steep stretch that takes you 0.5 mile up to the edge of Black Lake. The standard trail is to the left but sometimes it is easier to get off the trail because the snow cover is better on the steeper slope. Avoid running water and ice. Shortly before you reach Black Lake, Ribbon Falls should be a frozen spectacle. At 4 miles you reach Black Lake.

SEE MAP ON PAGE 62.

11. North Longs Peak Trail

ROUND TRIP	12.4 miles to Granite Pass
DIFFICULTY	Easy to challenging
SKILL LEVEL	Novice snowshoers; intermediate skiers
HIGH POINT	12,080 feet
ELEVATION GAIN	2,840 feet
AVALANCHE DANGER	None to high
MAP	Trails Illustrated #200, Rocky Mountain National Park
CONTACT	Rocky Mountain National Park

COMMENT: This trail is a rarity because of its beautiful views and relatively low use. Few people take it in the winter. The first 3 miles or so to the Boulder Brook Trail intersection has low to no avalanche danger most of the year. It also offers superb views on the return, of Glacier Gorge, Flattop Mountain and Hallet Peak, the Mummy Range, and the entire valley. This can be a fun ski on skinny or mid-width skis.

GETTING THERE: From Estes Park, continue west to the third traffic light, where you will see a sign for the park. Turn left at the sign and go up a hill, bear right at the stop sign, and then bear right at the intersection 0.5 mile after the next traffic light. You will see signs for the Beaver Meadows Visitors Center.

From the Beaver Meadows entrance, take the first left at 0.25 mile onto Bear Lake Road. Drive approximately 8 miles to the new Glacier Gorge parking lot. If this lot is full, park in the Bear Lake lot and walk back on the trail connecting the two, which is a pleasant, short jaunt of about 0.4 mile.

THE ROUTE: The trail travels west from the parking lot above the small gorge and then descends and crosses a bridge. It is about a 400-foot gradual gain past Alberta Falls to the intersection with the North Longs Peak Trail in 1.1 miles. Here The Loch Trail continues straight ahead, but you turn left. From this intersection it is 5.1 miles one way, or a total of 6.2 miles one way, to Granite Pass—an ambitious winter or summer round trip.

The trail goes downhill from the intersection for approximately 100 to 200 feet and you are immediately greeted by great views of the Mummy Range and valley as well as Glacier Gorge. This part of the trail is very open to sun and wind and can have sections that are in need of snow. Don't be dismayed, because you will soon be

The Mummy Range from the North Longs Peak Trail.

on a north-facing portion. Climb back out of the draw after crossing Glacier Creek. The trail levels out for a bit and enters a short new-growth forest of lodgepole and spruce. After another 0.25 mile or so you round the bend into the Boulder Brook drainage where you can get an impressive view of the summit of Longs Peak. You can also see the north shoulder of the mountain's massif soaring above and daring you to make the climb above tree line to Granite Pass.

At about 1.5 miles from the trailhead you will enter a more mature forest of taller trees; this is a reasonable turnaround point because the view is obscured until you near tree line. At about 2.25 miles the trail reaches approximately 10,000 feet. Going higher above tree line is only advisable if avalanche danger is minimal. It is safer in the late spring when the snow has consolidated. From here it is another 1 mile or so to a small stream crossing and the intersection with the Boulder Brook Trail on the left. This also makes a good turn around point for a great round-trip trek of approximately 6.6 miles.

To continue on to Granite Pass, go straight/right. At about 3.5 miles you cross Boulder Brook and begin climbing. This requires steep switch-backing about 1.5 miles through an avalanche zone that should only be crossed if avalanche danger is low. The switchbacks can be tricky in winter and require a map, compass, GPS, and good route-finding skills. After emerging above tree line the route can be wind-swept, with scarce snow.

The trail levels out at about 5 miles and climbs much more slowly for the next 0.25 mile before steepening again on the shoulder of Battle Mountain. At about 5.5 miles the ascent eases for the last 0.7 mile or so. The view from Granite Pass is a 360-degree wonder, but don't risk life or limb getting there. Turn around if avalanche conditions are dicey.

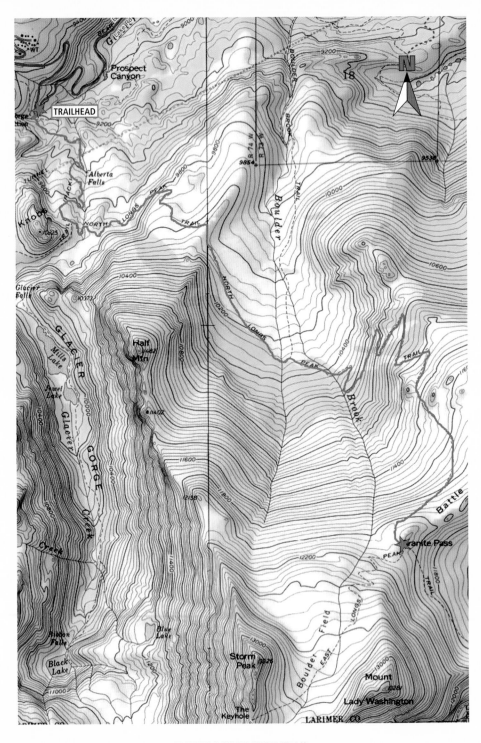

NORTH LONGS PEAK TRAIL

12. Bear Lake Loop

LOOP	1 mile
DIFFICULTY	Easy
SKILL LEVEL	Novice
HIGH POINT	9,495 feet
ELEVATION GAIN	20 feet
AVALANCHE DANGER	None
MAP	Trails Illustrated #200, Rocky Mountain National Park
CONTACT	Rocky Mountain National Park

COMMENT: The beauty of Bear Lake is being able to see stunning scenery with very little effort, which is why it is one of the most popular places in the park. The only downside is the number of people, but it is still worth the visit. All you have to do is walk 200 feet from your car uphill, and (on a clear day) you will see craggy Hallet Peak looming overhead from a dizzying height. The trail around the lake is flat, but don't forget that your visitors from the flatlands will definitely notice that the altitude is 9,500 feet (gasp). The snow on the trail is often very hard-packed, so snowshoes might be optional, but they always give better traction.

GETTING THERE: From Denver, take I-25 north 40 miles and exit at Loveland/US 34. Take US 34 west through Big Thompson Canyon 40 miles to Estes Park. Allow at least one hour and 30 minutes. Other routes from Denver include US 36 northwest through Boulder and Lyons for 60 miles to Estes Park; and I-25 north for 30 miles to Highway 66, west on Highway 66 for 15 miles to Lyons, and northwest on US 36 for 20 miles to Estes Park. When you reach Estes Park, continue west to the third traffic light, where you will see a sign for the park. Turn left at the sign and go up a hill, bear right at the stop sign, and then bear right at the intersection 0.5 mile after the next traffic light. You will see signs for the Beaver Meadows Visitors Center.

From the Beaver Meadows entrance, turn left/south in 0.25 mile onto Bear Lake Road and follow it 9 miles to its terminus to reach the Bear Lake parking lot.

THE ROUTE: The trail begins with a series of switchbacks for a half mile. Enjoy From the parking lot, you will see the ranger station on the left as you enter the trail and a description and map on the right. Continue uphill and you will see the trail to Nymph, Dream, and Emerald Lakes on your left; bear right. In about 50 feet you

Hallett Peak from the Bear Lake Loop Trail.

will see Bear Lake on your left, and, if you are lucky, Hallet Peak will be towering above you, straining your neck. This is one of the most photographed places in the park and it only took you 15 minutes to get here. If the weather is cooperating, take your photos on the way out; it can cloud up and start blowing and snowing quickly. At this point some people just return to their cars. I suggest circumnavigating the lake. I advise against walking out onto the lake. Just continue along the well-trodden path and you will see another trail on the right climbing steeply up to Bierstadt Lake and Flattop Mountain. Continue straight ahead and enjoy the varying views across the lake as you go counter-clockwise around the lake. Almost every step will give you a different perspective on the trees and frozen lake. The hill on the northwest side of the lake can be popular for sliding or sledding if there is enough snow. The hill is not too steep, so you can experiment with climbing and descending in your snowshoes in deeper snow while avoiding trees and rocks. Many a snowshoer and skier have discovered that even those pretty little aspen trees don't bend on impact with any part of your body. As you round the lake you will get a different view of the lower shoulder of Flattop Mountain, too. After you have made the circuit you will pass the Lakes trail again. If you and your family have the energy, venture up this gradually climbing trail as far as you can before returning to your vehicle. Maybe you will even make it to Nymph Lake.

Magical Glacier Gorge.

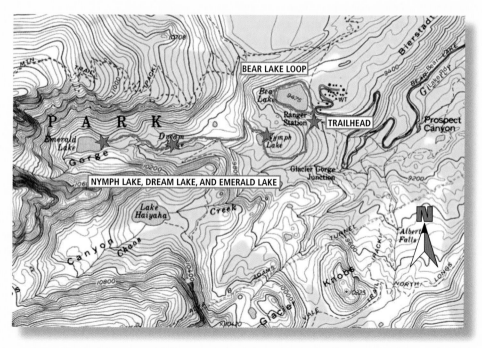

BEAR LAKE LOOP | NYMPH LAKE, DREAM LAKE, and EMERALD LAKE

13. Nymph Lake, Dream Lake, and Emerald Lake

ROUND TRIP	1 mile to Nymph Lake; 2.2 miles to Dream Lake; 3.6 miles to Emerald Lake
DIFFICULTY	Easy to moderate
SKILL LEVEL	Novice snowshoers; intermediate skiers
HIGH POINT	9,700 feet at Nymph Lake; 9,900 feet at Dream Lake; 10,100 feet at Emerald Lake
ELEVATION GAIN	225 feet to Nymph lake; 425 feet to Dream Lake; 625 feet to Emerald Lake
AVALANCHE DANGER	Low to moderate
MAP	Trails Illustrated #200, Rocky Mountain National Park
CONTACT	Rocky Mountain National Park

COMMENT: The trail to Nymph, Dream, and Emerald Lakes features some of the most beautiful scenery in the park. Because the trail is relatively short and easy to navigate, it is not difficult to understand why the lakes are also among the most popular in the park. The hard-packed snow on the lower trail can make snowshoes superfluous unless there has been fresh snow. From the parking lot, it is only 0.5 mile to Nymph Lake, so it is not a difficult trek.

This can be skied but is usually too hard-packed from heavy use so snowshoes are a better choice. Experienced skiers can use any style of ski on this route. The challenge for skiers is the hard-pack on the way down over the last mile because of the number of snowshoers packing it down. It can be icy.

GETTING THERE: From Estes Park, continue west to the third traffic light, where you will see a sign for the park. Turn left at the sign and go up a hill, bear right at the stop sign, and then bear right at the intersection 0.5 mile after the next traffic light. You will see signs for the Beaver Meadows Visitors Center.

From the Beaver Meadows entrance, turn left/south in 0.25 mile onto Bear Lake Road and follow it 9 miles to its terminus to reach the Bear Lake parking lot.

THE ROUTE: The trails in this area include many crisscrossed social trails, and it is Arriving early after a major snowstorm is best for skiing and not as important for snowshoeing if you don't mind lots of company on weekends. The trail heads south

Nancy Olsen on the Nymph Lake, Dream Lake, and Emerald Lake Trail.

and then curves west and north 0.5 mile to Nymph Lake. It is usually frozen solid and safe to cross at the height of winter, but err on the side of caution. You can loop around the lake to the right in or very near the trees to enjoy views of Hallet Peak, Thatchtop, and Flattop Mountain. Turning around at Nymph Lake is a nice, short family outing that can be combined with some off-trail walking on the way back to Bear Lake.

From the north side of Nymph Lake the trail continues uphill to the left. It requires a traverse over steep terrain that can be trying after a heavy, fresh snowfall. Once you emerge from the trees, if the snow is deep, the trail can be hard to find. Don't be drawn straight uphill to the right even though you are likely to see tracks going that way. That is a route that will probably lead you into avalanche danger. Bear left and stay at a fairly low angle. Stay above the picturesque valley spreading out on the left, and below the impressive rock cliffs looming on the right. A steady climb uphill is what you want, though there is more than one route to Dream Lake.

The route across Dream Lake.

The various paths eventually merge at the top, but bearing to the right after the initial slope is the most common route. On the return trip, the hillside that will be on the right is a nice place to run and jump through powder.

The trek from Nymph to Dream Lake is eye candy. Stately evergreens climb the mountainsides with branches and needles that seem etched in the crystal high-altitude atmosphere. You will soon have a striking view of Longs Peak. Just before you reach Dream Lake there is an intersection with the trail to Lake Haiyaha on the left; continue straight/right. In 0.6 mile from Nymph, moderate switchbacking gets you to the sleepy shoreline of Dream Lake. Weave your way through a few rocks, climb the last hillock, and then you can see the stunning setting of Dream Lake. This is definitely a terrific photo opportunity because of the exquisite surroundings: towering mountains and cliffs, scruffy wind-sculpted trees with gnarled roots, and the mists, clouds, and blowing and drifting snow of the high country in winter.

The 0.7-mile trail to Emerald Lake is straightforward. Track around the north side of Dream Lake and climb steadily over the rolling terrain with views on all sides. This can be a challenging section of trail in deep, untracked powder as you continue up Tyndall Gorge. At Emerald Lake the shoulder and cliffs of Flattop Mountain soar on the north, while Hallet Peak and Tyndall Glacier complete the panorama..

SEE MAP ON PAGE 71.

14. Flattop Mountain

ROUND TRIP	8 miles
DIFFICULTY	Moderate to challenging
SKILL LEVEL	Intermediate snowshoers/skiers to expert skiers
HIGH POINT	12,324 feet
ELEVATION GAIN	2,849 feet
AVALANCHE DANGER	Low to considerable on upper slopes; check with RMNP
MAP	Trails Illustrated #200, Rocky Mountain National Park
CONTACT	Rocky Mountain National Park

COMMENT: The addition of snow and snowshoes in winter make this challeng-ing summer hike unlikely for all but the very physically fit and more experienced winter adventurers. However, most people can handle snowshoeing at least part of the trail to enjoy some of the great views. The trail offers views of Bear Lake and the tops of Glacier Gorge and Longs Peak. If you get an early start and get lucky with the weather, summiting is a distinct possibility. This mountain has several popular ski routes aside from the main trail. You will want AT or tele skis for this route. Take the Lake Helene route to the northeast slope for good ski routes. The first mile can be very hard-packed and icy requiring carrying skis up and downhill. It is best skied after a major snowstorm. You need to be an advanced ski mountaineer to summit.

GETTING THERE: From Colorado Springs, take US 24 west to the Chipita Park/ From Estes Park, continue west to the third traffic light, where you will see a sign for the park. Turn left at the sign and go up a hill, bear right at the stop sign, and then bear right at the intersection 0.5 mile after the next traffic light. You will see signs for the Beaver Meadows Visitors Center.

From the Beaver Meadows entrance, turn left/south in 0.25 mile onto Bear Lake Road and follow it 9 miles to its terminus to reach the Bear Lake parking lot.

THE ROUTE: The trail ascends steeply on switchbacks, reaching a rock outcrop-ping Starting from the parking lot, walk to the right toward the lake. When you reach the shoreline you can see the impressive massif of Hallet Peak and the unim-pressive summit of Flattop behind. Go to the right and watch for the sign that takes

View of Flattop Mountain.

you first gradually uphill through the pretty aspen that frame both the lake and Hallet Peak. At the first intersection, about 0.2 mile, the trail to the left continues around Bear Lake; stay to the right. At the first major switchback, at 0.4 mile, you come to the Bierstadt Lake Trail straight ahead; take a left to stay on the Flattop Mountain Trail.

The next steep stretch parallels Bear Lake, affording you some of the best views of Longs Peak, Bear Lake, Glacier Gorge, and the glacier-carved U-shaped valleys. It's a perfect place for photographs because it will be a while until you break into the clear again. In about 0.25 mile the trail veers north into Engelmann spruce trees and you can see east into Mill Creek Basin. Overall you climb steadily for approximately 0.8 mile to reach the intersection with the Fern-Odessa Lake Trail. The rangers try to keep the trail sign uncovered, but deep snow can obscure most of it.

Going this far is a nice, quick trip for a family with kids. You could turn around and go back to circle Bear Lake, having enjoyed some spectacular views and gotten your heart rate up. Though the time will vary, making it this far and circling Bear Lake could easily be an hour-plus family jaunt with small children.

At the trail intersection, the Odessa Lake Trail goes straight ahead; stay to the left on the Flattop Mountain Trail, which switchbacks up. The trail climbs steadily, mostly in fir and spruce trees, until you reach the Dream Lake overlook, which is not obvious or well marked. Here once again are great views of both Longs and Hallet Peaks. Depending on the depth of the snow, just getting to tree line can easily take a couple of hours or more if you stop frequently for breaks and have to break trail through very deep powder. If you are determined, very fit, and on the move, and the snow isn't too powdery, you can make tree line in an hour or so, which is approximately 2.5 miles from the Bear Lake trailhead. When you reach tree line you likely will encounter wind, and possibly severe windchill. This is a good time to have a snack and decide if discretion is the better part of valor. The wind can blow some of the trail clear of snow, however, you can usually pick your way through to find more snow.

If you want to ski and the snow is good above tree line, track toward the northeast slope and ski down as far as the Fern Lake Trail. Going below that trail will take you into thick trees and willows and it is easy to get lost. From tree line you still have another 1.5 miles of very steep hiking to make the summit. Unless there has been a recent storm, the snow from tree line to the summit is often wind blown and sun crusted. If there has been a recent powder event with little wind, enjoy the rare ski to the top. If not, stick to snowshoes.

How long it takes from tree line to the summit is very dependent on the conditions. Turning around is highly recommended if it is snowing or if whiteouts are possible. The views are nonstop above tree line. As you near the summit there are breathtaking views of Bear Lake valley and the pointy false summit and actual summit of Hallet Peak. You can also see the Tyndall Glacier. On the flat, windswept summit that is your destination, you can see over the Continental Divide into the west side of the park and the trails that lead into the Grand Lake and Colorado River drainage.

Some people ski from the top toward Hallet Peak and then down the glacier, but this route has avalanched and caused fatalities.

FLATTOP MOUNTAIN | LAKE HELENE

15. Lake Helene

ROUND TRIP	6 miles
DIFFICULTY	Moderate
SKILL LEVEL	Intermediate snowshoers and skiers
HIGH POINT	10,620 feet
ELEVATION GAIN	1,145 feet
AVALANCHE DANGER	Low to moderate; check with RMNP
MAP	Trails Illustrated #200, Rocky Mountain National Park
CONTACT	Rocky Mountain National Park

COMMENT: This trail isn't for the fainthearted in the winter after heavy snow, but it is a spectacular route. It branches off from the Flattop Mountain Trail about 0.8 mile from Bear Lake. As with all of the routes in this book, you can bite off a smaller morsel to savor rather than attempting the whole route and still have a great time. There is a good approach for skiing the northeast slope of Flattop Mountain about 0.5 mile above the Flattop Mountain Trail turnoff on the west side. The slope is less than 25 degrees, so not extremely hazardous for avalanches.

GETTING THERE: From Estes Park, continue west to the third traffic light, where you will see a sign for the park. Turn left at the sign and go up a hill, bear right at the stop sign, and then bear right at the intersection 0.5 mile after the next traffic light. You will see signs for the Beaver Meadows Visitors Center.

From the Beaver Meadows entrance, turn left/south in 0.25 mile onto Bear Lake Road and follow it 9 miles to its terminus to reach the Bear Lake parking lot.

THE ROUTE: This hike starts from the visitor center's parking lot. The main trailhead is at the far end of the parking lot from the visitor center. The other trailhead is not so obvious. The trail starts from the entrance road to the parking lot where the road branches to the back of the visitor center for park personnel. The Revenuer's Ridge Trail is accessed from here; this is also the end of the Wapiti Nature Trail. The hike described here ends at this trailhead.

Start at the far end of the parking lot where there are interpretive signs, a trailhead sign, and a sign identifying the Wapiti Nature Trail #6. The nature trail goes to the left and the Rock Pond Trail #5 goes to the right. Take the right fork downhill and cross the Wapiti Nature Trail in 0.13 miles. Continue to a horseshoe bend on a ridge where there is a large boulder to sit on and enjoy the great views. Pass by the junction of the Preacher's Hollow Trail #4 (which nosedives into a canyon) and reach the Four Mile Overlook #44 junction after 1.1 miles. This trail goes into the Dome Rock State Wildlife Area and is good for long hikes and remote country. The Rock Pond Trail branches to the right, dropping more steeply into the canyon where Brook Pond and Rock Pond are located. After 2.1 miles, there is a 0.22-mile side trip to Brook Pond. It is worth the trip, as this is one of the most picturesque ponds in the park.

After the trail junction to Brook Pond, continue another 0.13 miles down to Rock Pond. At Rock Pond, go across the dam and find the new (as of fall 2010) Rock Canyon Trail #15. This single-track trail goes up a narrow canyon, where a bench is nestled among some boulders next to a small stream. This is a cool place to relax before the climb up the canyon.

The Rock Canyon Trail tops out at Geer Pond and, after 0.8 miles, reaches the junction of the Geer Pond Trail #25 and the Beaver Ponds Trail #26 on the north

Notchtop Mountain backdrop from the Lake Helene Trail.

A traverse on Lake Helene Trail.

side of Geer Pond. Continue northward for 0.5 miles on the Beaver Ponds Trail #26, passing another junction of the Geer Pond Trail, climbing one short, steep grade to Homestead Trail #12. Turn right onto Homestead and follow it for 0.7 miles up to Revenuer's Ridge Trail #1 near the Homestead Trailhead.

Take Revenuer's Ridge Trail to the south (right) 0.4 miles to the Lost Pond Trail. Go past the spur to the Lost Pond Trailhead and around a curve. The wide trail goes straight ahead, becoming the Livery Trail #20 to the equestrian trailhead. A single-track trail, Revenuer's Ridge, branches to the right. Continue on this trail to the Outlook Ridge Trail. Turn left (east), and go to the trailhead sign at the Outlook Ridge Trailhead. The Revenuer's Ridge Trail continues to the south (right) at the trailhead sign. Pass the Wapiti Nature Trail junction and arrive at the visitor center parking area to complete this hike.

SEE MAP ON PAGE 78.

Rocky Mountain National Park

Chapter 2

ROCKY MOUNTAIN NATIONAL PARK— SOUTHEAST

"If you know wilderness in the way you know love, you would be unwilling to let it go. . . This is the story of our past and it will be the story of our future."

—Terry Tempest Williams

Early morning on the approach to Chasm Lake.

South of Estes Park is the Longs Peak trailhead (not a park entrance). The peak was considered unclimbable from the time of its discovery by Stephen Long in 1820 until fearless, one-armed Grand Canyon navigator John Wesley Powell summited it in 1868 from the south side. His approach was especially remarkable because his party had to climb all the way up and over the Continental Divide through uncharted terrain from Grand Lake before attempting the summit. However, it is likely that Native Americans climbed the peak before him.

Longs Peak is one of those places you never tire of no matter how many times you have visited, summited, or attempted to summit it. Many an expert climber has spent an unplanned bivouac among its frigid granite cliffs praying for dawn. The towering northeast face of Longs Peak, known as the Diamond, is one of the most challenging technical climbs in North America. It requires superb high-altitude rock-climbing skills in radically variable weather between 11,000 and 14,000 feet. Former rescue ranger, the late Jim Detterline, climbed Longs over 400 times.

The true beauty of Longs Peak is the wide variety of trails that crisscross its massive expanse and makes it possible for trekkers of all skill levels to partake of its high-altitude glory. Winter months are less crowded because making the summit is impossible for all but a very select set of winter mountaineers. Another bonus is that even when there is little snow in Estes Park, this trailhead generally offers good snow because of its elevation of 9,500 feet. The trails also have excellent tree coverage that protects the snow below tree line. If it is late or early in the season you might have to do some intermittent hiking between snowshoeing.

The embrace of Wild Basin is unique and intimate as you stroll next to frozen waterfalls or make your way above tree line, where you can see 13,900-foot Mount Meeker and its soaring neighbors. You can venture as far as the Continental Divide and summit it or savor the icy lakes that are nestled below. You can also venture on to the flanks of Longs Peak up to the frozen, snow-covered tundra, where it wraps its arms around Chasm Lake. Enjoy. The options and sights are limitless in this winter wonderland. If you are lucky, you will be accompanied by elk, deer, moose, stellar jays, or mountain goats.

16. Estes Cone

ROUND TRIP	6 miles
DIFFICULTY	Moderate
SKILL LEVEL	Novice snowshoers
HIGH POINT	11,000 feet
ELEVATION GAIN	1,600 feet
AVALANCHE DANGER	Low
MAP	Trails Illustrated #200, Rocky Mountain National Park
CONTACT	Rocky Mountain National Park

COMMENT: This pleasant trek to Estes Cone offers striking views of Longs Peak and Mount Meeker as well as the Twin Sisters Peaks to the east. You can reach Estes Cone from either the Longs Peak trailhead or Lilly Lake trailhead. The Longs Peak trailhead is shorter, higher, and easier to snowshoe with more reliable snow because you will be starting at an elevation of 9,400 feet. It is generally a better route for snowshoes than skis. The final climb to the summit is not recommended for young children.

GETTING THERE: From Estes Park, take Highway 7—the Peak to Peak Highway— south 7.5 miles to the turnoff on the right/west side of the road for the Longs Peak Campground and trailhead. Go up the hill about a mile to the intersection with the campground road and bear left into the trailhead parking lot. From Denver, take I-25 north 40 miles and exit at Loveland/US 34. Take US 34 west through Big Thompson Canyon 40 miles to Estes Park. Allow at least one hour and 30 minutes. Other routes from Denver include US 36 northwest through Boulder and Lyons for 60 miles to Estes Park; and I-25 north for 30 miles to Highway 66, west on Highway 66 for 15 miles to Lyons. From Lyons, take a left on Highway 7 and drive west 14 miles then north 10 miles to the Longs Peak Campground road on the left. From Denver the route through Lyons is the best.

THE ROUTE: The trail begins at the Longs Peak Ranger Station, which is generally closed during winter months. The route starts on the Longs Peak Trail for about 0.5 mile of gradual uphill through the lodgepole pine forest. At the junction, trail signs say it is 2.7 miles to Estes Cone (the Longs Peak Trail goes left/south to Chasm Lake in 3.7 miles according to the trail sign). Turn right/north. Shortly you arrive at another junction. The trail to the right goes down into Tahosa Valley. Continue

View of snowy Estes Cone.

straight/left. At around 1 mile the trail veers to the northwest and levels off some-what before climbing gradually to Inn Brook at 1.25 miles. Just after crossing the brook, you reach the site of Eugenia Mine, where some aspen trees are mixed in with the pine. This is a good place for a snack and water break.

The trail then travels northeast downhill into Moore Park, reaching a trail junction at 1.7 miles. The trail to the right goes down into Tahosa Valley. Turn left to join the Storm Pass Trail. It goes northwest, gradually climbing to Storm Pass at 2.4 miles, where the trees begin to thin out and there is another trail junction. To the left, the Storm Pass Trail continues down to Sprague Lake; turn right/northeast to reach the rock summit of Estes Cone. Here the trail switchbacks more steeply uphill. The most challenging section is the last long switchback section because it climbs the last 1,000 feet in approximately 0.6 mile. This rocky part of the trail will reward you with the best views of Longs Peak and Mount Meeker.

Warning: If you make it to the summit area at 2.8 miles, you will have to shed your snowshoes and climb very carefully on the sometimes slick, wet, and icy rock to reach the top of the summit rocks. You can still have a very enjoyable outing by going as far as Storm Pass and walking up enough of the switchbacks to catch a few photo ops, or to the bottom of the summit rocks, then turning around. If you are fortunate you will catch a sunny day or fresh snow.

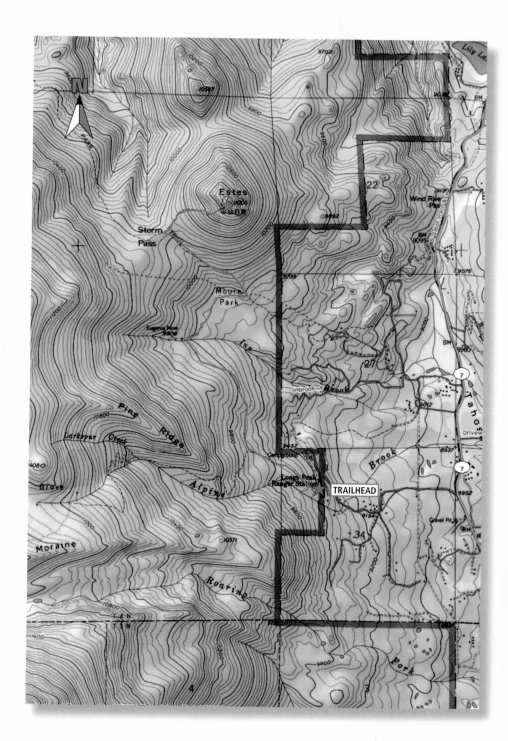

ESTES CONE

17. Chasm Lake

ROUND TRIP	8.4 miles
DIFFICULTY	Challenging
SKILL LEVEL	Intermediate to expert snowshoers or skiers
HIGH POINT	11,800 feet
ELEVATION GAIN	2,400 feet
AVALANCHE DANGER	Low to considerable, can be avoided; check with RMNP.
MAP	Trails Illustrated #200, Rocky Mountain National Park
CONTACT	Rocky Mountain National Park

COMMENT: This spectacular trek offers striking views of Longs Peak and Mount Meeker as well as the Twin Sisters Peaks to the east. The entire trail should be attempted only by those experienced in high-mountain, mid-winter travel above tree line. You have to cross one avalanche chute that could avalanche in high conditions. Check for avalanche conditions in the area before attempting the route and consider digging a snow pit if danger is moderate. It is usually safe, but the trail is easy to lose if it is not already broken, and even then people tend to blaze their own paths in the snow cover of winter when the standard route gets obliterated by drifts. It is a skiable route with AT or tele skis and advanced ski skills. You can ski the route toward Jim's Grove instead of toward the lake itself for more open, easier conditions. Since the area above tree line is sun exposed and wind scoured, conditions can vary dramatically. If the snow is old and the cover thin, you will be happier on snowshoes for the descent.

   TIP: From Lyons, take a left on Highway 7 and drive west 14 miles then north 10 miles to the trailhead on the left.

GETTING THERE: From Interstate 25, take exit 140, Nevada /Tejon. The second light off the exit ramp is Nevada. Follow the signs for Colorado 115 South and take exit 46, Lake Avenue. At the Broadmoor Hotel, bear right onto Lake Circle. Take the roundabout to head left on Mesa Drive. Mesa becomes Park Road, then becomes El Pomar Road. Follow the signs toward the Cheyenne Mountain Zoo. After 0.5 miles, turn right onto Old Stage Road. Check your odometer. Old Stage turns to dirt at 0.8 miles. Pass the Broadmoor stables at 5.6 miles, and turn left at 6.1 miles onto Forest Service Road 371 toward Emerald Valley Ranch. Follow this road 0.5 miles over a hill and look for a small parking space on the right next to a rock wall; pipe will be visible. There is only space for one to two vehicles.

A soggy spring day on the way to Chasm Lake.

THE ROUTE: The trail sets off and almost immediately passes the ruins of an old Walk 0.5 mile of gradual uphill through the lodgepole pine forest to an intersection where trail signs say it is 3.7 miles to Chasm Lake. The Storm Pass Trail splits off to the right/north where the trail sign says it is 2.7 miles to Estes Cone; continue straight/left (southwest). After the trail splits it steepens, climbing with occasional short switchbacks. Unfortunately one of the steepest sections of the trail is at the beginning when you aren't sufficiently warmed up to enjoy it. It climbs up 500 feet to 10,000 feet fairly quickly in thick tree cover and in a little less than 1 mile. It then levels a bit and climbs more gradually for the next 0.4 mile as the trees thin out allowing you coy views of the summit of Longs Peak looking down from on high, daring you to climb it. On a clear day you will enjoy an impressive view of The Diamond on Longs Peak.

As the trail starts to climb and switchback, it turns more due south, edging its way up past Goblin's Forest. You cross Larkspur Creek and then have to cross one potential avalanche chute to reach the small footbridge that crosses Alpine Brook. Don't dawdle.

In a good to average snow year the trail can be difficult to follow from this point on as it traverses south and then climbs steeply west up to 11,000 feet. Sometimes the snow is so old and hard-packed you won't need snowshoes. Don't hesitate to turn around if conditions become challenging. Soon the stunted trees reveal a spectacular view of the slope all the way to the summit. Once you are above tree line at 11,000 feet you have a panoramic view in all directions. In a thin snow year you might have to take off your snowshoes and hike because the intense sun can melt the snow off the very rocky ridge. Always keep an eye on the weather. The trail down might not be as straightforward as you remember; allow extra time for slower members of your party. Once above tree line you gradually make your way to a ridge and somewhat steep snowfield that you have to traverse to the south to reach the final stretch up Mills Moraine. Here, at about 2.8 miles, stay straight/left to veer to the south toward Chasm Lake.

Follow the ridge about a mile to 11,600 feet, then walk around a corner and be startled by the views of Longs Peak and Mount Meeker, with Peacock Pool almost 600 feet below. It can be a bit of a difficult and precarious ridge walk for a short 0.4 mile across another sometimes vertical snowfield, and then across Roaring Fork. Here a Rocky Mountain National Park hut was recently swept away in a major avalanche. It is then another 200 feet up to Chasm Lake, which is surrounded by soaring Mount Meeker and Longs Peak.

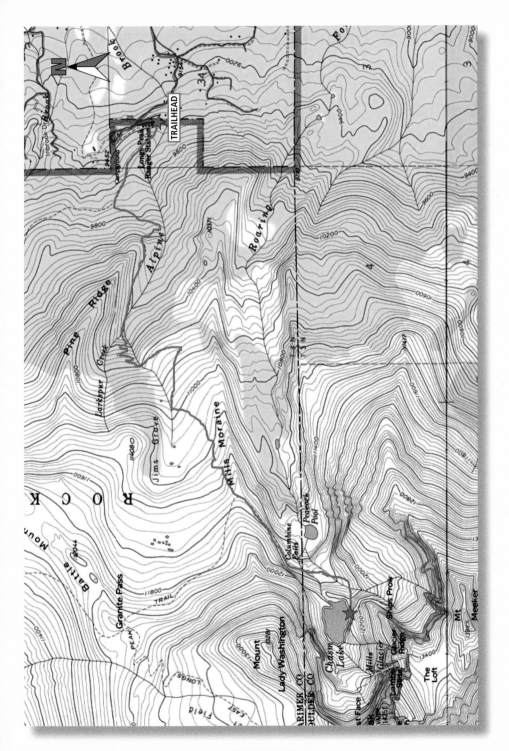

CHASM LAKE

18. Copeland Falls, Calypso Cascades, and Ouzel Falls

ROUND TRIP	3.8 miles to Copeland Falls; 6 miles to Calypso Cascades; 7.4 miles to Ouzel Falls
DIFFICULTY	Easy to moderate
SKILL LEVEL	Novice snowshoers; intermediate skiers
HIGH POINT	8,515 feet at Copeland Falls; 9,200 feet at Calypso Cascades; 9,450 feet at Ouzel Falls
ELEVATION GAIN	195 feet to Copeland Falls; 880 feet to Calypso Cascades; 1,130 feet to Ouzel Falls
AVALANCHE DANGER	None
MAP	Trails Illustrated #200, Rocky Mountain National Park
CONTACT	Rocky Mountain National Park

COMMENT: If you have young children who are not very ambitious, the short hike from the road closure near Copeland Lake to Copeland Falls might just be enough adventure for one day. For those ready for a little more distance and climbing, continue on to Calypso Cascades and Ouzel Falls, one of the most popular winter treks in Wild Basin. The trail features the subtle beauty of a frozen stream with snow-covered ice sculptures that can be enjoyed by adventurers of all ages and abilities. Call park headquarters to make sure the snow cover is adequate for snowshoes.

Since temperatures have warmed, this area rarely has enough snow for good ski conditions, so check with the park to be sure there is good coverage. It can be skied with skinny or mid-width skis. If you want to ski all the way to Ouzel or Thunder Lakes you will have challenging steep descents on skinny skis. Experienced skiers can use any style of ski on this route.

As of late 2011, the Air Force was restricting access to this part of the academy grounds to those with military IDs. This policy has varied many times in the last few years and it is hoped that full access will open again.

GETTING THERE: From Lyons travel west and north on Highway 7 to Allenspark. Wild Basin is between the small towns of Allenspark on the south and Meeker Park on the north. From Highway 7, drive west on the Wild Basin road; proceed past the lodge to Copeland Lake and around the lake to the left. The road narrows to almost single-car width. The road is closed near Copeland Lake (8,320 feet).

Copeland Mountain in Wild Basin.

THE ROUTE: Walk From the parking area, walk about 1.5 miles, either on the flat road or the adjacent horse trail on the left side of the road, to the summer trailhead at Wild Basin Ranger Station (8,500 feet; closed in winter). The trail, which is a bit more pleasant and interesting than the road, rolls gently and gains approximately 200 feet to the ranger station.

From the ranger station, proceed to the left through the parking lot to a route map and sign. Bear left and take the trail across the bridge. Take the well-marked side trail 0.4 mile from the ranger station to see Copeland Falls. The multi-level, subtle beauty of the frozen falling water is worth exploring with young children and camera in hand.

The trail continues up North Saint Vrain Creek, offering a lot of variety as it winds, rolls, and steadily climbs through a pretty mixed forest of aspen and a variety of evergreens. Parts of the trail are next to the beautiful frozen waterfalls and ice of the creek, however at times you move some distance from it. At about 2.5 miles there is a trail junction; continue straight/left.

Shortly you come to the bridge that crosses the creek about 0.4 mile below Calypso Cascades. This is a good spot for a snack break. It usually offers nice photo opportunities of the diorama of hillocks of snow and ice crystals that dress the creek. In approximately another 0.25-mile climb, you will reach the intersection of North Saint Vrain Creek and Cony Creek. Just a bit farther at the 3-mile mark is the magic of the Calypso Cascades.

At the cascades, the Allenspark Trail is on the left; bear to the right, and cross Cony Creek over two more bridges. Above the bridges are countless frozen-water cascades. At this point the trail levels for a bit and then steepens as it switchbacks straight uphill. From Calypso Cascades it is another steep 0.7 mile to Ouzel Falls. If you do not plan to go all the way to Ouzel Falls, it is worth going another 200 yards—even if it takes some gentle persuasion—to enjoy the views that open up of the west slopes of Longs Peak and Mount Meeker.

Once you get beyond the steep switchbacks you will soon cross Ouzel Creek and see Ouzel Falls in the near distance. In another 100 yards you reach an overlook at 3.7 miles with spectacular views of Longs Peak, Mount Meeker to the northwest, Meadow Mountain to the southeast, and Wild Basin and the North Saint Vrain Creek below to the north. The peaks are the primary attraction here; Ouzel Falls is unremarkable.

Ouzel Falls in Wild Basin.

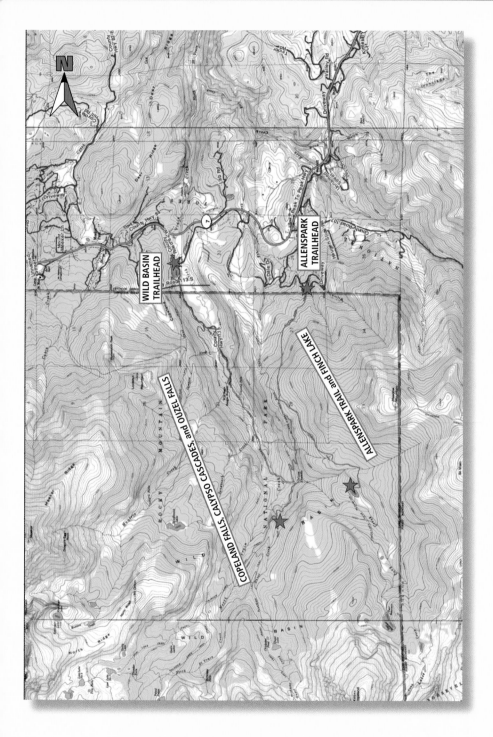

COPELAND FALLS, CALYPSO CASCADES, and OUZEL FALLS |
ALLENSPARK TRAIL and FINCH LAKE

19. Allenspark Trail and Finch Lake

ROUND TRIP	From Allenspark, 3.2 miles to overlook; 7 miles to Finch Lake
DIFFICULTY	Moderate to challenging
SKILL LEVEL	Novice snowshoers to intermediate skiers
HIGH POINT	9,760 feet at overlook; 9,912 feet at Finch Lake
ELEVATION GAIN	800 feet to overlook; 952 feet to Finch Lake
ROUND TRIP	From Wild Basin road closure, 7.6 miles to overlook; 11.4 miles to Finch Lake
DIFFICULTY	Moderate to challenging
SKILL LEVEL	Novice to falls, intermediate to expert skiers to Lake
HIGH POINT	9,760 feet at overlook; 9,912 feet at Finch Lake
ELEVATION GAIN	1,440 feet to overlook; 1,592 feet to Finch Lake
AVALANCHE DANGER	None to low. Can be avoided, check with RMNP backcountry office
MAP	Trails Illustrated #200, Rocky Mountain National Park
CONTACT	Rocky Mountain National Park

COMMENT: This trek offers two starting points that take you high above Wild Basin. You can begin at either the Wild Basin road closure at Copeland Lake, climbing up from the Wild Basin Valley, or the Allenspark trailhead higher up. The Allenspark trailhead is about 640 feet higher than the trailhead on the Wild Basin road and is about 2 miles shorter. From either, you snowshoe to an overlook where the two trails intersect, continuing up to Finch Lake if desired. You don't have to snowshoe all the way to the lake to enjoy a great view of Wild Basin. It is an interesting short side trip (out-and-back) to climb to the ridge above Wild Basin. At the overlook you are rewarded with spectacular views from above of this glacier-carved valley and the peaks that surround it. Mount Meeker and Chiefs Head Peak are just a couple of the many visible gems.

You can ski this trail on skinny skis but mid-width would be more comfortable on the descent. It would be easier to snowshoe to Finch Lake though many have skied it with good snow.

Mount Meeker view from the Allenspark Trail.

GETTING THERE: From Lyons travel west and north on Highway 7 to Allenspark. Wild Basin is between the small towns of Allenspark on the south and Meeker Park on the north. From Highway 7, drive west on the Wild Basin road; proceed past the lodge to Copeland Lake and around the lake to the left. The road narrows to almost single-car width. The road is closed near Copeland Lake (8,320 feet).

From the parking area, walk about 1.4 miles, either on the flat road or the adjacent horse trail on the left side of the road, to the Finch Lake–Pear Lake trailhead on the left before you reach the ranger station. It is about a 1.5-mile trek from this trailhead and about 3.8 miles one way from the road closure to the overlook near the top of the ridge, with an approximately 1,440-foot climb on switchbacks to reach the ridge. Upon arriving you have great views of Meeker, Longs, Chiefs Head, Pagoda, and the entire Wild Basin stretched before your feet. At this point you could turn around and have a satisfying round trip. To continue to Finch Lake, see below.

Allenspark Trail to overlook: From Highway 7, follow signs for the Allenspark/Ferncliff business route. When you reach the center of this small town, near the post office and church, turn west on CR 90. Stay on this road as it meanders for several miles. When you see Meadow Mountain Drive, turn right and reach the trailhead and parking lot in approximately 200 feet. The road from this point might not be passable in winter unless you have four-wheel drive.

North Saint Vrain Creek on Finch Lake Trail from Wild Basin.

THE ROUTE: The Allenspark Trail is more scenic than the trail from the Wild Basin valley floor; it is a steady climb with some variation all the way to the overlook. At about 0.8 mile there is a trail on the right—a short connector to the Wild Basin Trail. Continue straight/left. After approximately the first mile there are breaks in the trees and you start getting nice views of Chiefs Head, Pagoda Mountain, Meeker, and a bit of Longs Peak. The last 0.5 mile to the overlook provides even more nice views, with the grand finale, the overlook itself, at 1.6 miles, where you get a 180-degree view of the peaks and the valley.

Overlook to Finch Lake: This is a challenging addition to either of the routes. From the trail junction at the overlook, the Allenspark Trail continues straight ahead, and the trail down to the right goes to Wild Basin Road; take the Finch Lake–Pear Lake Trail to the left (southwest). You reenter the trees and climb steadily toward the lake, passing through a small section of trail that was burned in the 1978 fire. In about 1 mile you cross a stream. After the first stream crossing, you dip into and out of the drainage and reach another stream crossing in about 0.5 mile. The trail then follows a small ridge 0.4 mile down to the lake in 1.9 miles from the overlook.

SEE MAP ON PAGE 96.

Indian Peaks Area

Chapter 3

PEACEFUL VALLEY

"I am glad I shall never be young without wild country to be young in. Of what avail are forty freedoms without a blank spot on the map?"

—Aldo Leopold, *A Sand County Almanac* (1949)

Sawtooth Mountain from Beaver Reservoir near Coney Flats.

True to its name, Peaceful Valley is a tranquil riparian area northwest of Boulder just outside of the Indian Peaks Wilderness. Enjoy spectacular views of jagged Sawtooth Mountain and its soaring 12,000-foot unnamed neighbor that guard Buchanan Pass on the south and north respectively. Meander the Middle Saint Vrain Creek drainage and experience a mixture of high mountain meadows, rock outcrops, and a variety of evergreen and aspen trees. At 8,500 feet this heavily forested area below tree line offers some of the lowest and easiest trails with consistent snow.

The area absorbs a lot of weekenders because it offers many snowshoeing routes to choose from. Begin just before the Peaceful Valley Campground at a trailhead known by several monikers: Middle Saint Vrain, Buchanan Pass, and Peaceful Valley. This gives you the option of using either Middle Saint Vrain Road or the Buchanan Pass Trail for an out-and-back or loop. Other options would be to start at trailheads near Beaver Reservoir off of CR 96 to explore Coney Flats Trail or the Sourdough Trails.

Peaceful Valley can be reached from Nederland, Lyons, or Estes Park.

Ski touring in the Rainbow Lakes area.

20. Buchanan Pass Trail and Middle Saint Vrain Creek

ROUND TRIP	10.8 miles to tree line
DIFFICULTY	Easy to moderate
SKILL LEVEL	Novice snowshoers; intermediate skiers
HIGH POINT	9,880 feet at tree line
ELEVATION GAIN	1,360 feet to tree line
AVALANCHE DANGER	None to low
MAP	Trails Illustrated #102, Indian Peaks, Gold Hill
CONTACT	Boulder Ranger District, Roosevelt National Forest

COMMENT: This is an easy trek on a heavily used trail that starts on a road and then parallels it while passing through rolling, forested terrain. It is wise to arrive early to avoid the large, midday weekend crowds. This trail is good for snowshoers of all ages and skill levels and it is a good place to go on windy days because of the heavy tree cover that shields you from the wintry blasts once you get beyond Camp Dick Campground.

The first mile is sun and wind exposed and usually has crusty snow, but after that the tree cover usually provides good snow protection making the skiing better in the trees. This route can be skied with skinny or mid-width skis if you have good ski skills. Skiing out on the trail and back on the road can work well with skis if you want a quicker descent on the road. The road is sometimes hard-packed and icy so you will want metal edges on your skis. If you are on snowshoes stay on the trail for an out and back.

GETTING THERE: From Denver, take I-25 to Highway 66 and go west 16 miles to Lyons. From Fort Collins drive US 287 south to Highway 66 and go west to Lyons. From Boulder, take Highway 36north to Highway 66, and then turn west on 66 to Lyons.

From Lyons, turn south on Highway 7 and drive 14 miles to Highway 72, the Peak to Peak Highway, then turn south on Highway 72 toward Nederland. The Peaceful Valley area is west of Highway 72 a couple of miles south of Raymond. From Nederland, drive north on Highway 72 about 5 miles past Ward.

Mountain view from Buchanan Pass Trail.

On Highway 72 heading south, when you see the turnoff for Peaceful Valley about 3.5 miles south of Raymond, you are close, but don't take the Peaceful Valley turnoff. Take the second turnoff on the right (west) after Peaceful Valley. Look for signs for Peaceful Valley Campground, Forest Access, or Camp Dick. The highway marker is a small brown sign with a tent symbol on it. Turn onto FR 114. The turnoff is approximately 6 miles north of Ward.

THE ROUTE: At the beginning of this route the snow can be a bit thin. Some of the best views for photography are at the beginning of the trail and in the Peaceful Valley Campground. If it is pictures of peaks you want, snap away at Mount Audubon and Sawtooth Peak here, because in about a mile you will reach heavy forest. For the first mile the route follows the road between Peaceful Valley Campground and Camp Dick Campground, crossing Middle Saint Vrain Creek twice. Past the gate at the far end of the road, the unpaved road continues along the south side of the creek; take the trail, which crosses to the creek's north side on a small footbridge. The snow improves dramatically once you enter the trees. The streamside and short hill are a pretty setting here, and after 1 mile of walking it is a good place for a water break and/or photos.

At around 2 miles you will pass through some open meadows. Enjoy the warm sunshine before entering the cool forest. Some nice rock outcrops are good for lounging in the sun while you have a snack. It is a very wide valley. The road and trail climb very gently, offering a variety of mountain scenery. There is a side trail for horses that, because it is less traveled, offers powder rather than the hard-packed snow on the main trail. Though the horse trail is not shown on maps, it is within view of the main trail. It offers more rolling terrain and rock outcrops to climb for variety.

On the main trail at 2.5 miles, cross a side stream; at 3 miles is another open meadow. The challenging spots on the horse trail are at about the 3-mile mark where the trail narrows around a rock and above a drop into the creek, where there is a bypass with extra climbing. The main trail crosses another side stream at 3.5 miles. At 4.5 miles the end of the road crosses the creek and joins the trail. It is about 0.4 mile farther to the Indian Peaks Wilderness boundary and a trail junction. A tree line of sorts, another 0.5 mile beyond the wilderness boundary, offers nice views but a very long return trek unless you are on skis.

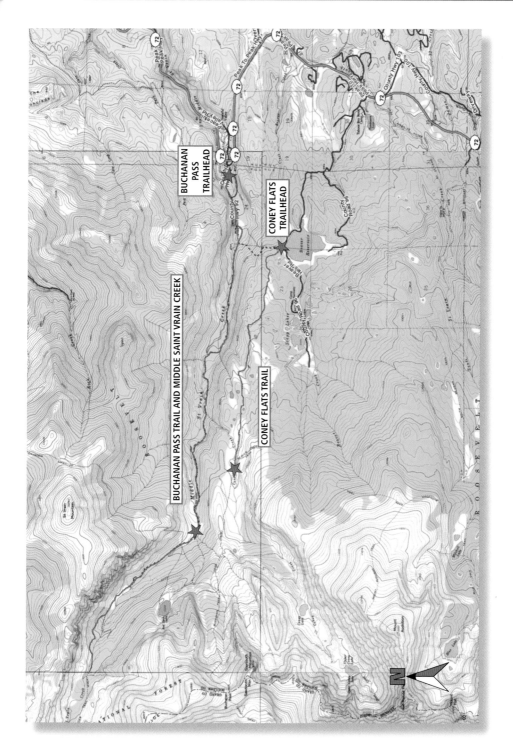

BUCHANAN PASS TRAIL and MIDDLE SAINT VRAIN CREEK

21. Beaver Reservoir-Coney Flats Trail

ROUND TRIP	7 miles to tree line
DIFFICULTY	Easy to moderate
SKILL LEVEL	Novice snowshoers; intermediate skiers
HIGH POINT	9,800 feet
ELEVATION GAIN	600 feet
AVALANCHE DANGER	None to low
MAP	Trails Illustrated #102, Indian Peaks, Gold Hill
CONTACT	Boulder Ranger District, Roosevelt National Forest

COMMENT: This relatively easy, out-of-the-way trail is primarily in the trees but does offer some nice views along the way of St.Vrain and Meadow Mountain. There are some great views of the Indian Peaks from Beaver Reservoir including Sawtooth. If the weather is iffy and you want peak pictures, take them before using the trail in case the weather socks in. Go as far as you like before turning around. This trail has become more popular with skiers than with snowshoers. This is a rolling and climbing "skinny" or mid-width ski trail. If you want to go all the way to Coney Lake, mid-width, AT, or tele skis would be a better choice.

GETTING THERE: From Interstate 25, take exit 141 (US 24/Cimarron Street) From Denver, take I-25 to Highway 66 and go west 16 miles to Lyons. From Fort Collins drive US 287 south to Highway 66, and go west to Lyons. From Boulder, take Highway 36north and then Highway 66 west to Lyons, or from Boulder take Canyon Boulevard/Highway 119 west to Nederland.

From Lyons, turn south on Highway 7 and drive 14 miles to Highway 72, the Peak to Peak Highway, then turn south on Highway 72 toward Nederland. The Peaceful Valley area is west of Highway 72 a couple of miles south of Raymond. From Nederland, drive north on Highway 72 about 5 miles past Ward. In 3 miles past the Peaceful Valley turnoff, past the Middle Saint Vrain/Camp Dick Campground turnoff, look on the west side of the highway for the one sign for CR 96 and the Tahosa Boy Scout Camp. The CR 96 turnoff is approximately 2.5

Mount Meeker view from the Allenspark Trail.

miles north of Ward and the Brainard Lake Recreation Area. Drive west on CR 96, passing the entrance to the Boy Scout camp, the Sourdough trailhead on the south side of the road in 2 miles, and the spillway of Beaver Reservoir at 2.75 miles. Then look for the trail on the right/north side of the road. You can turn around at a wide spot about 0.25 mile west and then park as close as you can get to the trailhead gate.

THE ROUTE: The first 0.9 miles of the hike are on the old exit of Cave of the Winds, A trailhead sign gives the distance to Coney Flats as 4 miles, one way. You can have an excellent ski or snowshoe in less than that distance. The main 507

Trail passes the Cutoff Trail to Camp Dick that is on the right in less than 100 yards, bear straight/left. If you want to take the Cutoff Trail down to Camp Dick, be ready for a steep, windy descent that is easy on snowshoes but challenging on skis. The main trail climbs after the Cutoff Trail and then descends and climbs again repeatedly. You will see several false trails coming in from the left and right, ignore them. The main trail is heavily used, with some 507 signs. After 0.5 mile the 507B Trail option will be on your left. It is less heavily used and generally more powdery than the main trail. It also winds and climbs a bit more steeply, rejoining the main trail in about 1 mile. Less-experienced skiers should stay on the main trail. If you want a short loop, go up the main trail and back on the 507B Trail. The trail rolls as it climbs, so you will climb at least 300 to 400 feet in the first 1.4 miles where you will reach a large sign that says skiers and hikers go right/ straight, bikers and cars left. If you want a view, venture into the trees to the right of the trail and you can see Saint Vrain and Meadow Mountains on a clear day. Some turn around here for a nice, short family outing. The main trail descends a bit more steeply for 0.25 mile before leveling then continuing to roll up and down hill. If you want a longer, steeper climb and descent adventure, go left on the Coney Flats Road at the large sign, rather than straight on the main trail. You will wind uphill and down dale and rejoin the main trail in 1.8 miles versus 1.2 miles. Don't attempt it unless you have excellent route finding skills since it isn't as heavily used or well marked. When the Coney Flats Road rejoins the trail you will be 0.6 mile from the Coney Flats/Creek Trailhead. Go straight for Buchanan Pass, or left for the Coney Creek Trail. Coney Creek goes toward Coney Lake below avalanche terrain; the pass climbs much more steeply though safely. A hard right will take you down to the Middle Saint Vrain Road/Trail where you might see snowmobiles. You will have a 6.4-mile round trip from this intersection if you turn around. On a clear day, you will have some nice views to savor for your efforts, but probably some wind, too.

SEE MAP ON PAGE 101.

22. North Sourdough Trail

ONE WAY	1.25 miles to Middle Saint Vrain Creek
DIFFICULTY	Easy to moderate
SKILL LEVEL	Novice snowshoers; intermediate skiers
HIGH POINT	9,140 feet at trailhead
ELEVATION GAIN	540 feet
ONE WAY	1.5 miles via Beaver Reservoir Cutoff Trail
DIFFICULTY	Easy
SKILL LEVEL	Novice snowshoers; intermediate skiers
HIGH POINT	9,200 feetd
ELEVATION GAIN	60 feet
ONE WAY	5 miles to Red Rock trailhead
DIFFICULTY	Moderate to challenging
SKILL LEVEL	Novice snowshoers; intermediate skiers
HIGH POINT	10,000 feet
ELEVATION GAIN	860 feet
AVALANCHE DANGER	Low
MAP	Trails Illustrated #102, Indian Peaks, Gold Hill
CONTACT	Boulder Ranger District, Roosevelt National Forest

COMMENT: From Beaver Reservoir you can take the North Sourdough Trail either north or south. The snow is generally better to the north. The route to the south, between Beaver Reservoir and Red Rock trailhead, is often plagued by spotty snow and is quite rocky early or late season. If there has just been a major spring snowfall in the area it will be okay. The route south from Beaver Reservoir to Red Rock Lake is best done one-way with a vehicle shuttle. More accessible, popular access points for the South Sourdough Trail are in the Brainard Lake Recreation Area at Red Rock trailhead, or farther south at Rainbow Lakes trailhead. The South Sourdough Trail from Red Rock trailhead to Rainbow Lakes has more reliable snow and is better for skiing.

Snowshoers on the North Sourdough Trail.

GETTING THERE: From Denver, take I-25 to Highway 66 and go west 16 miles to Lyons. From Fort Collins drive US 287 south to Highway 66, and go west to Lyons. From Boulder, take Highway 36 North and then Highway 66 west to Lyons, or from Boulder take Canyon Boulevard/Highway 119 west to Nederland. From Lyons, turn south on Highway 7 and drive 14 miles to Highway 72, the Peak to Peak Highway, then turn south on Highway 72 toward Nederland. The Peaceful Valley area is west of Highway 72 a couple of miles south of Raymond. From Nederland, drive north on Highway 72 about 5 miles past Ward. In 3 miles past the turnoff for Peaceful Valley and past the Middle Saint Vrain/Camp Dick Campground turnoff, look on the west side of the highway for the one sign for CR 96 and the Tahosa Boy Scout Camp. The CR 96 turnoff is approximately 2.5 miles north of Ward and the Brainard Lake Recreation Area. Drive west on CR 96, passing the entrance to the Boy Scout camp. The Sourdough trailhead is 2 miles west of Highway 72, about 0.25 mile before Beaver Reservoir, on the south side of the road. Another access point is at the Coney Flats trailhead, on the right/east side of the road a little more than 0.75 mile farther. It is called the Beaver Reservoir Cutoff Trail on some maps.

THE ROUTE: From the Sourdough trailhead, the trail to the north is a short route to Middle Saint Vrain Creek. In 0.25 mile it crosses Beaver Creek, and at about 0.75 mile the Beaver Reservoir Cutoff Trail comes in on the left. Continue straight to reach Middle Saint Vrain Creek. You can also turn left onto the hilly, heavily forested Beaver Reservoir Cutoff Trail at 0.75 mile, which takes you uphill to the Coney Flats Trail in another 0.75 mile. It can be a fun, short trip with a car shuttle, or you can take your snowshoes off and walk 0.75 mile on the road back to your car to close the loop at 2.25 miles.

From the Sourdough trailhead, the trail to the south climbs between two hills, crosses a gated road at about 0.75 mile, and intersects with the Baptiste Ski Trail at about 1.4 miles, and with the Wapiti Ski Trail at about 2.4 miles. It travels downhill and then uphill until a trail junction at about 3.1 miles. From there the South Saint Vrain Trail goes straight/right up to Brainard Lake. Go left on the South Saint Vrain Trail toward the Red Rock trailhead.

In about a mile is another trail junction at 4.2 miles. The South Saint Vrain Trail continues straight/left; go right on the Sourdough Trail and cross South Saint Vrain Creek. In about another mile you will reach the Red Rock Lake trailhead at a little over 5 miles. It is a long, very hilly trek.

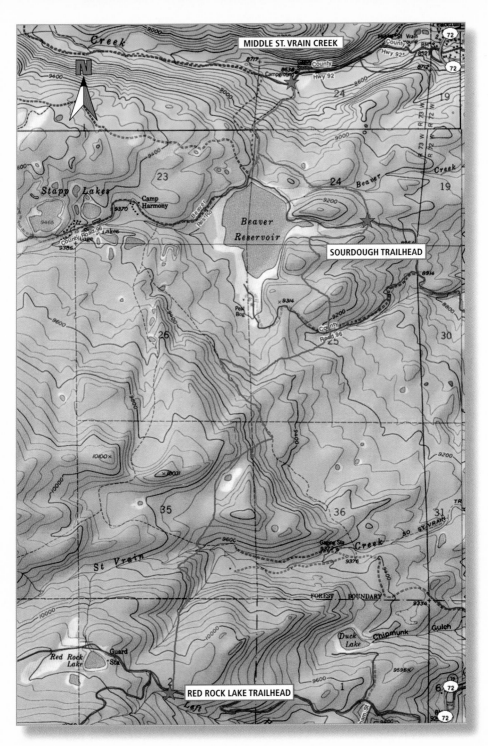

NORTH SOURDOUGH TRAIL

Indian Peaks Area

Chapter 4
BRAINARD LAKE RECREATION AREA

"Twenty years from now you will be more disappointed by the things that you didn't do, than by the ones you did do. So throw off the bowlines. Sail away from the safe harbor. . . Explore. Dream. Discover."

—Mark Twain (1835-1910)

Paiute Peak and Mount Audubon from Red Rock Lake snowshoers-only trail.

Brainard Lake Recreation Area bordering the Indian Peak Wilderness Area is one of the most popular places in the state for snowshoeing and cross-country skiing. When you see the stunning setting, you will know why. The Indian Peaks are a formidable and thoroughly enticing backdrop that makes it worthwhile to endure the popularity of this place. This glacier-carved Continental Divide mountain "wall" was once proposed to become part of Rocky Mountain National Park to protect the area, but it was feared the designation would cause it to be overrun with people. It is hard to imagine that it could be used more heavily than it is; however, it absorbs a large number of people very well because of the number of trail options. Weekday visits are highly recommended. If that isn't possible, then early arrival for a parking space is suggested, though the new parking lots help ease the situation.

The Forest Service strives to spread out the users and maintain the wilderness appeal of the area. First, the USFS asks that, if at all possible, you leave your pets at home. The heavy usage in the relatively small area would be much more palatable if there were fewer dogs. There are three trails that are designated dog-free: Little Raven, Waldrop, and the Colorado Mountain Club (CMC) Trail. The USFS also has some separate trails for skiers and snowshoers so that snowshoers don't have to walk in skiers' tracks and skiers don't have to zoom around the slower snowshoers.

Directions: From Boulder, take Canyon Boulevard/Highway 119 west 14 miles to Nederland. At Nederland, turn right/north on Highway 72, the Peak to Peak Highway, and go approximately 9 miles. The town of Ward is on the right/east side of the road. Watch for the Brainard Lake Recreation Area turnoff immediately on the left/west side of the road after the Ward turnoff

Snowshoers enjoying a balmy spring trail day near Brainard Lake.

23. South Sourdough Trail

ROUND TRIP	12 miles
DIFFICULTY	Moderate (one-way or out-and-back) to challenging (round trip)
SKILL LEVEL	Novice snowshoers; intermediate skiers
HIGH POINT	10,200 feet
ELEVATION GAIN	From Red Rock trailhead to Rainbow Lake, gain of 500, loss of 900 feet From Rainbow Lakes trailhead, gain of 1,000 feet, loss of 400 feet
AVALANCHE DANGER	Low
MAP	Trails Illustrated #102, Indian Peaks, Gold Hill; USGS Ward
CONTACT	Boulder Ranger District, Roosevelt National Forest

COMMENT: The South Sourdough Trail, though popular, has much less traffic than other trails in and around the Brainard Lake Recreation Area. You won't get quite the stunning views of the Indian Peaks Wilderness, but you will get beautiful views of the foothills and plains. From the Red Rock trailhead you can go either north or south. Both routes offer a rolling, hilly, sheltered trail. The route to the south is a bit easier than going north toward Beaver Reservoir. You can just go south for as far as you like and then turn around. You can easily have an enjoyable hour or two with an out-and-back route. Going all the way to the Rainbow Lakes Trail is a half-day or full-day adventure with a descent to the Rainbow Lakes parking area at the end. The Brainard Lake–Red Rock end is higher, so starting at the Rainbow Lakes end is a climb of 1,000 feet. This trail is well marked with blue diamonds and arrows. This trail is equally popular with skiers and snowshoers. It is an advanced ski trail because of some steep sections and tight turns. Experienced skiers can use any style of ski on this route.

GETTING THERE: Take From Nederland, turn right/north on Highway 72, the Peak to Peak Highway, and go approximately 9 miles. The town of Ward is on the right/east side of the road. Watch for the Brainard Lake Recreation Area turnoff immediately on the left/west side of the road after the Ward turnoff. From Highway 72, drive west on the Brainard Lake Road to the gate closure in about 3 miles. The Sourdough Trail is just east of the gate closure, crossing the road at the Red Rock trailhead parking area.

South Sourdough Trail near Rainbow Lakes Trailhead.

For Rainbow Lakes access from Boulder, take Canyon Boulevard/Highway 119 west 14 miles to Nederland. At Nederland, turn right/north on Highway 72, the Peak to Peak Highway, for approximately 6 miles. Turn west on the Rainbow Lakes campground road, also marked for the University of Colorado Mountain Research Station. The parking lot is approximately 1 mile on the south/left side of the road.

THE ROUTE: From the campground sign, cut through the first campsite to the bridge From the Red Rock trailhead parking area on Brainard Lake Road: Go toward the summer entrance and turn left. Take the Sourdough Trail south and go downhill to cross Left Hand Creek. The trail then climbs as it rolls to introduce you to the Sourdough routine. The trail gradually ascends and in about 0.4 mile the Little Raven Trail goes off to the right; continue straight/left in thick trees. The trail rolls up and down, and twists while gradually climbing for another 0.8 mile where it reaches the trail's high point at 10,200 feet. Enjoy the trees, the intermittent views, and the roller coaster as the trail rolls along at around 10,000 feet. It then climbs to another stream crossing at about 1.75 miles. The trail levels and continues due south for 0.75 mile affording nice views. Then it turns sharply west/right at about 2.6 miles. In another mile it drops to Four Mile Creek, and then the Peace Memorial Bridge at around 3.5 miles. This is a good turnaround point for an out-and-back, or you can turn around before descending 100 feet into the drainage to save the climb back out. The trail switchbacks into the drainage to cross Four Mile Creek, then climbs back up and continues due south another 0.75 mile or so. At about 4 miles the trail winds to the east and then south for

1 mile, descending the ridgeline to the Rainbow Lakes Road at 6 miles.

From the Rainbow Lakes parking area: This starting point will provide you with an 800-foot climb, from around 9,200 feet to around 10,000 feet, over the first 2.5 miles. The high point of the trail, 10,200 feet, is at the north end. You will then gain and lose at least another 200 feet along the way on the roller coaster, dropping into and out of a couple of creek drainages. The trail is north of the parking area. It travels gradually uphill west, levels, and resumes with a steeper climb. Bear right at the first

Weathered Sourdough Trail sign.

arrow, and then left at the next one as the trail turns west and opens up to a view of Niwot Ridge and Mountain at around 9,400 feet. The trail turns sharply left/south, and begins a series of steeper switchbacks, paralleling the University of Colorado Mountain Research Station road. At 1 mile it levels at the top of the switchbacks at 9,600 feet and tracks north, crosses a power line with views of the Peak to Peak Highway, and then travels west along the ridge with views of Niwot Mountain as it climbs to around 9,700 feet. In an open aspen area the trail turns sharply north/right and climbs up to 9,800 feet, then descends briefly before climbing up to a Sourdough Trail sign that says it is still 5 miles to the other end at the Red Rock trailhead (sigh). There is a flat stretch for 0.3 mile to the north, and then a steep uphill to the northwest that ends at almost 9,900 feet, with a short descent to the Peace Memorial Bridge at Four Mile Creek. This is a good place to turn around, giving you almost a 5-mile round trip, unless you want to climb higher and see a few views of Golden Gate Canyon State Park in the distance as the trail tracks north. The trail climbs again, turning sharply left/south to begin switchbacks up to 10,000 feet. Once you reach 10,000 feet you will enjoy another roller coaster ride with intermittent views.

LITTLE RAVEN TRAIL

This short connector trail between the South Sourdough Trail and Left Hand Reservoir Road is a fun, challenging sidelight for experienced skiers with excellent ski skills. You will want wider AT or tele skis for the descent, though it can be done on skinny skis. You can access the trail from Left Hand Reservoir Road, about 1 mile from the winter trailhead. Trek left at the first intersection and be ready for a steep twisty descent down to the South Sourdough Trail. You can also access it by going south on the Sourdough Trail from the Red Rock trailhead in the Brainard winter parking lot.

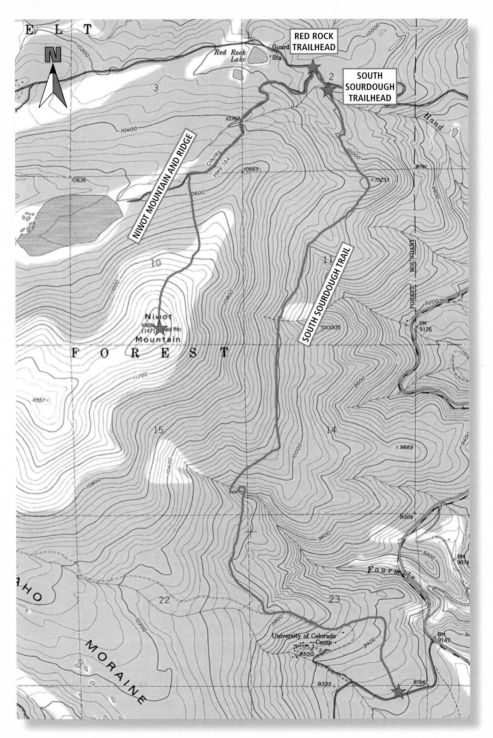

SOUTH SOURDOUGH TRAIL | NIWOT MOUNTAIN and NORTH NIWOT RIDGE

24. Niwot Mountain and Ridge

ROUND TRIP	6 miles
DIFFICULTY	Challenging
SKILL LEVEL	Intermediate to expert snowshoers and skiers
HIGH POINT	11,557 feet
ELEVATION GAIN	1,557 feet
AVALANCHE DANGER	Low to moderate
MAP	Trails Illustrated #102, Indian Peaks, Gold Hill
CONTACT	Boulder Ranger District, Roosevelt National Forest

SKI ICON

COMMENT: This high ridge towering to the south of the Brainard Lake area can offer an interesting winter adventure. It has a grand view of the majestic Indian Peaks and Longs Peak without requiring you to travel the length of Brainard Lake Road. There are two approaches to Niwot Ridge, but one of them—the western approach from Long Lake—is not recommended because of high avalanche hazard. You can reach the eastern approach from either the Left Hand Reservoir Road or the Sourdough and Little Raven Trails. There is no marked trail on this approach to the ridge top, so good route finding and bushwhacking skills are required, plus a topo map and compass. This climb is best attempted on a calm day. Niwot Mountain and Ridge are often windswept, so be prepared for hiking as well as snowshoeing. Most of the slopes are low-angle, and avalanche-hazard areas can be avoided. You will want AT or tele skis for this rare adventure. You need a major snowstorm and no wind, a rare combination for this route. It is usually wind scoured and crusty, but occasionally you can get lucky and then you can experience lots of nice turns.

GETTING THERE: From Nederland, turn right/north on Highway 72, the Peak to Peak Highway, and go approximately 9 miles. The town of Ward is on the right/east side of the road. Watch for the Brainard Lake Recreation Area turnoff immediately on the left/west side of the road after the Ward turnoff. From Highway 72, drive west on the Brainard Lake Road to the gate closure in about 3 miles. The Red Rock trailhead parking lot is just east of the gate closure. Left Hand Reservoir Road is at the entrance station west of the Red Rock trailhead parking lot. The Sourdough Trail is across the road from the parking area. The route described here takes the trails on the way up and then the road, which is about 0.3 mile shorter, on the way down.

Clouds over Niwot Mountain.

THE ROUTE: Take the Sourdough Trail south and cross Left Hand Creek. The trail rolls gently approximately 0.5 mile to reach the intersection with the Little Raven Trail. There should be a sign marking the Little Raven Trail. Turn right/west onto the Little Raven Trail (the South Sourdough Trail continues straight/left). The Little Raven Trail alternates between steep and moderate climbing. As it nears Left Hand Reservoir Road it levels out a bit and climbs more slowly. In approximately 0.6 mile you will reach the intersection with Left Hand Reservoir Road at 1.1 miles. Turn left/southwest onto the road (to the right is your return path). There is a sign on the right for the Little Raven Trail, which goes on to Brainard Lake; stay on the road. Climb approximately 150 yards up the Left Hand Reservoir Road to an old gravel pit or mine on the south side of the road, where you leave the road for the ridge at about 1.2 miles.

Climb up the hill to the left/east side of the mine, then bear southeast/left when you enter the trees. You climb steeply and gain about 200 feet in the first 0.25 mile through thick trees. After 0.15 mile you are on a more gradual ascent path at around 10,600 feet and about 1.5 miles from the trailhead; pick the best route and angle to the southwest. After climbing another 0.25 mile and another 200 feet to 10,800 feet you will encounter stunted pine trees at 1.7 miles. At this point you already have great views of Longs Peak to the north and Mount Toll, Pawnee Peak, and Mount Audubon to the west. If the wind is howling, turn around.

If it is one of those rare days, note carefully where you have emerged from the trees and pick your way southwest up the ridge for 0.5 mile. Look back frequently so you'll know where to reenter the trees on your return. At about 2.3 miles, angle south toward the rock shelter visible on the top of the ridge. It offers a nice windbreak for a snack or photos. The Niwot Mountain summit is the high point at the east end of the ridge at 11,471 feet. Continue about a mile southwest along the ridge to the second high point at 11,557 and 3.25 miles. If you are in a high point–bagging mood, you can continue slightly northwest another mile to 11,679 feet. You must turn around before the Boulder watershed boundary.

On the return when you reach Left Hand Reservoir Road, stay on it. About 0.1 mile after the intersection to the right with the Little Raven Trail, cross Left Hand Creek. The road continues with some nice views to the north and then descends for a mile back to Brainard Lake Road.

SEE MAP ON PAGE 113.

25. Red Rock Lake and Brainard Lake

ONE WAY	0.75 mile to Red Rock Lake
DIFFICULTY	Easy
SKILL LEVEL	Novice skiers and snowshoers
HIGH POINT	10,100 feet
ELEVATION GAIN	100 feet
ONE WAY	2.2 miles to Brainard Lake via road
DIFFICULTY	Easy
SKILL LEVEL	Novice skiers and snowshoers
HIGH POINT	10,300 feet
ELEVATION GAIN	300 feet
ONE WAY	2.3 miles to Brainard Lake via snowshoers-only trail
DIFFICULTY	Moderate
SKILL LEVEL	Novice snowshoers
HIGH POINT	10,300 feet
ELEVATION GAIN	300 feet
LOOP	1.2 miles around Brainard Lake
DIFFICULTY	Easy
SKILL LEVEL	Novice
HIGH POINT	10,370 feet
ELEVATION GAIN	70 feet
AVALANCHE DANGER	None
MAPS	Trails Illustrated #102, Indian Peaks, Gold Hill; USGS Ward
CONTACT	Boulder Ranger District, Roosevelt National Forest

COMMENT: One of the reasons the Brainard Lake Recreation Area is popular is its proximity to Denver and Boulder; another is its ease of use for family or novice outings. It is almost impossible to get lost, and the views of the surrounding Indian Peaks are spectacular. The Red Rock Lake Trail is a very short, easy, and scenic out-and-back for families with very young children that can also be a warm up for a trip to Brainard Lake. Brainard Lake Road can be snowshoed as an out-and-back to Brainard Lake—or any distance short of the lake. The road rolls gently and the snow is usually packed down firmly by midmorning. You pay for the convenience, however, by encountering the greatest number of dogs and people on the road. If you don't like furry friends or lots of people, or if you want to avoid having skiers zoom up and around you, then the snowshoers-only trail is for you. It is a pleasant and fairly easy tromp through the trees that shelter you from the wind, with some viewpoints. You can also do a loop between Red Rock Lake and Brainard Lake by combining the road and the snowshoers-only trail. You can have a nice kick and glide ski tour around Brainard Lake on "skinny" Nordic skis. There are a variety of ski and snowshoe trails that are a bit more challenging and interesting.

GETTING THERE: From Nederland, turn right/north on Highway 72, the Peak to Peak Highway, and go approximately 9 miles. The town of Ward is on the right/east side of the road. Watch for the Brainard Lake Recreation Area turnoff immediately on the left/west side of the road after the Ward turnoff. From Highway 72, drive west on the Brainard Lake Road to the gate closure in about 3 miles. Do not confuse this with the Red Rock trailhead just east of the gate that is the entry point for the superb but challenging Waldrop, Saint Vrain Creek, and Sourdough Trails.

Some of the Indian Peaks from frozen Brainard Lake.

Family sled outing at Brainard Lake.

THE ROUTE: From the west side of the Alvarado Trailhead parking area, follow the Walk from the Red Rock trailhead parking area west to the Brainard Lake Road closure and walk around the gate. Take Brainard Lake Road west. In 100 yards, just past the CMC Trail, the snowshoers-only trail is on the left (described below); stay right, on the road. As you walk up Brainard Lake Road, in about another 50 yards the Red Rock Lake Trail/side road is on the left. Waldrop North Trail is on the right.

RED ROCK LAKE TRAIL: Go left for a nice, short, easy side excursion to the south side of Red Rock Lake. It gives you a spectacular view of the peaks without having to walk all the way to Brainard Lake. The Red Rock Lake area is the best place for photos until you reach Brainard Lake. If you have very young children and want a short excursion, this detour to Red Rock Lake may be enough of an outing.

The Red Rock Lake Trail climbs a bit steeply from Brainard Lake Road through trees; bear right at any intersections. The trail levels and rolls gently before descending to the lake at 0.3 mile. Once you reach the lake you can go to the right to follow the east edge of the lake back to Brainard Lake Road. At the road, if you feel a bit more adventuresome and don't mind a small hill, continue along the north edge of the shoreline around the lake toward the west. You are rewarded with additional views of the peaks and a nice view of Red Rock Lake. Be careful that you are not walking on the lake itself because the ice might be thin and the shoreline is narrow. When you reach the west end of the lake, bear right and climb the short hill. Turn left/west on the Red Rock Lake Road to return to Brainard Lake Road.

BRAINARD LAKE ROAD: Back at the trail intersections near the gate closure the road climbs gradually northwest; in 0.5 mile you cross Red Rock Lake's outlet stream. The Brainard Lake Road climbs slightly, curving southwest and then leveling off, reaching the midpoint intersections with the snowshoers-only trail at 1.25 miles. The south branch is on the left first and then the north branch is on the right.

The road resumes climbing southwest, and in 0.5 mile reaches the side loops for Pawnee Campground. In another 0.25 mile, at approximately 2 miles, you will reach the stunning high-mountain panorama at Brainard Lake snowshoers-only trail. On the south side of Brainard Lake Road 100 yards from the closure gate, the south leg of the trail starts off gradually climbing. At about 0.25 mile the trail goes around the north side of a small lake, enters thicker tree cover, then steepens as it goes along another mile. This definitely is not an early or late-season trail because it needs several feet of snow and very cold weather to make passable the small streambed that comprises part of it. The next segment of the trail opens up and offers nice views of the majestic peaks that surround Brainard Lake. At approximately 1.25 miles the trail reaches Brainard Lake Road.

Cross the road, walk about 100 yards west, and continue on the north leg of the trail on the north/right side of the road. On this trail segment you get to avoid the crowd on the road and enjoy the solitude of the trees. There are not as many viewpoints, but there is a spectacle at Red Rock Lake, and another at the mid-point. The trail starts off gradually for the first 100 yards and then turns left up a steep hill. Don't be dismayed. It levels out after the first 0.25 mile and you have a nice view of Niwot Ridge as a reward for making the very short climb. The trail is quite moderate after that; the hill tops out at around 10,200 feet and then you actually lose some elevation. It parallels the road from atop the hill and then eventually drops down almost next to it before swinging west into the Pawnee Campground at 1.8 miles. Early in the season the campground might have some usable picnic tables if you are hungry. After the campground you cross through the Pawnee Picnic Area and might be tempted to go directly to Brainard Lake. Stay on the trail, which takes you back onto the road and to Brainard Lake in 0.5 mile, where you can enjoy the full panorama of the Indian Peaks.

BRAINARD LAKE LOOP: From the end of either the road or the snowshoers-only trail, you can continue on the road around the lake to enjoy views of the Indian Peaks or reach the roads to the trailheads for Mitchell and Blue Lakes and for Long Lake and Lake Isabelle. From where Brainard Lake Road first reaches the lake, go right (counterclockwise). In 50 yards the north leg of the snowshoers-only trail comes in from the right; in another 25 yards you cross the lake's outlet stream. You will see the Arickeree Picnic Area, and in another 25 yards a trail goes off to the right. At a little over 0.3 mile you cross Mitchell Creek and less than 100 yards later is the Mitchell Creek Picnic Area, which is at the intersection with the road to Mitchell, Blue, and Long Lakes and Lake Isabelle on the right at 0.4 mile.

At the west end of the lake where the other trailheads split off you are in the trees. From there you can turn right to proceed to another trailhead; stay straight/left on the road to continue around the lake. At 0.7 mile the Niwot Cutoff Trail comes in from the right. You soon have nice views to the north and west across Brainard Lake. Now the road climbs a small hill in 0.4 mile to the start of the loop.

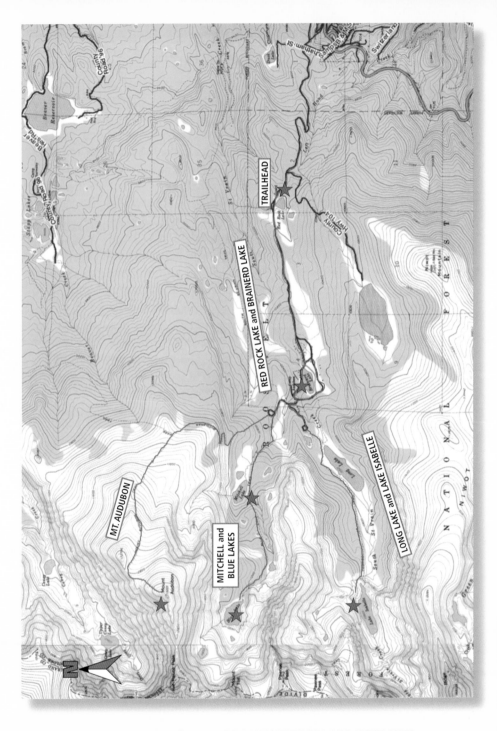

**RED ROCK LAKE and BRAINARD LAKE | MITCHELL AND BLUE LAKES
MOUNT AUDUBON | LONG LAKE and LAKE ISABELLE**

26. Mitchell and Blue Lakes and Mount Toll

ROUND TRIP	7.2 miles to Mitchell lake; 10 miles to Blue Lake
DIFFICULTY	Moderate to challenging
SKILL LEVEL	Novice to Mitchell Lake, intermediate to expert to Blue Lake
HIGH POINT	10,700 feet at Mitchell Lake; 11,300 feet at Blue Lake; 12,979 at Mount Toll
ELEVATION GAIN	700 feet to Mitchell Lake; 1,300 feet to Blue Lake; 2,900 feet to Mount Toll
AVALANCHE DANGER	Low to Considerable (on Mount Toll)
MAP	Trails Illustrated #102, Indian Peaks, Gold Hill
CONTACT	Boulder Ranger District, Roosevelt National Forest

COMMENT: You need good weather and snow conditions and/or to get an early start to make the round trip to Mitchell Lake from the Brainard Lake Road gate closure. It is worth the trip to see the setting of this large, high-mountain lake and the backdrop of the Indian Peaks. If conditions permit, you can continue on the Mitchell Lake Trail 1.4 miles to Blue Lake. This is a tougher trek than the trek from Long Lake to Lake Isabelle but is spectacular. Fortunately, the return is mostly downhill except for one small hill. Toll Mountain is best skied in the spring after the snow has stabilized since it is definitely steep enough to avalanche at any time. You need expert ski skills and AT or tele skis to ski it. Most people who ski it don't climb all the way to the summit. You can make it to either Mitchell or Blue Lake on skinny skis but the descent is more fun on wider skis.

GETTING THERE: From Nederland, turn right/north on Highway 72, the Peak to Peak Highway, and go approximately 9 miles. The town of Ward is on the right/east side of the road. Watch for the Brainard Lake Recreation Area turnoff immediately on the left/west side of the road after the Ward turnoff. From Highway 72, drive west on the Brainard Lake Road to the gate closure in about 3 miles. The Red Rock trailhead parking lot is just east of the gate closure.

THE ROUTE: Cross the road to the trail and climb through forest and over some From the Brainard Lake gate closure follow Brainard Lake Road 2 miles one way (or the snowshoers-only trail 2.3 miles one way) to reach the lake, then follow the loop 0.4 mile around the lake to the turnoff for summer trailheads at 2.4 miles. At the well-marked turnoff for Mitchell and Long Lakes on the right/north side of Brainard Lake Road, the trailhead road turns to the north and in 0.1 mile forks; take the right hand branch (the left branch goes to Long Lake and Lake Isabelle). In about 100 yards the road crosses Mitchell Creek, and Waldrop North Trail comes in from the right here. At 0.25 mile from the turnoff the South Saint Vrain Trail comes in from the right, and the road curves left (west). Meander through a thick tree cover gradually uphill to the summer trailhead parking lot (10,500 feet) at 0.4 mile (a 200-foot elevation gain) from the turnoff from Brainard Lake Road, 2.9 miles from the gate closure.

From the summer trailhead the trail levels before climbing steadily next to Mitchell Creek. You will continue in trees most of the way. In about 0.3 mile, at the boundary for Indian Peaks Wilderness, a path comes in from the left at 3.2 miles. Shortly after, the trail opens up and you will see several nice views of the pointed summit of Mount Toll. In a little more than 0.3 mile you cross the southern shore of a little lake at 3.5 miles, and about 0.1 mile after, at 3.6 miles, you reach the shoreline of Mitchell Lake. After the first shoreline access to Mitchell Lake you will cross its outlet and continue to climb around its southern shore. There are several more opportunities to descend to the lakeshore and enjoy the views of Mount Toll, Paw-

Mount Toll from the Blue Lake Trail.

Mitchell Lake from the Mount Audubon Trail.

nee Peak, and Shoshoni Peak. Reach the inlet stream from Blue Lake at 3.9 miles. If you don't want to go all the way to Blue Lake but would like a nice view above the trees, continue on the trail and climb the steep hill just west beyond Mitchell Lake. It is worth the price of admission to see the view back to the east.

Continuing up to Blue Lake, the trail is steeper throughout, although there are a few flat stretches. It is not a good early season trail. At 4.1 miles you will cross the stream, and then again at 4.2 miles. After the first steep hill beyond Mitchell Lake, you are well out of the trees. On a clear day you have a steady diet of nice views all the way of Niwot Ridge. Numerous waves of ridges roll away under your feet as you climb one false summit ridge after another. Several little lakes to your left are not yet Blue Lake.

Finally, at 5 miles from the gate closure you reach the southeastern shore of Blue Lake at its outlet; the lake is above tree line in a glacial cirque beneath Mount Toll and Pawnee Peak. If you want to ski Mount Toll you will have to circumnavigate Blue Lake. Crossing the lake for a direct approach can be risky in the spring when ice is melting. As with many of the trails in this book, even if you turn around short of Blue Lake, you will have had a very enjoyable adventure. Just remember that the return trip will seem longer. Be conservative in your turn around time.

SEE MAP ON PAGE 120.

27. Mount Audubon

ROUND TRIP	14.8 miles for the summit
DIFFICULTY	Challenging
SKILL LEVEL	Expert, with winter mountaineering skills
HIGH POINT	13,223 feet
ELEVATION GAIN	2,700 feet
AVALANCHE DANGER	Low to moderate
MAP	Trails Illustrated #102, Indian Peaks, Gold Hill
CONTACT	Boulder Ranger District, Roosevelt National Forest

COMMENT: You have to have good weather and snow conditions and/or get a very early start to make the round trip to the top of Mount Audubon from the Brainard Lake Road gate closure. The easiest way to achieve the summit is to climb it before the road closes for the season, or as soon as it opens, saving around 6 miles roundtrip. The late spring approach guarantees more complete snow coverage. An alternative strategy for speed is to ski to the trailhead with your snowshoes on your pack, and then snowshoe when skiing is no longer tenable. Skiing all of the way on the road is another very viable alternative. The higher reaches of Mount Audubon are often blown free of snow, so expect to alternate between snowshoeing or skiing and hiking. The summit is 7.4 miles one-way from the gate closure. Excellent route-finding skills and fitness are required to see the stunning view of the Indian Peaks from the top. You will want AT or tele skis for this route that features lots of steep descents on the return. There is a good, relatively safe, slope for taking turns on the south side to the west the main trail one half miles after the trail steepens. There are also some skiable slopes on the east side of the trail that are steeper and more avalanche prone.

GETTING THERE: From Boulder take Canyon Boulevard/Highway 119 west 14 miles to Nederland. At Nederland, turn right/north on Highway 72, the Peak to Peak Highway, and go approximately 9 miles. The town of Ward is on the right/east side of the road. Watch for the Brainard Lake Recreation Area turnoff immediately on the left/west side of the road after the Ward turnoff. Go west on Brainard Lake Road 3 miles to the winter road closure.

THE ROUTE: From the trailhead, hike a spur trail 0.6 miles to connect with the From the Brainard Lake gate closure, follow Brainard Lake Road 2 miles one way

The Venable Creek Trail.

PHOTO BY DAN ANDERSON

(or the snowshoers-only trail 2.3 miles one way) to reach the lake, then follow the loop 0.4 mile around the lake to the turnoff for summer trailheads at 2.4 miles. If you don't want to ski on the road, you can take the Waldrop North Trail to the South Saint Vrain Trail for a direct but rolling route. At the well-marked turnoff for Mitchell and Long Lakes on the right/north side of Brainard Lake Road, the trailhead road turns to the north and in 0.1 mile forks; take the right-hand branch (the left goes to Long Lake and Lake Isabelle). In about 100 yards the road crosses Mitchell Creek, and Waldrop North Trail comes in from the right here. At 0.25 mile from the turnoff, the South Saint Vrain Trail comes in from the right and the road curves left/west. Meander through a thick tree cover gradually uphill to the summer trailhead parking lot (10,500 feet) at 0.4 mile (200-foot elevation gain) from the turnoff from Brainard Lake Road, which is 2.9 miles from the gate closure.

The Mount Audubon trailhead is at the north/right end of the summer parking, separate from the Mitchell/Blue Lakes trailhead. You will be traveling west and northwest as you gradually climb to a head wall at around 10,600 feet. It is around a mile to reach the headwall, where you turn right/north and climb more steeply on switchbacks. The long switchbacks will take you up about 200 feet where the trail levels a bit. You will see the summit to the southwest, and most of the route ahead. The skiable south facing slope is to the west; east facing slopes to the east. The sign for the Buchanan Pass Trail is in 0.5 mile. In another 0.25 mile, switchbacks begin again around 10,900 feet and then the trail travels more gradually as it traverses northwest almost a mile. Some skiers prefer to turn to the west and ski the steep south slopes rather than going for the summit. They are steep enough to avalanche. If you stay on the main trail you will see steep cliffs that drop off to the north, and a very steep slope to the summit. There are multiple cairn routes (if they aren't completely buried under the snow) to the summit that is west and then southwest from the bottom of the slope. Pick what looks like promising snow cover as you go, making your own switchbacks. The snow depth will vary dramatically, but you will be glad for the extra traction from snowshoes though you will have to avoid some rocks. Unless there has been a recent storm and no wind, it is unlikely that you will have great snow all the way to the summit for skiing. You can still get in a good round trip regardless of your turn around point.

SEE MAP ON PAGE 120.

28. Long Lake and Lake Isabelle

ROUND TRIP	6.3 miles to Long Lake; 9.3 miles to Lake Isabelle
DIFFICULTY	Moderate to challenging
SKILL LEVEL	Intermediate snowshoers and skiers
HIGH POINT	10,600 feet at Long Lake; 10,800 feet at Lake Isabelle
ELEVATION GAIN	600 feet to Long Lake; 800 feet to Lake Isabelle
AVALANCHE DANGER	Low
MAP	Trails Illustrated #102, Indian Peaks, Gold Hill
CONTACT	Boulder Ranger District, Roosevelt National Forest

COMMENT: Long Lake enjoys a stunning setting, and the trek has its own rewards. Lake Isabelle, another 1.5 miles beyond, is reached on one of the more beautiful trails in the Front Range. It is a steady climb from Long Lake but not particularly steep until you are very near Lake Isabelle. From this lake you can also safely venture another 0.5 mile up the Pawnee Pass Trail before entering an avalanche hazard area.

Skiing to Lake Isabelle on mid-width or Nordic skis is worthwhile, or you can circle Long Lake by using the Jean Lunning Trail on the south side as part of the loop.

GETTING THERE: From Boulder, take Canyon Boulevard/Highway 119 west 14 miles to Nederland. At Nederland, turn right/north on Highway 72, the Peak to Peak Highway, and go approximately 9 miles. The town of Ward is on the right/east side of the road. Watch for the Brainard Lake Recreation Area turnoff immediately on the left/west side of the road after the Ward turnoff. Go west on Brainard Lake Road 3 miles to the winter road closure.

THE ROUTE: From the north side of the Alvarado Trailhead parking area, head From the Brainard Lake gate closure, follow Brainard Lake Road 2 miles one-way (or the snowshoers-only trail 2.3 miles one-way) to reach the lake, then follow the loop 0.4 mile around the lake to the turnoff for summer trailheads at 2.4 miles. At the well-marked turnoff for Long and Mitchell Lakes on the right/north side of Brainard Lake Road, the trailhead road turns to the north and in 0.1 mile forks; take the left hand branch (the right goes to Mitchell and Blue Lakes). The road gradually climbs southwest 0.4 mile to the summer trailhead parking lot (10,500 feet) at 2.9 miles from the gate closure.

Winter respite at Long Lake.

From the trailhead you have nice views of Niwot Ridge along the way to Long Lake. On the left is a short connector to the Jean Lunning Trail, which is mostly in the trees and doesn't offer the great views of the Pawnee Pass Trail; stay straight/right. When you reach the lake at about 3.2 miles, there is a spectacular and unique view of the Indian Peaks. If it is a windy day, hang on to your hat to enjoy the view for any length of time. If it isn't windy, the lakeshore is a delightful place for a lunch or snack break.

As you continue west and then southwest along the shore of Long Lake for 0.5 mile, you are rewarded with superb views almost all the way, since most of the trail has openings through the trees to Niwot Ridge. There is a trail junction at 4 miles with the other end of the Jean Lunning Trail to the left; for Lake Isabelle, stay straight/right. In about 0.4 mile beyond the intersection you come to a very nice, open meadow area at 4.4 miles that affords a terrific view of the ridge and some of the peaks beyond. It is a good place for a rest break because it has southern exposure and is still relatively sheltered from the wind. After this, the trail steepens considerably and switchbacks up through trees 0.25 mile to Lake Isabelle at 4.6 miles. The view from here of this section of the Indian Peaks is nothing less than stunning.

OTHER TRAILS TO EXPLORE

From Lake Isabelle you can continue higher up the Pawnee Pass Trail, but stop when the trail starts to near the ridgeline with cliffs above. This area is very avalanche-prone. The route is safe up to that point. You need an early start to make this a fun trip on short winter days.

Along the way notice what may be a glacial terminal moraine with a meadow on the uphill side. The meadow may once have been a lake.

SEE MAP ON PAGE 120.

29. Rainbow Lakes and Arapaho Glacier Overlook Trail

ROUND TRIP	8 miles to the lakes
DIFFICULTY	Easy to moderate
SKILL LEVEL	Novice snowshoers or skiers to lakes; intermediate to Overlook
HIGH POINT	10,100 feet
ELEVATION GAIN	800 feet
AVALANCHE DANGER	Low
MAP	Trails Illustrated #102, Indian Peaks, Gold Hill
CONTACT	Boulder Ranger District, Roosevelt National Forest

COMMENT: Greenhorn Mountain is the highest point in its namesake wilderness The majestic high alpine terrain of the Arapaho Glacier Overlook and Rainbow Lakes is heavily trod in the summer but not as heavily used in the winter, making it a treat for snowshoers and skiers. Access Rainbow Lakes and encounter the massive spectacles of Niwot and Caribou Ridges, brooding Bald and Pomeroy Mountains, and the high and distant summit ridge of the Arapaho Peaks. The area is south of the busy Brainard Lake area and west of a bustling parking lot that is at the south end of the Sourdough Trail. The Rainbow Lakes road beyond the Sourdough parking lot is impassable in the winter, but a trek on the road to the Rainbow Lakes trailhead will reward you with views of the area's rugged peaks.

The Rainbow Lakes are in a spectacular high-mountain setting, nestled next to the soaring tundra of the glacier-carved Caribou ridgeline. The road is closed to winter travel, so it can be used for a nice snowshoe or ski toward the trailhead. You will have good views of both the Caribou and Niwot Ridges and some of the towering Indian Peaks on the way, though making it all the way to the lakes and back is a long day unless you are very fleet of foot or fast on skis. Snowshoeing or skiing just part of the road is a worthwhile adventure since it climbs very gradually and offers mountain views. Sections of the road might be snow-free because of wind and sun, so be prepared to carry your snowshoes or skis for short parts of the road. You can use skinny Nordic skis for this outing and if someone breaks trail for you it can be a round trip ski and glide. If you want to add to the adventure, start early, and have lots of stamina, take the side trail on the north toward the Arapahoe Glacier

Indian Peaks from Rainbow Lakes Road.

Overlook. The road is an advanced beginners ski route but the Glacier Trail requires expert ski skills but can easily be snowshoed.

GETTING THERE: From Boulder, take Canyon Boulevard/Highway 119 west 14 miles to Nederland. At Nederland, turn right/north on Highway 72, the Peak to Peak Highway, and go approximately 6 miles. Turn west on the Rainbow Lakes Campground road, also marked for the University of Colorado Mountain Research Station. The parking lot is approximately 1 mile on the south/left side of the road.

THE ROUTE: Leave the trailhead on good trail and work up to the saddle, gaining You will have to park in the Sourdough Trail parking lot and walk 0.5 mile to the Rainbow Lakes road closure. It is 3 miles one way just to the Rainbow Lakes trailhead, and another mile to the first of the lakes, The road to the University of Colorado Mountain Research Station is on the right at 0.6 mile. Rainbow Lakes road is on the left/south side of the research road through the closure gate 0.5 mile from the parking lot, and turns sharply south for a mile, then climbs gradually to 9,600 feet. At about 1.25 miles the road turns west. You will see views through the aspen on the left. At 1.5 miles towering Pomeroy and Klondike Mountains come into view as the road descends toward North Boulder Creek. At about 2.25 miles it crosses North Boulder Creek. The road then climbs back up to 9,700 feet, then to 9,900 feet as it nears the trailhead. The trailhead is at the end of the road at the western edge of the Rainbow Lakes Campground. The Glacier Overlook Trail is at the very end of the campground road loop next to the trailhead map.

If you make it to the trailhead, the lakes trail rolls gently for another mile to the lakes to the northwest alongside a creek. You'll have some nice views along the way. In a mile you reach the lakes, which are surrounded by Caribou and Arapaho Ridges at around 10,000 feet. The real treat is the view from the lakes if you make it that far. Don't dawdle too long, as you have a long trek back. As mentioned, you can skip the lakes and go for the Arapaho Glacier Overlook Trail. It is 12 miles round trip to the overlook but only 4 miles round trip to the spectacular overlook of the Boulder watershed and a view of Mount Albion. You will want AT or tele skis for this route, and the longer days of spring.

RAINBOW LAKE

Nederland Area

Chapter 5

NEDERLAND FOOTHILLS

"If we had the courage to follow those unknown canyons. . . we might walk right into Eden."

—James C. Work, *Windmills, the River & Dust: One Man's West* (2005)

Aspen grove on the Caribou Ranch Trail.

The Nederland area, 19 miles from Boulder, offers a variety of trails at the foot of the Indian Peaks. The magnificent backdrop of the Continental Divide invites the uninitiated into the high foothills and mountains of the Front Range. Enjoy the windswept meadows, frozen sparkling lakes and streams, and the aspen and conifer forests. Nederland is surrounded by Roosevelt National Forest and is within easy driving distance of Golden Gate Canyon State Park, Eldora Mountain Resort, the easy Magnolia Trails, and Rollinsville's East Portal of the Moffat Tunnel, offering trails of varying difficulty for winter adventures. The rolling Magnolia Trails network is minutes from town. Golden Gate Canyon offers the scenic and short Raccoon Trail. Eldora has three easy to moderate trails with Indian Peaks views. Rollinsville's East Portal trails offer forest excursions to austere, high mountain lakes. The town of Nederland also features more than the famous Frozen Dead Guy and the annual winter festival celebrating him; there are a dozen excellent restaurants, bakeries, coffee shops, and a brewpub to fortify the body for recreating the hearty soul. There are also affordable and unique lodging options, and service by RTD buses if you don't want to make the short commute from Boulder by car.

The best way to get to Nederland is to drive west up Boulder Canyon/Highway 119 from Boulder.

Marmot inspecting visitors to his lair near James Peak.

30. Caribou Ranch

ROUND TRIP	3.1 miles; DeLonde Homestead 1.2 miles; Blue Bird Loop 1.9 miles
DIFFICULTY	Easy
SKILL LEVEL	Beginner snowshoers and novice skiers
HIGH POINT	8,300 feet
ELEVATION GAIN	200 feet
AVALANCHE DANGER	None
MAP	Trails Illustrated #102, Indian Peaks, Gold Hill
CONTACT	Boulder County Open Space and Boulder Ranger District, Roosevelt National Forest

COMMENT: The Boulder County Open Space area called Caribou Ranch includes the historic DeLonde Homestead with a striking aspen- and pine-ringed high mountain meadow, as well as the nineteenth-century Blue Bird Mine complex. The ranch was used as a site to film movies between 1936 and 1971, including the 1966 remake of *Stagecoach* starring Bing Crosby and Stephanie Powers. Most of the historic buildings have been preserved. You can see into the close quarters the miners used. Enjoy a stream, waterfall, diverse trees, and animals. This trail has enough snow only after a major easterly upslope or the snows of mid-winter. Wait until after January unless you hear Nederland has good snow cover. Restrictions: Dogs and bicycles are prohibited and the ranch is closed from April 1st through June 30th to protect calving elk and migratory birds. This can be an easy Nordic skinny ski tour after a major Front Range storm, but not before.

GETTING THERE: From Nederland, go through the roundabout straight and bear right onto Peak to Peak Highway 72 north. Travel 2 miles to CR 126; turn left/west on CR 126 and go 1 mile to the Caribou Ranch parking lot.

THE ROUTE: From the trailhead, hike a spur trail 0.6 miles to connect with the You will travel northwest from the parking area and go gradually uphill in thick trees. In 0.5 mile you will crest the ridge and have a sweeping view of part of the ranch and the hilly, forested terrain. This section of the trail is often blown free of snow. You will descend a short hill and reenter the trees, coming to a comely small meadow and another section of sun-exposed trail. You might have to carry your snowshoes. The trail turns sharply north and goes downhill with a historical

Delonde Homestead at Caribou Ranch.

marker about the Switzerland excursion train. You will reach an intersection in 0.25 mile. If you are not sure you want to hike the entire loop, turn right and go down a short hill to begin a counter-clockwise circuit. This will take you to the historic DeLonde Homestead, beaver pond, and Blue Bird Mine complex at the beginning of your trek. There are plaques about the movie, mining, and the resort history of the ranch as well as the wildlife. You will reach the homestead in approximately 0.5 mile. You can make a slight detour to the southeast to see the beaver pond and wildlife description before continuing north toward the mine. The next section is uphill through rocky terrain for over 0.5 mile. You might have to carry your snowshoes. You will see signage for Boulder Creek, and then the Blue Bird Mine. If you visit the mine, continue past the structures for 0.25 mile to reach the streamside picnic area and a small, possibly frozen waterfall. When you go back downhill, look to your left for the trail—it is easy to miss the trail and end up on the service road.

When you return to the trail from the mine, continue for another 1.5 miles back to the trailhead by traveling west/right; or make your trek a shorter route by retracing your steps. It is worth completing the entire circuit so you can enjoy the meadow and the stately stands of aspen. If you continue west, the trail crests a small hill and then goes downhill before leveling. There is a viewpoint less than 0.5 mile on the left that is good for photos. When you round the bend in the trail, it travels southeast and begins a gentle climb back to where you started.

SIDEBAR: Caribou Ranch
There is a nearby barn on private property near the open space also called Caribou Ranch that was famous as a music recording studio in the 1970s and used by Elton John, U-2, John Lennon, Joe Walsh, some of the Eagles, Stephen Stills, and other well-known musicians. It burned down in 1985 and the property was then used for a gated, high-end real estate development. The rest of the ranch was purchased by Boulder County and became the Caribou Ranch Open Space.

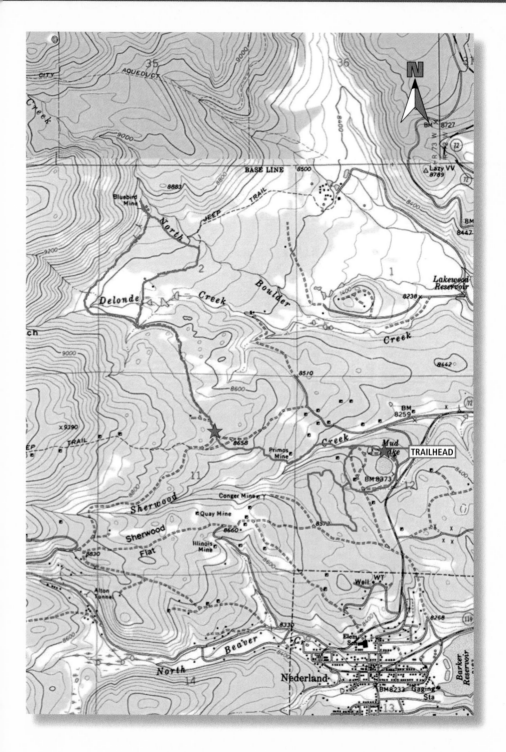

CARIBOU RANCH | MUD LAKE OPEN SPACE

31. Mud Lake Open Space

ROUND TRIP	2.4 miles via: Kinnickinnick Loop, 1.1 miles; Tungsten Loop, 0.8 miles; and Caribou Ranch connector trail, 0.5 mile
DIFFICULTY	Easy
SKILL LEVEL	Beginner snowshoers; intermediate skiers
HIGH POINT	8,300 feet
ELEVATION GAIN	200 feet
AVALANCHE DANGER	None
MAP	Trails Illustrated #102, Indian Peaks, Gold Hill
CONTACT	Boulder County Open Space and Boulder Ranger District, Roosevelt National Forest

COMMENT: This is a beautiful, lightly used Boulder County Open Space area featuring stately aspen, a frozen lake, and even a sliding area for kids. It is an easy figure-eight loop in gently rolling terrain that also features a pine, fir, and spruce forest with views of Bald and Pomeroy Mountains. This trail has enough snow only after a major easterly upslope or after the snows of mid-winter because of its 8,200-foot elevation. Wait until after January, unless you hear Nederland has good snow cover from a major early season storm. This can be an easy Nordic ski after a major Front Range storm. Restrictions: Dogs are allowed on leash at Mud Lake, but not Caribou Ranch. Don't venture on to the lake surface unless you are absolutely sure it is frozen solid.

GETTING THERE: A high-clearance, four-wheel-drive vehicle is recommended to From Boulder take Canyon Boulevard/Highway 119 west 16 miles to Nederland. Go straight through the roundabout and bear right onto Peak to Peak Highway 72 north for 2 miles to CR 126; turn left/west on CR 126 for 0.5 mile. Turn left into the Mud Lake parking lot.

THE ROUTE: From the parking lot, follow the Lily Lake Trail for 1 mile—the first. The trailhead is on the northwest edge of the parking lot. There is a map at the trailhead. You will travel uphill 50 yards to an intersection with the Tungsten Trail. Go left immediately to reach lovely, usually frozen Mud Lake. Waterfowl will be there early in the season or until it freezes solid. You can circumnavigate the lake for a very short, easy stroll, or follow the entire, slightly hilly Tungsten loop for an almost 1-mile jaunt and enjoy the views from both sides of the lake. Be

Jeremiah and Lylah Johnston, fun at Mud Lake.

sure to trek over to the east side of the lake for the best photography. You will see a sweeping view of the lake with Pomeroy Mountain (a sub-peak of South Arapaho Peak) in the background.

If you want a more extended adventure with a bit more uphill and nice views, add the 1.1 miles of the Kinnickinnick Loop. You will climb around 200 feet to include it but the trail is not very steep and well worth it. Traveling counter-clockwise on Kinnickinnick from Tungsten will mean you will climb the steepest (northwest) section first and then have a mellow downhill. As you wind your way uphill on gentle switchbacks you will see a bench at the top of the hill. This is also an excellent spot for pictures of Pomeroy and Bald Mountains, and you might even see Mount Audubon peaking over the top in the distance if it is a clear day. If you prefer a mellower climb first, go clockwise (southeast), and enjoy a beautiful stand of aspen on the way up. If you want to lengthen the enjoyment, include the Caribou Ranch connector trail to add another mile roundtrip. It is a beautiful gradual hill route, with pretty meadows and ponderosa pine and is frequented by deer, elk, and even moose. You might have to shed your snowshoes to cross Sherwood Creek on the wooden bridge. This trail section is more sun-exposed, so snow cover might be thin until the middle of the winter. The trail intersections are well marked but the trails themselves are not continuously marked. Most of the winter these well-used trails will be obvious but if you are the first to arrive after heavy snow you might have to route find. It is difficult to get lost because the open space is relatively small. Just remember which direction the parking lot is and that it is generally uphill from the lot and downhill to get back to it.

SEE MAP ON PAGE 135.

32. West Magnolia Trails

ROUND TRIP	7 miles of non-motorized trails; 8 miles of roads 1.5 miles on trails 925A and 342; 1 mile on trails 925A and 925B; 1 mile on trail 355A
DIFFICULTY	Easy
SKILL LEVEL	Beginner skiers and snowshoers
HIGH POINT	8,900 feet
ELEVATION GAIN	400 feet
AVALANCHE DANGER	None
MAP	Trails Illustrated #102, Indian Peaks, Gold Hill
CONTACT	Boulder Ranger District, Roosevelt National Forest

COMMENT: This is a large network of easy trails in gently rolling terrain in an aspen, pine, fir, and spruce forest with views of South Arapaho Peak, Bald and Pomeroy Mountains, as well as the Eldora Mountain Resort. The loops can be confusing, but it is very difficult to get lost. These trails have enough snow only after a major upslope or after the snows of mid-winter. Wait until after January, unless you hear Nederland has good snow cover from an early season storm. If you are very ambitious you can ski from West Magnolia campground all the way to Rollinsville. After a major storm, this area can be good for easy Nordic skiing.

GETTING THERE: From Boulder, take Canyon Boulevard/Highway 119 west 16 miles to Nederland. Go left/south through the roundabout onto Peak to Peak Highway 72 for 2.7 miles to Magnolia Road/CR 132W; turn right/northwest, and you will see a small parking area on the right. Or, continue west for another mile, and park outside of the second forest gate that is closed for the winter. Walk southwest around the gate and you will see the trailhead on the right/west side of the summer parking lot.

THE ROUTES:
TRAILS 925A/B, 342A, AND 926A

From the first parking area, you will see a sign for the 925A trail on the left/west uphill side of the trailhead. This goes gradually uphill into the trees to the north and then west. In a little over 0.25 mile you will come to the intersection with the 925B and 925F trails. If you continue straight you will end up on the 925F trail, which will take you over a hill and through the trees to Magnolia Road in about 1 mile. If you

Spring snow on West Magnolia Trails.

go right/north on the 925B trail you will go downhill and around back to the parking area in only 0.75 mile. If you go downhill on 925B and then left on 342A you will enjoy a longer additional 0.75-mile loop through a beautiful aspen grove called Aspen Alley. You can loop the grove on 342A and 926A, and then return uphill to the parking area.

TRAIL 355A

These trails/roads are from the summer trailhead that is 1 mile west of Highway 119: 355A, 355, 926E and F, and Hobbit.

This is an easy, rolling out-and-back that travels west from the trailhead. You will probably want to continue onto the 926E and F trail to extend your trip through the forested rolling, rocky hills. There will be nice views to the north of Eldora Mountain Resort and South Arapaho Peak. When 355A dead ends into campground loop 355, turn right to pick up 926 E and F. They will take you to a small ridge top and then back around to 355, which is primarily the summer campground road. Trail 355 can also be used to extend your trek through the thick, lodgepole pine forest. If you want to go farther, take 355-I past the 355 campground road, and south onto Hobbit I. Hobbit I and II are more difficult to discern in deep snow. Give it your best effort, and if you lose the Hobbit trails, you can retreat onto the portion of 355 that is nearby. Just keep a general sense of which direction you came from or, better yet, carry a compass for orienting yourself.

SIDEBAR: The Switzerland Trail

The Switzerland Trail was a narrow-gauge railroad line that operated around the turn of the twentieth century between Nederland and Ward carrying supplies and ore to and from mining camps and the mills, and then tourists between towns in the Front Range and the mining camps from 1883 to 1919. It was one of the primary means of transportation for people and goods into the mines and mountain towns it served. The rail bed is now popular for hiking and biking.

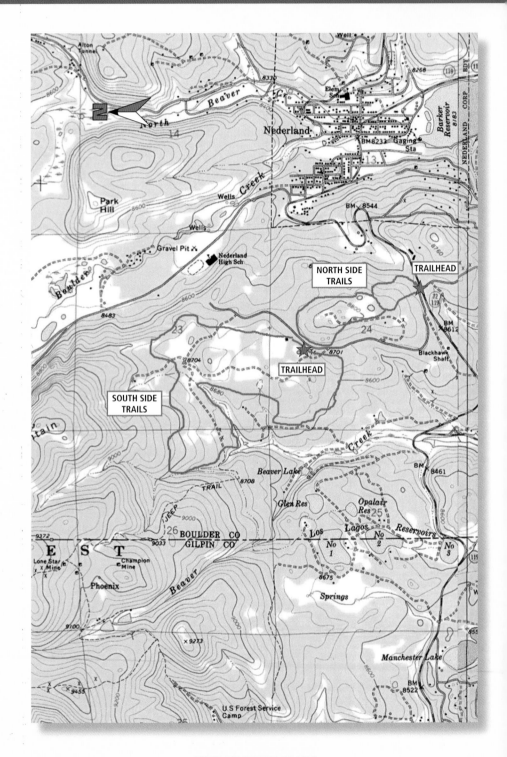

WEST MAGNOLIA TRAILS

Nederland Area

Chapter 6

ELDORA MOUNTAIN RESORT AND HESSIE

"Storms are fine speakers, and tell all they know, but their voices of lightning, torrent, and rushing wind are much less numerous than the nameless still, small voices too low for human ears; because we are poor listeners."

—John Muir, *The Mountains of California* (1894)

The view of Neva Mountain from Fourth of July Trail.

Nederland is a charming former mining community that is 19 miles west of Boulder. The Eldora Mountain Resort is approximately 5 miles west of Nederland and is 1,200 feet higher, with the base at 9,400 feet. Avoid driving Interstate 70 to the larger ski areas by visiting Eldora Mountain Resort; Boulder Canyon is a short, scenic drive in comparison. There is RTD bus service from Boulder to Eldora seven days a week so take advantage of this option so you so not have to drive on very well-maintained but snowy roads. The additional elevation and proximity to the Continental Divide means that the resort receives much more snow than Nederland or Boulder. A warm, sunny day in Boulder can be a snowy powder day at the Eldora Mountain Resort most of the winter. Oddly enough, even the town of Eldora just downhill from the resort and west of Nederland is also in a different climate zone and often gets more snow and wind than even its snowy, windy neighbor Nederland. This means that snowshoers, Nordic skiers, and downhill skiers can rely on good snow cover most of the winter. The area is a bit more wind-prone than breezy Boulder, but the snowshoe and Nordic trails have excellent tree cover that provides good shelter from the breezes you will experience in the downhill area and parking lot. The snowshoe trails often have some of the best powder snow because they are protected from wind and sun.

If you want to snowshoe or ski, but want the predictability of a resort with warm lodges, food, and well-marked trails and are willing to pay for it, then Eldora's snowshoe and Nordic trails are for you. Fortunately, the trail passes for access to the Nordic Center trails are only a fraction of the cost of a downhill lift ticket, even at Eldora's less expensive prices. The resort offers four lovely trails in the trees (with more planned) that also feature some great views of the Indian Peaks and the Continental Divide. You can also access the free but somewhat more challenging Jenny Creek national forest trail from Eldora. The Nordic Center is the starting point for the trails, and it is a good place for warming and snacks. You can ride a shuttle bus to two other lodges with more complete food and beverage service. There is a bar in the main lodge for après trail activities. There is also a wide variety of coffee shops, excellent restaurants, and pubs in Nederland as well as lodging and entertainment. Nederland has a vibrant local music scene, with several bands that tour nationally, and often appear locally for a pittance. Book a night in a local lodge and avoid the commute.

Eldora is easily reached from Nederland, which is 17 miles west of Boulder. From Boulder take Canyon Boulevard/Highway 119.

33. Jenny Creek Trail

ROUND TRIP	3.2 miles to Jenny Creek; 10.6 miles to Yankee Doodle Lake; 9 miles to Guinn Mountain Hut
DIFFICULTY	Moderate to Jenny Creek; Challenging to Yankee Doodle Lake
SKILL LEVEL	Novice snowshoers, intermediate skiers for Jenny Creek; intermediate for Yankee Doodle Lake
HIGH POINT	9,700 feet at Jenny Creek; 10,900 feet at Yankee Doodle Lake; 10,900 feet at Guinn Mountain Hut
ELEVATION GAIN	650 feet to Jenny Creek; 1,450 feet to Yankee Doodle Lake; 1,600 feet to Guinn Mountain Hut
AVALANCHE DANGER	None
MAP	Trails Illustrated #102, Indian Peaks
CONTACT	Boulder Ranger District, Roosevelt National Forest

COMMENT: This popular trail begins at Eldora Mountain Resort next to the Nordic Center and is free of charge. The resort trails require a trail pass. The Eldora Nordic Center offers snack foods, beverages, and restrooms. Once you wind your way through the ski area, you will be traveling through a peaceful, thick lodgepole pine forest. You will be treated to some shining mountaintops of the Indian Peaks gleaming through the treetops on your roller coaster trail adventure. There are two Jenny Creek Trails, one at the bottom of Dead Man Hill in the Eldora Mountain Resort Nordic area, and the other a USFS Access Trail that starts next to the beginner ski runs. The access trail can be hard-packed snow unless there has been a recent snowstorm. Both trails have good tree cover that protects them from wind. You can ski this route on skinny, AT, or tele skis. If you're going to the Guinn Hut you will need tele skis or AT skis with skins for the steep ascents and descents or will have to be a skinny ski expert. Eldora Mountain Resort is planning to eventually install an alpine ski lift at the bottom of Dead Man Hill that will dramatically alter the Nordic area and their Jenny Creek trail. Restrictions: No dogs are allowed on the resort trails or on the adjacent USFS Jenny Creek Trail.

GETTING THERE: From Boulder, take Canyon Boulevard/Highway 119 west 16 miles to Nederland. Go left/south through the roundabout onto Peak to Peak Highway 72 for around 1 mile, and turn right onto CR 130. In approximately 2 miles, turn left on CR 140 uphill to Eldora Mountain Resort. Park outside of the resort on the left where

South Arapaho Peak from the Jenny Creek Trailhead.

the access trail is marked. Then walk into the resort and turn left toward the Nordic Center where you will see the access trail next to the easiest ski run.

THE ROUTE: The trail starts at the west end of the parking area. A large part of You will go uphill next to the Ho Hum beginner ski run. There is a Forest Service access sign next to the trail. About 50 yards uphill there is another USFS sign on the left, actually pointing downhill; don't take the trail on the left, but continue straight uphill west-southwest. Once the trail levels out at the top of the slope, go right/west around the back of the chairlift and continue uphill. You will be next to the downhill ski run. You will see the trail turning to the left/south and there will be a blue Forest Service access sign. Snowshoe on the right side of the ski trail, not in the ski trail, since skiers might be coming down the steep hill at high rates of speed. You also don't want to damage the ski trail. It is always more fun to snowshoe in powder instead of hard pack. Uphill another 100 feet you will see a large brown sign pointing you right/west for the Jenny Creek and Guinn Mountain Trails. You will encounter one of the steepest hills, but the trail goes up much more gradually after it. There are brown USFS trail markers every 100 yards or so and some blue diamonds. You will climb gradually up to around 9,700 feet, high on a ridge above the Jenny Creek valley below with nice views before the trail descends down to the creek, bottoming out at around 9,500 feet.

This is a good turnaround point, unless you want to make the long steep climb up Guinn Mountain to the Guinn Mountain Hut. When the trail reaches the creek bottom, it intersects with Jenny Creek Road and the Guinn Mountain Trail. Bear right/northwest to take the Guinn Mountain Trail, which climbs steeply uphill. It is another 2 miles one way in the trees to the hut. For Yankee Doodle Lake, take Jenny Creek Road another 2.7 miles one way. You will be paralleling and then intersecting the Rollins Pass Road that is heavily used by snowmobiles. The Guinn Mountain Hut is a better destination, if you don't mind a very steep climb, because you can take shelter if a storm blows in or even plan to spend the night. The Guinn Mountain/Arestua Hut is maintained by the Colorado Mountain Club, and is on a first-come, first-served basis. You can check the reservation calendar on the CMC Boulder Group website and clicking on the reservations link.

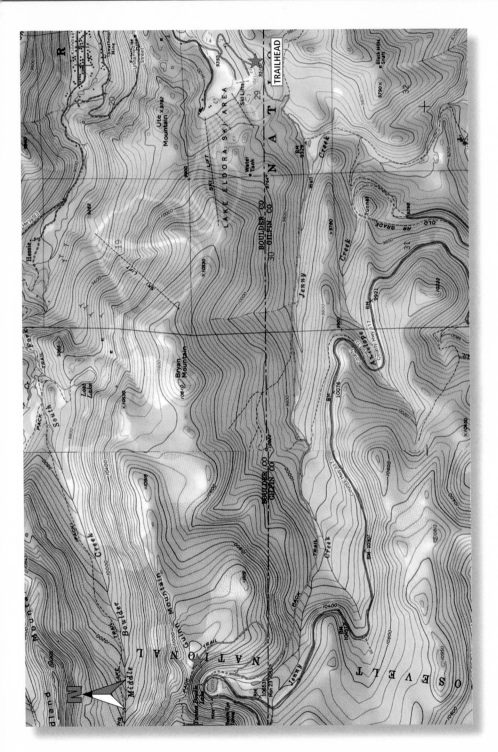

JENNY CREEK TRAIL

34. Fourth of July Trail/Road

ROUND TRIP	7 miles
DIFFICULTY	Easy to Moderate
SKILL LEVEL	Novice skiers and snowshoers
HIGH POINT	9,700 feet
ELEVATION GAIN	800 feet
AVALANCHE DANGER	Low to considerable; can be avoided
MAP	Trails Illustrated #102, Indian Peaks, Gold Hill
CONTACT	Boulder County Open Space and Boulder Ranger District, Roosevelt National Forest

COMMENT: The Hessie valley is a beautiful riparian area of Middle Boulder Creek located just west of the town of Eldora. You will see rock formations and many peak views. It is a good route for family excursions, as even hiking part of the trail is worthwhile. The Fourth of July Road will take you above the Hessie valley for a sweeping view of the valley and the north side of the Eldora Mountain Resort. You will also see the peaks of Bryan (10,810 feet) Chittenden (10,860 feet), Guinn (11,200 feet), Woodland (11,205 feet), and a more distant unnamed 12,000-foot mountain before entering the tree-lined portion of the road where you will have great views of South Arapaho Peak (13,397 feet). The first 3.5 miles of the road is avalanche safe. As you near the steep flanks of Klondike and Bald Mountains, and especially South Arapaho Peak, the avalanche danger increases. There have been fatal avalanches near the Fourth of July trailhead, so traveling that far is not wise unless avalanche danger is low. But you can have a nice long snowshoe or ski and be in no avalanche danger. This is a very popular route. Either plan to arrive early or visit during the week to avoid crowds and garner a close-in parking spot. You can ski the road with Nordic or wider skis. The descent after you turn around is not steep.

GETTING THERE: From Nederland, go left/south through the roundabout onto Peak to Peak Highway 72 for around 1 mile, and turn right onto CR 130. In approximately 2 miles, you will see the turnoff on the left for CR 140 uphill for Eldora Mountain Resort; don't turn, go straight. The town of Eldora is another 2 miles west. The Hessie trailhead is beyond the closed or impassable road on the west side of town. Parking is limited. Pay attention to the No Parking signs, or you will be towed.

Fourth of July Road.

THE ROUTE: From the parking area, walk beyond the warehouse toward the water. Your distance to the trail might vary a bit depending on where you can park. In any case, you will have at least a 0.75-mile stroll on the Fourth of July Road to reach the Hessie intersection. You will see the north side of the Eldora Mountain Resort to the south as you stroll along the road. At the fork, stay on the Fourth of July Road as it goes straight uphill and the Hessie road/trail goes left downhill. The next 0.5 mile is one of the steepest sections of the road and also the most sun-exposed, so you might have to shed your snowshoes. It climbs more gradually after this and has some almost flat sections and the snow will improve. As you climb 200 feet, enjoy the views to the south and west; this is the one of the best view sections of the road. In about 0.25 mile there is an open view as the trees part at around 9,200 feet. You will see the slopes of Bryan and Guinn Mountains above Lost Lake. You will also see the numerous snow-capped mountains.

As the road levels somewhat and the snow improves, enjoy the rugged flank of Crittenden Mountain while climbing to 9,300 feet. You will only gain another 200 feet over the next mellow 0.75 mile with a forest of aspen, mixed conifers, and Klondike Mountain's rocky cliffs as your view. The higher you go, the thicker the aspen get—reaching for the sky with their slender branches and defying heaven to be any nicer. Around 9,400 feet the trail levels as you cross a tributary of the creek. This section of the road can be very icy. An S-turn climbs more steeply to 9,500 feet, where you see seasonal cabins in the Grand Island community. The road then goes downhill and mellows as the aspen trees open up with head-on views of Klondike and Bald Mountains. Rounding another curve while the trail rolls, you will be startled to see a view of soaring South Arapaho Peak on the left/northwest side of the road. The road/trail climbs steeply to 9,700 feet as it sidesteps along the steep slopes of Klondike Mountain. The reward is another striking view of 13,000-foot-high South Arapaho Peak. You can also see the steep slopes of Bald and South Arapaho create avalanche hazards for the road in about 0.5 mile. Either turn around now, or savor the additional 1-mile loop, and begin your descent.

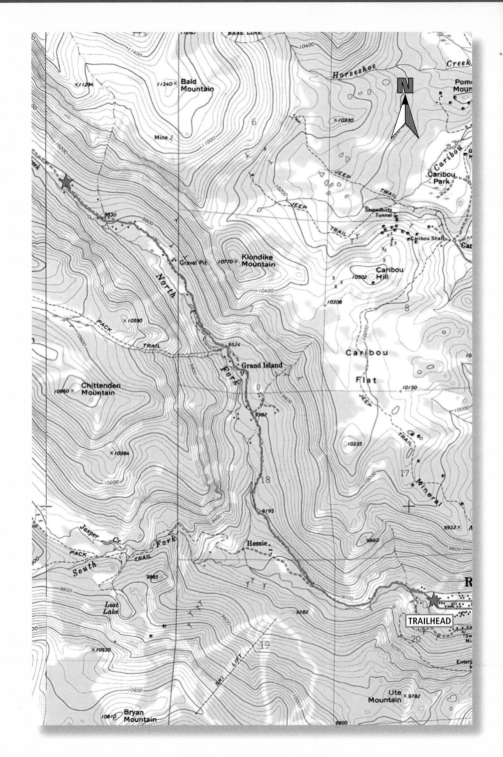

FOURTH OF JULY TRAIL/ROAD

35. Lost Lake Trail

ROUND TRIP	5.5 miles
DIFFICULTY	Moderate
SKILL LEVEL	Novice snowshoers; intermediate skiers
HIGH POINT	9,800 feet
ELEVATION GAIN	823 feet
AVALANCHE DANGER	Low to considerable; can be avoided
MAP	Trails Illustrated #102, Indian Peaks, Gold Hill
CONTACT	Boulder County Open Space and Boulder Ranger District, Roosevelt National Forest

COMMENT: The Hessie valley is a beautiful riparian area of Middle Boulder Creek, located just west of the town of Eldora. You will see rock formations, peak views, and moose if you are lucky. It is a good route for family excursions, since snowshoeing or skiing just part of the trail is worthwhile. This is one of two Lost Lake trails covered in this book. The other is North Fork Trail near Estes Park. This is a much shorter and easier route and is relatively close to the Denver-Boulder area, making it very popular. Either plan to arrive early or visit during the week to avoid crowds and garner a close-in parking spot.

This trail has some narrow steep sections so mid-width skis would be better than skinny skis, though skinny skis are fine for most of the route. You will want a major Front Range storm before visiting, since much of the trail and road are sun exposed.

GETTING THERE: From Nederland, go left/south through the roundabout onto Peak to Peak Highway 72 for around 1 mile and turn right onto CR 130. In approximately 2 miles you will see the turnoff on the left for CR 140 uphill for Eldora Mountain Resort; don't turn, go straight. The town of Eldora is another 2 miles west, and the Hessie trailhead is beyond the closed or impassable road on the west side of town. Parking is limited. Pay attention to the No Parking signs, or you will be towed.

THE ROUTE: Hike south on the Rainbow Trail. Cross a bridge after 0.6 miles and Your distance to the trail might vary a bit depending on where you can park. In any case, you will have at least a 0.75-mile stroll on the Fourth of July Road to reach the Hessie intersection. You will see the north side of the Eldora Mountain Resort to

Jasper Mountain massif from Lost Lake.

the south as you stroll. At the fork, the Fourth of July Road goes straight uphill; you will bear left downhill on the Hessie road/trail. It is another 0.7 mile to the town site sign that notes you are at 9,000 feet. Continue straight ahead on the level trail as you enter trees. You will see some cabins on the right; bear left. In about 0.3 mile you will cross Middle Boulder Creek on either the footbridge or the frozen surface. You will then see signage for the various trailheads for numerous lakes that are all 1 mile away. Now the real fun begins as the trail begins to climb more steeply in about 0.25 mile and switchbacks to the northeast before turning west-northwest. This part of the trail can be windswept with exposed rocks or have deep drifts to navigate. The steep slopes to the north pose a slight avalanche risk; they generally don't collect enough snow for large releases. The trail climbs 400 feet in less than a mile before leveling. Expansive views of the valley are your reward. You will enjoy a less steep 0.25 mile of trail in the trees and will reach another stream crossing and trail intersection. You are now only 0.5 mile from Lost Lake but you still have another 400 feet of climbing. Fortunately you are warmed up. (If some members of your party are breathless, this is a good turnaround point.) Once you renew your determination you will reach the lake in short order. You will see signs for the various lakes; bear left onto the Lost, Woodland, and King Lakes Trail. The other route to the right goes to Jasper and Devil's Thumb Lakes. You will climb 200 feet in 0.3 mile (gasp), and then the trail climbs more gradually. The trail for Woodland and King Lakes goes straight/right; turn left uphill for the Lost Lake Trail. Continue to bear left for Lost Lake. When you reach the lake, bear left and go around the south side of the lake. Avoid the north side below avalanche chutes that have buried and killed people. The south side of the lake is very safe. Travel around it far enough to see the spectacular views of Chittenden Mountain (10,860 ft.), Bald Mountain (11,342 ft.), South Arapahoe (13,397 feet) massif, and Jasper Mountain (12,923 feet) ridge.

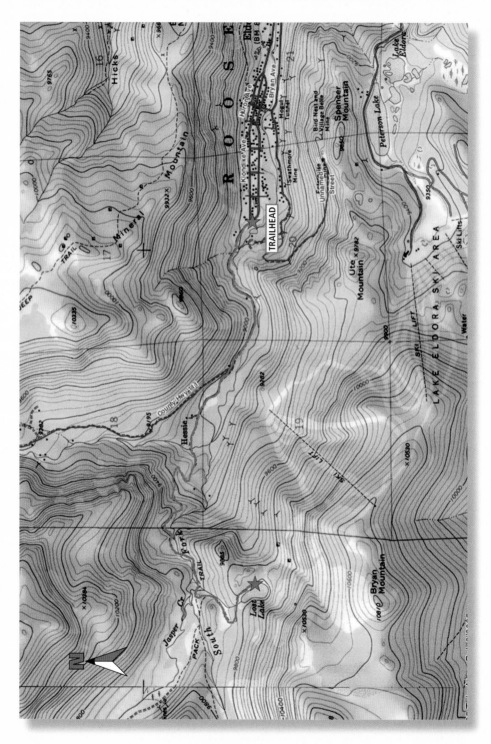

LOST LAKE TRAIL

36. Woodland Lake Trail

ROUND TRIP	10 miles
DIFFICULTY	Difficult
SKILL LEVEL	Intermediate snowshoers and skiers
HIGH POINT	10,800 feet
ELEVATION GAIN	1,800 feet
AVALANCHE DANGER	Low to none
MAP	Latitude 40° Boulder Nederland Trails
CONTACT	Boulder Ranger District, Roosevelt National Forest

COMMENT: The Hessie valley is a beautiful riparian area of Middle Boulder Creek, located just west of the town of Eldora. You will see rock formations, peak views, and moose if you are lucky. It is a good route for family excursions, since snowshoeing or skiing just part of the trail is worthwhile. Either plan to arrive early or visit during the week to avoid crowds and garner a close-in parking spot.

This trail has some narrow steep sections so mid-width skis would be better than skinny skis, though skinny skis are fine for most of the route. You will want a major Front Range storm before visiting since much of the trail and road are sun exposed.

GETTING THERE: From Nederland, go left/south through the roundabout onto Peak to Peak Highway 72 for around 1 mile and turn right onto CR 130. In approximately 2 miles you will see the turnoff on the left for CR 140 uphill for Eldora Mountain Resort; don't turn, go straight. The town of Eldora is another 2 miles west, and the Hessie trailhead is beyond the closed or impassable road on the west side of town. Parking is limited. Pay attention to the No Parking signs, or you will be towed.

THE ROUTE: The trail starts in a small valley but quickly climbs to a ridge top, Your distance to the trail might vary a bit depending on where you can park. In any case, you will have at least a 0.75-mile stroll or ski on the Fourth of July Road to reach the Hessie intersection. You will see the north side of the Eldora Mountain Resort to the south. At the fork, the Fourth of July Road goes straight uphill; you will bear left downhill on the Hessie road/trail. It is another 0.7 mile to the town site sign that notes you are at 9,000 feet. Continue straight ahead on the level trail as you enter trees. You will see a collapsed cabin on the right; bear left. In about 0.3 mile you will cross Middle Boulder Creek on either the footbridge or the frozen surface. You will then see signage for the various trailheads for numerous lakes that are all 1 mile away. Now the real fun begins as the trail begins to climb more steeply in about 0.25 mile and switchbacks to the northeast before turning west-northwest. This part of the trail can be windswept with exposed rocks or have deep drifts to navigate. The steep slopes to the north pose a slight avalanche risk; they generally don't collect enough snow for large releases. The trail climbs 400 feet in less than a mile before leveling. Expansive views of the valley are your reward. You will enjoy a less steep 0.25 mile of trail in the trees and will reach another stream crossing and trail intersection. (If some members of your party are breathless, this is a good

Skiers enjoying a powder day in a winter wonderland..

turnaround point.) You will see signs for the various lakes: 1.5 miles to Lost Lake, 4 miles to Woodland Lake, 5 miles to King Lake, 4 miles to Jasper, and 5 miles to Devil's Thumb. Bear left across the footbridge onto the Lost, Woodland, and King Lakes Trail. The other route to the right goes to Jasper and Devil's Thumb Lakes. You will climb 200 feet in 0.3 mile (gasp), and then the trail climbs more gradually and levels. The trail for Woodland and King Lakes goes straight/right; Lost Lake Trail is left. Continue to bear right. Enjoy the spectacular view of Jasper Peak from the Meadow.

Cross the next footbridge or the frozen stream and trek to the next trail intersection at just under the 2-mile mark and around 9,500 feet. Stay left for Woodland and King Lakes. Enjoy great views and a pretty wetland lake in the next 0.25-mile climb, a place where you could declare victory and turn around if the snow conditions are unfavorable. The trail goes left back into the trees and then takes a sharp right northwest to another stream crossing; if it is mid-winter you might be able to skip the bridge. The trail levels at the Indian Peaks Wilderness boundary and climbs more gradually as it crosses more meadows next to the stream. There is a frozen waterfall on the right before a trail intersection with a sign saying left for Woodland Lake.

At 9,600 feet the trail climbs more steeply at 100 feet per 0.1 mile. You have a great overview of the glacial moraine. At 9,900 feet the trail levels again briefly and crosses a narrow footbridge to the south. It then turns west and back to the south sharply. You climb some steep switchbacks up to 10,000 feet, then decide if you want to ski down the switchbacks if you are on skis. You will continue up to 10,300 feet before leveling with another frozen water feature. Hopefully the wetland will be frozen and covered with deep snow. The trail then turns south across a meadow, then enjoy a ridgeline view at 10,600 feet. You will then climb to an even more spectacular view of the ridge at 10,800 feet as you edge the frozen lake. Climb above the lake at 11,000 feet for an even better panorama.

WOODLAND LAKE TRAIL

37. Lakes Loop Trail

ROUND TRIP	2 miles to Lakes Loop; 1.5 miles out-and-back to Peterson Lake
DIFFICULTY	Easy to moderate
SKILL LEVEL	Beginner snowshoer
HIGH POINT	9,380 feet
ELEVATION GAIN	286 feet for Lakes Loop; 139 feet for Peterson Lake
AVALANCHE DANGER	None
MAP	Eldora Mountain Resort and Nordic Center
CONTACT	Eldora Mountain Resort

COMMENT: The Eldora snowshoeing trails are in the heavily forested Nordic Center area and offer a variety of terrain generally protected from wind. The Lakes Loop can be used as an easy, short, and scenic out-and-back that meanders out to two pretty, frozen lakes. If you snowshoe the entire loop, it is a moderate route with some steep hills. If you want a predictable environment and don't mind paying for it, then snowshoeing within a ski area is a good option. You will have well-marked trails with warming and snack facilities nearby. The fee for adults, at the time this book was written, was $21, $16 for seniors The resort also rents snowshoes. Restrictions: No dogs are allowed on the resort trails or on the adjacent USFS Jenny Creek Trail.

GETTING THERE: From Boulder, take Canyon Boulevard/Highway 119 west 16 miles to Nederland. Go left/south through the roundabout onto Peak to Peak Highway 72 for around 1 mile, and turn right onto CR 130. In approximately 2 miles, turn left on CR 140, uphill to Eldora Mountain Resort. When you enter the resort, turn left toward the Nordic Center.

THE ROUTE: The Tower Trail is a short—but steep—climb to a fire tower and lookLakes Loop is a rolling trail that passes by two ponds and is one of the easiest options. It rolls gently through the trees along the edge of the resort that borders CR 140. Pick up a trail map at the Nordic Center. The map is oriented with north on the bottom and south on the top. Go east/left from the Nordic Center and take the first snowshoe trail going to the right, next to the Dixie Cup Trail. The trail then climbs a short, steep hill as it crosses the Dixie Cup Trail. It parallels and then shares the

View from the Lakes Loop.

hilly Roller Coaster Trail to the Stadium. At the Stadium (a flat Nordic skiing practice area) the Lakes Loop Trail splits to the left/north while the Twisted Trail goes south/right. The Lakes Trail heads off into the trees, away from the Nordic trails on gently rolling terrain and then descends a steeper hill to Peterson Lake. The trail rolls along the edge of Peterson Lake and then gradually veers right toward Eldora Lake. A short section of this trail is exposed and can be windy and rocky. At the end of Peterson Lake there is a private cabin. It is possible to use the sheltered entryway for a snack break. Don't venture onto the ice of Peterson's Lake, as widely varying temperatures make it unreliable and dangerous. Beyond the cabin, the trail turns south and parallels the ski area boundary. There is private property to the east. The trail then passes between the dry lakes and Lake Eldora. Upon reaching Lake Eldora you can retrace your steps back to the Nordic Center for a short, relatively easy out and back. If you want a view of the Arapaho Peaks, persist for the next short hill climb before turning around.

If you are more ambitious you can continue on the loop's uphill portion. The trail climbs up to cross the Dixie, Annie B, and Mill Iron Nordic ski trails, climbing around 100 feet. The trail then climbs steep switchbacks up to a flat spot with nice views of the Arapaho Peaks to the northwest. The trail then continues to climb to reach its high point and views east through the trees of Nederland and Barker Reservoir near the Sawmill ski trail. The trail gradually ascends a saddle and then traverses the hill to the northwest, then begins a series of descents, crossing paths and joining with the Twisted snowshoe trail. You will cross the Gandy Dancer/Dixie/17th Avenue ski trail intersection and continue to descend. You will skirt the open meadow of the Stadium and join the Roller Coaster Trail back to the Nordic Center.

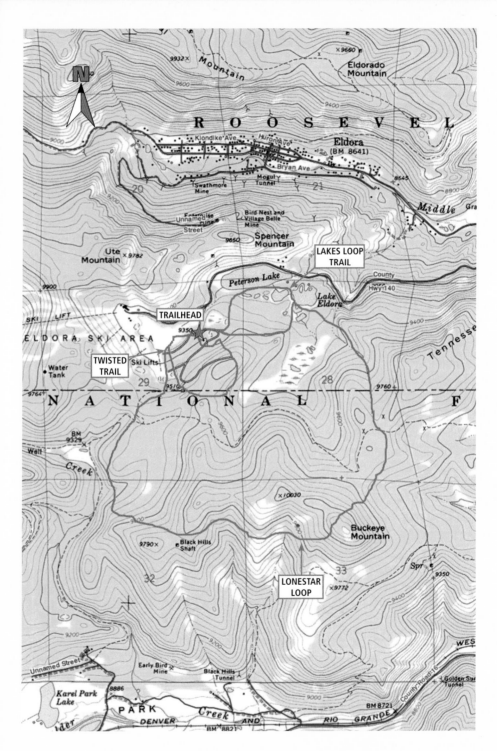

LAKES LOOP TRAIL | TWISTED TRAIL | LONESTAR LOOP

38. **Twisted Trail**

ROUND TRIP	Twisted 1.5 miles
DIFFICULTY	Moderate
SKILL LEVEL	Beginner snowshoer
HIGH POINT	9,600 feet
ELEVATION GAIN	300 feet
AVALANCHE DANGER	None
MAP	Eldora Mountain Resort and Nordic Center
CONTACT	Eldora Mountain Resort

COMMENT: This trail loop features a great view of South Arapaho Peak and the Continental Divide. It includes some steep stretches during its 300-foot climb through nicely forested terrain. This trail is a short moderate loop and can be extended by adding in any of the other snowshoe trails (Lakes or Lonestar loops) that intersect this loop. The Eldora snowshoeing trails are in the heavily forested Nordic area, and offer a variety of terrain, generally protected from wind. If you want a predictable environment, and don't mind paying for it, then snowshoeing within the ski area is a good option. You will have well-marked trails, with warming and snack facilities nearby. The fee for adults, at the time this book was written, was $21, $16 for seniors The resort also rents snowshoes. Restrictions: No dogs are allowed on the resort trails or on the adjacent USFS Jenny Creek Trail.

GETTING THERE: From Boulder, take Canyon Boulevard/Highway 119 west 16 miles to Nederland. Go left/south through the roundabout onto Peak to Peak Highway 72 for around 1 mile, and turn right onto CR 130. In approximately 2 miles, turn left on CR 140, uphill to Eldora Mountain Resort. When you enter the resort, turn left toward the Nordic Center.

THE ROUTE: This description assumes a start from the east trailhead. If you wish Pick up a trail map at the Nordic Center. The map is oriented with north on the bottom and south on the top. Start off east/left from the Nordic Center and take the first snowshoe trail going to the right, next to the Dixie Cup Trail. The trail then climbs a short, steep hill as it crosses the Dixie Cup Trail. It parallels, and then shares the hilly Roller Coaster Trail with Nordic skiers to the Stadium meadow. Since you will be sharing the first part of this trail with Nordic skiers, try to stay

South Arapaho Peak from the Twisted Trail.

out of their tracks if possible, and if tracks are obvious. At the Stadium, which is a flat Nordic skiing practice area, the Lakes Loop Trail splits to the left/north while the Twisted Trail goes south/right. The Twisted Loop goes right/south along the edge of the Stadium meadow and climbs gradually and then more steeply through rolling terrain, crossing the Gandy Dancer Trail. This trail intersection actually has multiple Nordic trails intersecting and signed, so you'll have to look carefully for the snowshoe trail. The Nordic trails do say No Snowshoers, and the skiers are not allowed on the snowshoe trails in order to avoid potential collisions. From there the steep uphill begins in earnest, but the views are worth the effort on clear days. You will crest the steep hill and then cross the Woodcutter and Sawmill ski trails. When you are near the Twin Twisted Tree Nordic ski trail, turn around and you will enjoy a peak-a-boo view of South Arapaho Peak before going being relieved to be going steeply downhill. If the snow is consistent and you see no boulders or stumps showing through, you can venture off trail for some powder. You will cross the 17th Avenue and Cheater's Corner Nordic trails on your very direct route back to the Nordic Center. You will end up on top of the beginner alpine ski runs, where you will enjoy another great view of South Arapaho and the entire resort below you before tracking to the right/east and going downhill to the Nordic Center.

SIDEBAR: Eldora Expansion
There are currently plans to expand the ski area into the Hessie valley, though there is much opposition to the idea because of potential wildlife disruption and consumption of water from Middle Boulder Creek. It is a lovely, quiet area now, so the additional road and ski equipment will likely disturb the serenity.

SEE MAP ON PAGE 157.

39. Lonestar Loop Trail

ROUND TRIP	4.3 miles
DIFFICULTY	Challenging
SKILL LEVEL	Intermediate to advanced snowshoers
HIGH POINT	10,030 feet
ELEVATION GAIN	834 feet
AVALANCHE DANGER	None to low
MAP	Eldora Mountain Resort and Nordic Center
CONTACT	Eldora Mountain Resort

COMMENT: The Lonestar Loop and Sunrise Trails parallel each other—one for snowshoers and the other for skiers. Both are challenging routes that feature spectacular ridge top views of the Continental Divide. You can, of course, just snowshoe or ski parts of the trails and have a shorter, less challenging excursion. Both trails travel very close to the Tennessee Mountain Cabin if you want an overnight stay. Reservations for this cabin are made through the Nordic Center at Eldora Mountain Resort. The Eldora snowshoeing and Nordic trails are in the heavily forested Nordic area and are generally protected from wind. If you want a predictable environment, then snowshoeing within a ski area is a good option. You will have well-marked trails with warming and snack facilities. The fee for adults, at the time this book was written, was $21, $16 for seniors The resort also rents snowshoes. Restrictions: No dogs are allowed on the resort trails or on the adjacent USFS Jenny Creek Trail.

The Lonestar Loop and Rising Sun Trail are used by both snowshoers and skiers. The west side Setting Sun and Lonestar Trails are separate. Sections of the Rising And Setting Sun Trails are steep so using AT or tele skis and skins is advised.

GETTING THERE: From Nederland, go left/south through the roundabout onto Peak to Peak Highway 72 for around 1 mile, and turn right onto CR 130. In approximately 2 miles, turn left on CR 140, uphill to Eldora Mountain Resort. When you enter the resort, turn left toward the Nordic Center.

THE ROUTE: Sign the trail register and proceed through the gate. Merge onto the Lonestar is the most challenging snowshoe trail in the resort and the Rising and Setting Sun Trails are the most difficult cross-country ski trails. They gain over 800 feet while rolling up, down, and sideways with a path toward the Tennessee Mountain Cabin. If you go clockwise, and are doing the entire loop, you will finish going

Rocks along St. Charles Trail.

downhill in the most scenic section. You will use either the Lakes Loop snowshoe trail to access the Lone Star Loop. Pick up a trail map at the Nordic Center to see the alternatives. The map is oriented with north on the bottom and south on the top. If you want to start with a more gradual uphill, and finish on a long downhill, go counter-clockwise on the Twisted Loop to start. You get the best views at the beginning, although you have to turn around to see them as you go uphill. Here is a counter-clockwise description of the Lonestar snowshoe trail: From the Nordic Center go toward the beginner alpine slope and take a sharp left uphill next to the Tenderfoot lift. You will see a US Forest Service sign for Jenny Creek Trail access on the left. You will climb steeply uphill, ascending 100 feet, next to the slope. Ignore the first trail on the left. Once you reach the top of the hill, stop and look over your shoulder at South Arapaho Peak. The trail flattens as you go straight into the trees. Follow the snowshoe sign and enjoy a short climb followed by a level section as you cross the 17th Avenue ski trail. The Jenny Creek US Forest Service access trail departs to the right/west. You then have another short ascent and then the trail descends and levels out crossing the Twin Twisted Tree Nordic ski trail. At this point, the Twisted snowshoe trail splits off to the east, while the Lonestar Loop goes straight uphill to the south. After ascending this hill, Lonestar descends to cross the Sawmill Nordic trail. It then climbs gradually, paralleling the Rising Sun and Setting Sun Nordic trails on the way up. It then descends again through a wooded stretch. After crossing the Rising Sun Nordic trail, you will climb gradually and then steeply, crossing the Setting Sun Nordic trail. This is the longest, steepest uphill. Turn around and enjoy the spectacular views behind you of the distant peaks. When you reach the top of the ridge the view opens up to a sweeping 180-degree view of the Continental Divide, with James Peak to the southwest and the Arapaho Peaks to the northwest. This is a great place for a snack break. The trail stays on the ridge top, and rolls as it runs east to the west slope of Buckeye Mountain before plunging downhill to intersect the Rising/Setting Sun ski trails. There is a rolling stretch and then you intersect the Rising Sun Trail again in a saddle between Buckeye and Tennessee Mountains. From there you can turn left and continue downhill to the base area or go right/uphill to the Tennessee Mountain Cabin. Rob's Shortcut is a more efficient approach with better protection for the snow. The Lonestar Loop turns north and combines with the Rising Sun Nordic trail and then plunges 0.75 mile downhill. You exit Lonestar between the Beavers Revenge and Mill Iron Nordic ski trails. Bear right and look carefully for the signs for the Lakes Loop snowshoe trail to take you back to the Nordic Center.

SEE MAP ON PAGE 157.

40. Rising Sun and Setting Sun Trails

ROUND TRIP	4.3 miles
DIFFICULTY	Challenging
SKILL LEVEL	Intermediate to advanced snowshoers
HIGH POINT	10,030 feet
ELEVATION GAIN	834 feet
AVALANCHE DANGER	None to low
MAP	Eldora Mountain Resort and Nordic Center
CONTACT	Eldora Mountain Resort

COMMENT: The East Spanish Peak, the smaller and most eastern outlier of the The Sunrise and Sunset Trails can combine for a spectacular, challenging loop. The Sunrise and Lonestar snowshoe trails combine for the ascent. The Sunset and Lonestar Trails parallel each other—one for snowshoers and the other for skiers. Both are challenging routes that features spectacular ridge top views of the Continental Divide. Skiing downhill is easier on the west side Sunset Trail since you won't have to watch for snowshoers. Sections of the Sunrise and Sunset Trails are steep, so using AT or tele skis and skins is advised. You could ski them on skinny skis if you are an expert and it is a powder day. If you are an expert skier who likes to ski in trees, go to the top of the Lonestar snowshoe trail and ski down through the trees, watching for the Setting Sun Trail.

You can, of course, just ski part of the trails and have a shorter, less challenging excursion. Both trails travel very close to the Tennessee Mountain Cabin if you want an overnight stay. Reservations for this cabin are made through the Nordic Center at Eldora Mountain Resort. The Eldora snowshoeing and Nordic trails are in the heavily forested Nordic area and are generally protected from wind. If you want a predictable environment, then snowshoeing or skiing within a ski area is a good option. You will have well-marked trails with warming and snack facilities. The fee for adults at the time this book was written was $25, $16 for seniors for a Nordic pass. The resort also rents snowshoes and skinny skis. Restrictions: No dogs are allowed on the resort trails or on the adjacent USFS Jenny Creek Trail.

GETTING THERE: From Walsenburg, travel east on US 160 to Highway 12. Turn From Nederland, go left/south through the roundabout onto Peak to Peak Highway 72 for around 1 mile, and turn right onto CR 130. In approximately 2 miles, turn left

View of South Arapaho Peak from the Setting Sun trail.

on CR 140, uphill to Eldora Mountain Resort. When you enter the resort, turn left toward the Nordic Center.

THE ROUTE: The Lonestar snowshoe trail is the most challenging snowshoe trail in the resort and the Rising Sun and Setting Sun Trails are the most difficult cross-country ski trails. They gain over 800 feet while rolling up, down, and sideways with a path toward the Tennessee Mountain Cabin. They are moderate for experienced backcountry skiers. If you go clockwise, and are doing the entire loop, you will finish going downhill in the most scenic section. From the Nordic Center start on the Dixie/Beaver's Revenge Trails if you are on skis. Pick up a trail map at the Nordic Center to see the alternative routes. The map is oriented with north on the bottom and south on the top. When you reach the top of the Beaver's Revenge Trail look on the left for the Rising Sun Trail. It is a steady and sometimes steep heavily forested trail. You will climb at least a mile before the Lonestar snowshoe trail separates off to the right; continue straight to the intersection of the Rising Sun and Rob's Shortcut Trail. If you want to see the cabin, detour off on Rob's Trail. The Rising Sun Trail turns sharply to the right and goes downhill and then uphill to the intersection with the Setting Sun Trail. Go straight for the Setting Sun Trail or take a sharp right to continue downhill on Rising Sun. Setting Sun is the best descent. The middle section of Rising Sun traverses uphill after ¼ mile. The Setting Sun Trail descends through a wooded stretch and then offers spectacular views of the Continental Divide with James Peak to the southwest and the Arapaho Peaks to the northwest through the trees. This is a great place for a snack break. You will eventually intersect the Rising Sun Trail and then end up on the uphill Sawmill Trail, intersecting with the Twisted Tree and Jasure ski trails. Turn right and climb the short hill up Twisted for another nice descent down to the Gandy Dancer Trail. Take Gandy Dancer back to 17th Avenue Trail and the Nordic Center.

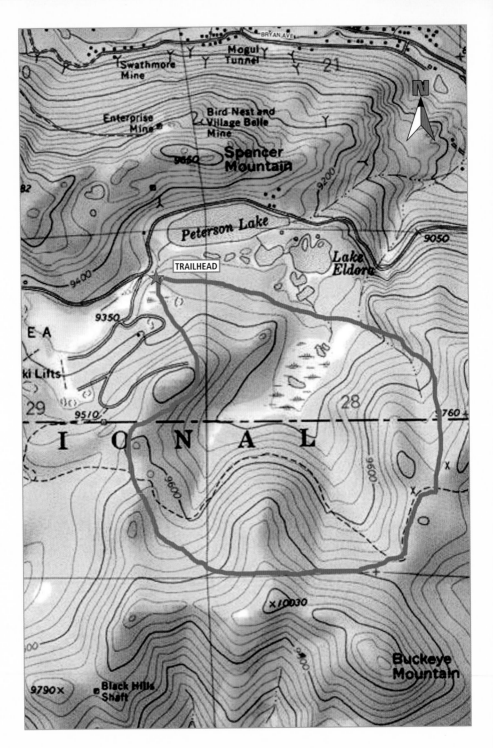

RISING SUN AND SETTING SUN TRAILS

Nederland Area

Chapter 7

ROLLINSVILLE AREA

"We are all one in nature. Believing so, there was in our hearts a great peace and a welling kindness for all living, growing things."

—Luther Standing Bear, *Land of the Spotted Eagle* (1933)

Rollinsville is a mountain town created to serve not only the numerous mines and miners, but also as a railroad stop on the way to the famous Moffat Tunnel that bored under James Peak and the Continental Divide toward Winter Park. It is now the entryway to the Moffat Road and the popular trailheads 10 miles west at or near the East Portal, of one of the highest (9,239 feet) and longest (6.2 miles) railroad tunnels in the world. You are likely to see coal and freight trains plying their way through the expansive and beautiful mountain valley, or even Amtrak's California Zephyr going to or from the West Coast. The tunnel was holed through in 1926 in a blast triggered by US President Calvin Coolidge. The fist railroad traffic went through in 1928. It is still a very busy, often clogged route for Union Pacific and Burlington Northern-Santa Fe trains.

The Mammoth Gulch, Rogers and Heart Lake, and Forest Lakes Trails are on the way to or at the East Portal of the tunnel. Two of the trails are highly scenic routes to high mountain lakes, while Mammoth Gulch features spectacular views of the riparian and glacier-carved valley. All of these trails are skied and snowshoed.

There is a bar/restaurant and a quick-stop grocery in Rollinsville, which is 4.5 miles south of Nederland.

Rogers Pass Lake and Heart Lake trailhead.

41. Rogers Pass Lake and Heart Lake

ROUND TRIP	8.2 miles
DIFFICULTY	Moderate to challenging
SKILL LEVEL	Beginner to the meadow; intermediate/advanced to Rogers Pass and Heart Lakes
HIGH POINT	11,340 feet
ELEVATION GAIN	2,100 feet
AVALANCHE DANGER	None to low
MAP	Trails Illustrated #103 Winter Park, Central City, Rollins Pass, Boulder County Trails, Colorado Front Range Recreation Topo Map
CONTACT	Boulder Ranger District, Roosevelt National Forest

COMMENT: Snowshoe or ski any portion of this popular trail, and you will have an enjoyable trek in a stately old-growth forest with a few ridge top views along the way. You will need a long day to make it all through part of the James Peak Wilderness to Rogers Pass and Heart Lakes but they are magnificent jewels, cupped by the soaring mountaintops of the Continental Divide. The trail has many steep sections, making it an intermediate to advanced ski trail. You will need AT or tele skis with climbing skins. Downhill traction makes it easier but slower for snowshoers. This is a very popular trail on weekends with lots of dogs. It is marked with intermittent blue diamonds. Restrictions: You will be in the James Peak Wilderness Area, so no open fires are permitted, and dogs must be kept on leash. Please do keep your dogs firmly under voice control for their safety, as you might encounter fast downhill skiers.

GETTING THERE: From Nederland, go left/south through the roundabout onto Peak to Peak Highway 119 south for 4.5 miles to Rollinsville; turn west/right on narrow, gravel Gilpin CR 16 then drive 8 more miles to the Moffat Tunnel and the East Portal trailhead. The road is plowed and there is a large parking area and pit toilet restrooms.

THE ROUTE: Go around the right/north side of the tunnel on the South Boulder Creek Trail (#900). Until the creek is covered and frozen you might have to shed your snowshoes to get over a couple of footbridges early or late in the season. The snow is often thin for the first mile of the trail because of sun and wind exposure early and late in the season, but fine mid-winter. Once you enter the thick tree cover you will have good consistent snow. At 1.2 miles you will reach the intersection with

Rogers Pass Lake and Heart Lake trailhead.   PHOTO BY GREG LONG

the Forest Lakes Trail; continue straight ahead. In another 0.3 mile you will reach a fork in the trail as it steepens. In about 0.25 mile the trail turns sharply right uphill on a switchback that goes north/northeast, many people miss this turn. At around another 0.4 mile you might see the Crater Lakes Trail (#819) on the right; continue straight ahead. You will see another false trail on the right as the trail levels briefly then goes steeply over 10,000 feet, crossing a tributary of South Boulder Creek and turning due south. Take a minute to enjoy the old-growth forest of stately trees, many of which are draped in Spanish moss. Look to the left and you can see the snow-capped high ridgeline tracking west, often with spindrift looking like wispy clouds being blown over the top. You will be protected from the wind by the thick tree cover. A somewhat less steep section will catapult you up to 10,300 feet where there will be a stream crossing and the trees will open up with more views to the south of the high ridge as well as the ridge to the north. You will pass through a lot of pretty glades as the trail climbs more gradually over the next mile to around 10,400 feet. You can enjoy another sunny break in the trees with a small meadow on the right. The trail goes south and actually levels and goes temporarily downhill. Then the trail swings west, and the next mile to Heart Lake is much steeper, climbing 700 feet (gasp). Look for potential side trails to the lakes that are both at just over 11,000 feet. Heart is at 11,300 feet and Rogers Pass is at 11,100 feet. Take a long lunch break, and enjoy the ride down.

ROGERS PASS LAKE and HEART LAKE

42. **Forest Lakes Trail**

ROUND TRIP	6.5 miles to lower lake; 7 miles to upper lake
DIFFICULTY	Moderate
SKILL LEVEL	Intermediate snowshoers and skiers
HIGH POINT	10,820 feet at lower lake; 11,020 feet at upper lake
ELEVATION GAIN	1,400 feet at lower lake; 1,620 feet at upper lake
AVALANCHE DANGER	None to low
MAP	Boulder County Trails, Colorado Front Range Recreation Topo Map
CONTACT	Boulder Ranger District, Roosevelt National Forest

COMMENT: Forest Lakes is a scenic jaunt to two high mountain lakes with good views of the Continental Divide for the last 1.5 miles. Snowshoeing or skiing any portion of this route will be rewarding. This is a much easier and shorter route than the trek to Rogers Pass and Heart Lakes. You will want AT or tele skis to ski it. It requires advanced ski skills, since it is a fast and steep descent on skis. It opens up to views and sun earlier than the Rogers Pass/Heart Lakes route, but that also means portions of the south-facing route melt off faster. This trail is not as well marked with blue diamonds as the Rogers Pass/Heart Lakes route. Restrictions: You will be in the James Peak Wilderness Area, so no open fires are permitted, and dogs must be kept on leash. Please do keep your dogs firmly under voice control for their safety, as you might encounter fast downhill skiers.

GETTING THERE: From Nederland, go left/south through the roundabout onto Peak to Peak Highway 119 south for 4.5 miles to Rollinsville; turn west/right on narrow, gravel Gilpin CR 16; drive 8 more miles to the Moffat Tunnel and the East Portal trailhead. The road is plowed and there is a large parking area and pit toilet restrooms.

THE ROUTE: Climbing a short series of switchbacks leads quickly to the top of the Go around the right/north side of the tunnel on the South Boulder Creek Trail (#900). Until the creek is covered and frozen you might have to shed your snowshoes to get over a couple of footbridges. The snow is often thin for the first mile of the trail because of sun and wind exposure early and late season, but it will be fine in mid-winter. Once you enter the thick tree cover you will have much better snow. At 1.2 miles you will reach the intersection with the Forest Lakes Trail (809); go northeast/right, having climbed around 400 feet. The trail is initially an old road that

Early snowshoe season outing at Forest Lakes.

traverses a steep slope, climbing 300 feet in around 0.75 mile. You will climb 200 feet and cross Arapaho Creek in about 0.5 mile. There is a footbridge. Use it if the creek is not completely frozen over. You will have intermittent views of the riparian valley as you climb through the thick trees. The road ends as the trail swings northwest and rolls more gradually uphill through a mixed forest. The trail breaks from the trees and has excellent views of the high mountain ridgeline on your left from the pretty glade at around 10,000 feet. This section of the trail is a bit hard to follow with its multiple social ski trails, but you will have the ridgeline on your left for orientation. Keep traveling northwest toward the lakes. The trail climbs more gradually for the next 0.75 mile. When you pass the intersection with the Arapaho Lakes Trail, you will be around 1 mile from the lower lake and will reach 10,400 feet gradually. Some people like to see the Arapaho Lakes too, and will ski the avalanche-hazard bowls above the lakes. The last 0.5 mile is steeper, as the trail climbs another 200 feet in short order. Enjoy the beautiful lake with the Continental Divide ridgeline as the backdrop. If you continue on to the upper lake, you might hear snowmobiles on the Rollins Pass Road, which is only 0.25 mile beyond it.

Some skiers like to ski the trees on the left side of the trail after you cross the bridge on the descent. Pick your route carefully since the trees can be very tight if you turn off too soon. Go at least ¼ mile before taking to the trees.

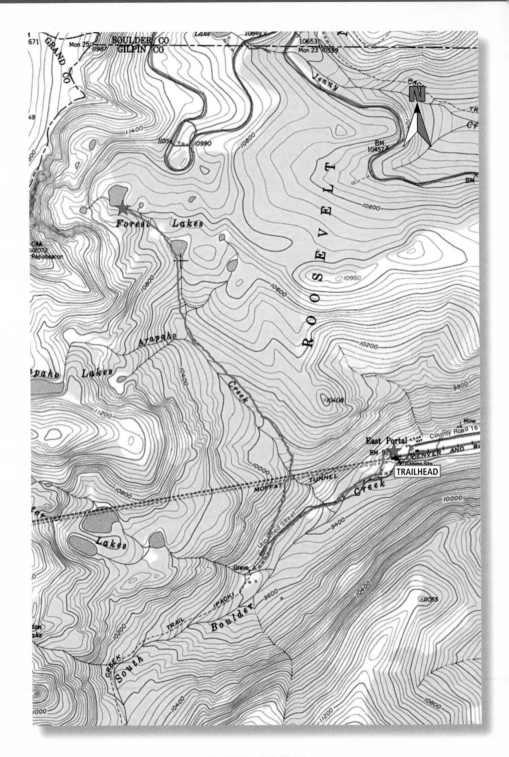

FOREST LAKES TRAIL

43. Arapaho Lakes Trail

ROUND TRIP	6 miles to lower lake; 6.5 miles to upper lake
DIFFICULTY	Difficult
SKILL LEVEL	Intermediate snowshoers; expert skiers
HIGH POINT	11,220 feet at lower lake; 11,500 feet at upper lake
ELEVATION GAIN	1,700 feet to lower lake; 1,900 feet to upper lake
AVALANCHE DANGER	Moderate to high on the ridgeline above the lakes
MAP	Boulder County Trails, Colorado Front Range Recreation Topo Map
CONTACT	Boulder Ranger District, Roosevelt National Forest

COMMENT: The Arapahoe Lakes Trail is one of the best trails in the area for skiing through trees. It is a much steeper climb than Forest Lakes, but if you like tree skiing and don't mind tight trees requiring quick turns you will love it. You will climb to the top of a ridge overlooking the second lake with a spectacular view of the 12,000-foot ridgeline of unnamed peaks. One is informally called Radio Beacon Peak. Most people don't descend down to the upper lake from the overlook, and the slopes above it are highly hazardous for avalanches until spring consolidation. Snowshoeing or skiing any portion of this route will be rewarding. This is a much shorter route than the trek to Rogers Pass and Heart Lakes. You will want AT or tele skis to ski it. It requires advanced ski skills since it is a fast and steep descent on skis. This trail is not as well marked with blue diamonds as the Rogers Pass/Heart Lakes route. Restrictions: You will be in the James Peak Wilderness Area, so no open fires are permitted, and dogs must be kept on leash. Please do keep your dogs firmly under voice control for their safety, as you will encounter fast downhill skiers.

GETTING THERE: From Nederland, go left/south through the roundabout onto Peak to Peak Highway 119 south for 4.5 miles to Rollinsville; turn west/right on narrow, gravel Gilpin CR 16; drive 8 more miles to the Moffat Tunnel and the East Portal Trailhead. The road is plowed and there is a large parking area and pit toilet restrooms.

THE ROUTE: The Levsa Trail is a 1-mile loop hike from the campground. Go around the right/north side of the tunnel on the South Boulder Creek Trail (#900). Until the creek is covered and frozen you might have to shed your snowshoes to get over a couple of footbridges. The snow is often thin for the first mile

Skiers enjoying the stunning view on a frosty powder day.

of the trail because of sun and wind exposure early and late season, but it will be fine in mid-winter. The Arapaho Lakes descent requires deep, mid-winter snow cover since it travels over fallen trees and stumps. Once you enter the thick tree cover you will have much better snow. At 1.2 miles you will reach the intersection with the Forest Lakes Trail (809); go northeast/right, having climbed around 400 feet. The trail is initially an old road that traverses a steep slope, climbing 300 feet in around 0.75 mile. You will climb 200 feet and cross Arapaho Creek in about 0.5 mile. There is a footbridge—use it if the creek is not completely frozen over. You will have intermittent views of the riparian valley as you climb through the thick trees. The road ends as the trail swings northwest and rolls more gradually uphill through a mixed forest. The trail breaks from the trees and has excellent views of the high mountain ridgeline on your left from the pretty glade at around 10,000 feet. This section of the trail is a bit hard to follow with its multiple social ski trails, but you will have the ridgeline on your left for orientation. Keep traveling northwest toward the lakes. The trail climbs more gradually for the next 0.75 mile. When you reach the intersection with the Arapaho Lakes Trail, you will be around 0.75 mile from lower Forest Lake. The trail levels and descends slightly to Arapaho Creek. The 819 Trail turns sharply left/west and ascends rapidly as the trees thicken. Keep the creek on your right as you ascend through the tall, thick, mixed forest of ponderosa and lodgepole pine. If you bear left you will reach the shore of the lower lake. Most skiers want to bear right to surmount the overlook of the upper lake and massif, so they can take a few more turns on the steep slope.

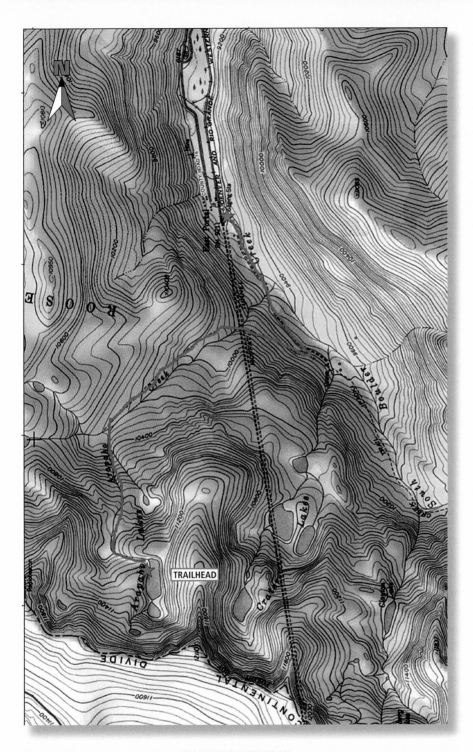

ARAPAHO LAKES TRAIL

44. Mammoth Gulch Road

ROUND TRIP	3 miles
DIFFICULTY	Moderate
SKILL LEVEL	Novice snowshoers and skiers for the road; intermediate ski skills for Nebraska Hill
HIGH POINT	9,700 feet at intersection; 10,200 feet
ELEVATION GAIN	850 feet to 1,300 feet
AVALANCHE DANGER	Low to moderate
MAP	Trails Illustrated #103, Winter Park, Central City, Rollins Pass, Boulder County Trails, Colorado Front Range Recreation Topo Map
CONTACT	Idaho Springs Ranger District, Roosevelt National Forest

COMMENT: What is in summer a four-wheel-drive road becomes a scenic route for snowshoeing or skiing in the winter. You will see sweeping views of the Continental Divide ridgeline and James Peak. You might see Amtrak and other trains barreling by on the nearby east-west railroad tracks. The primary challenge is very limited parking and an aggressive sheriff who will ticket you. You will need a four-wheel-drive vehicle to park unless it is early or late season. Carpool, and have a backup plan around the East Moffat trails in case there is no off-road parking available. You can ski this route on any style of skis if you are an experienced skier, but it is not good for beginners. If you want to take some turns on the Nebraska Hill bowl that is northwest of the road you will want AT or tele skis; it is steep enough to avalanche.

GETTING THERE: From Nederland go left/south through the roundabout onto Peak to Peak Highway 119 south for 4.5 miles to Rollinsville; turn west/right on narrow, gravel Gilpin CR 16. Drive approximately 6 more miles to the whistle-stop town of Tolland. The Mammoth Gulch Road is the first road on the left/south after Tolland.

THE ROUTE: After starting out on the easy, wooded gradient, the trail continues This route offers three fairly straightforward out-and-back routes. You will gradually climb up around 800 feet on the road for about 1.5 miles before it starts to level out a bit. At the intersection, you have three choices: 1) Forest Trail 183: you can take this trail on the west side downhill, losing around 200 feet of elevation into a very pretty meadow

View from Mammoth Gulch Road.

and mixed conifer/aspen area. Once you have bottomed out in the former reservoir in Mammoth Gulch there are no trail markers and route finding becomes an issue. If you can carefully retrace your route, you can wander around as you please and then ascend back up to the main road/trail. 2) Go straight ahead toward the head of Mammoth Gulch, below Kingston and James Peaks. The road climbs gradually to around 10,000 feet over the next 2 miles where you will reach avalanche terrain. Nebraska Hill is to the right, you can ski into the gulch, northwest of the road for low-angle, relatively safe terrain before you reach the steep slopes of Nebraska Hill that can be hazardous. This is a good turnaround point unless you are a winter mountaineer with avalanche experience. If you are, and avalanche danger is low, you can continue up valley to Echo Lake below James Peak. This Echo Lake is not the same as the Mount Evans Echo Lake. 3) Take the sharpest left and the steeper uphill option that stays on CR 4N. In 0.5 mile it climbs to another intersection where you go left again if you want to summit Baltimore Ridge (10,260 feet), or climb another mile up to an intersection with Moffat Road at 10,500 feet. The Moffat Road is the safer approach for James Peak, other than St. Mary's Lake accessed from Interstate 70. (The description for snowshoeing up James Peak in this book is from St. Mary's Lake.)

If you want more certainty, stay on the main trail/road in choice 2 above, which will continue to climb very gradually, with some level spots. Because the road eventually tracks under avalanche terrain and dead-ends in a drainage below James Peak, take a topographical map so you know when you are below the steep avalanche terrain. The top of this gulch is surrounded by avalanche slopes, which are best avoided until the snow is very stable.

SIDEBAR: Packing Your Snowshoes

Snow conditions can vary from light, fluffy power to windswept rocks and gravel in a matter of 100 yards in the Front Range of Colorado. Always have a way of comfortably carrying your snowshoes. Obviously for short stretches you will just carry them in your mittens, but for a long stretch of bad conditions or a snow-free approach route, it is a good idea to have some system of attaching your snowshoes to your pack with straps so that they won't bang around and annoy you.

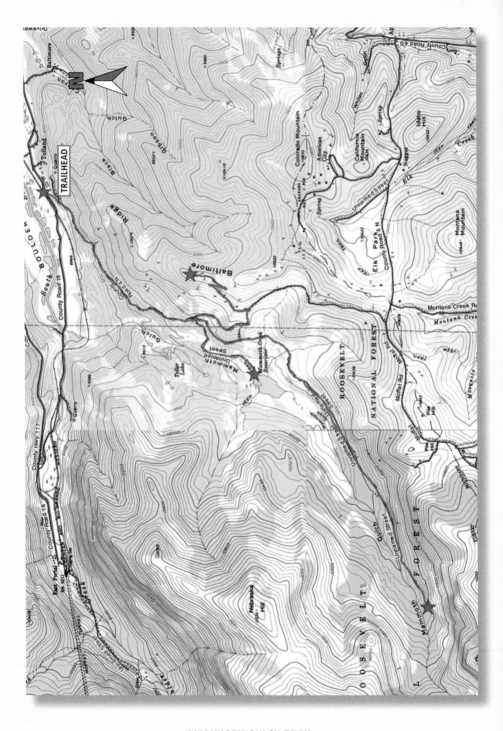

MAMMOTH GULCH TRAIL

45. Raccoon Loop Trail

ROUND TRIP	2.5 miles
DIFFICULTY	Moderate
SKILL LEVEL	Beginner snowshoers; experienced skiers
HIGH POINT	9,400 feet
ELEVATION GAIN	500 feet
AVALANCHE DANGER	None
MAP	Golden Gate Canyon State Park, Colorado Front Range Recreation Topo Map
CONTACT	Golden Gate Canyon State Park

COMMENT: The Raccoon Trail is one of many beautiful trails in Golden Gate Canyon State Park. The trailhead is a grand overlook of the Continental Divide and Indian Peaks. This trail is one of the best choices for snowshoeing or skiing because it is over 9,000 feet high and protected by trees. This doesn't mean it always has enough snow, so check with the park or be prepared to carry your snowshoes. Visiting after a major Front Range upslope storm is ideal. The worst case is a superb winter hike. If you start at the overlook you will enjoy the aforementioned spectacular peak view. The trail then goes downhill and you will end on an uphill to get back to the overlook. If you start at the campground, you will end your trek on a downhill. This description starts from the overlook. You can use any style of skis if you are an experienced skier, but it is not for beginners.

RESTRICTIONS: Dogs must be kept on leash. A Colorado State Parks pass, daily or annual, is required to use this trail.

GETTING THERE: From Nederland take Highway 119 south for 10 miles to Gap Road/CR 2, which is 5 miles south of Rollinsville. There is a large brown state park sign as well as other park signage. You can access the trail from either Reverend's Ridge Campground or the overlook. For the overlook, continue uphill past the campground turnoff for another 1.5 miles; it will be on your left. The county road is plowed and there is a parking area with pit toilets.

From Golden, take Highway 93 north to Golden Gate Canyon Road and turn left. Go 13 miles to the visitor center. Continue 4 miles on Highway 46, 4 miles to turn right/north onto Highway 119. In approximately 4 miles, turn right onto Gap Road/CR 2. Yes it does. Trailhead is far from it.

Looking toward the top of Grayback Peak.

THE ROUTE: Start by enjoying the view from the visitor center deck; it is one of the best choices for photos. From the overlook parking area you have two choices for this loop: northeast/clockwise travel, or south/counter-clockwise. In both cases you will be going downhill at the start and uphill at the end. I suggest a clockwise route since the initial downhill this direction is a bit more gradual. The trail is to the right of the deck and turns southwest through switchbacks. You will have some peak views as the trail rolls gently through the mixed forest to an intersection in about 0.7 mile. If you go left/straight you will be on the Elk Trail to Bootleg Bottom (1.2 miles); turn right/west-northwest and continue downhill in a pretty glade that Robin Hood would enjoy. You will bottom out in about 0.5 mile and the trees open up with a nice meadow on your left. You will see the side trail to the campground on your left; in 100 yards take a sharp right and S-turn to stay on the Raccoon Trail. You will see a private cabin on your right. This is an excellent spot for photos of the rock formations silhouetted by the stately aspens. You will edge along the magnificent aspen grove and then encounter the steepest part of the trek. The trail climbs 200 feet, quickly gaining part of the 500-foot climb that has just begun. This part of the trail is sun exposed and might have thin snow. The trail levels and then climbs steeply again. Turn around to enjoy the peak views behind you before climbing some more. After you have climbed almost 400 feet and another 0.5 mile, the trail levels, descends, and takes a sharp right/southeast turn through aspen trees. It turns right again downhill then goes left uphill to reach the park road. The trail parallels the road back to the overlook. If you see the side trail on the right, take it to enjoy more spectacular views for the last 0.25 mile.

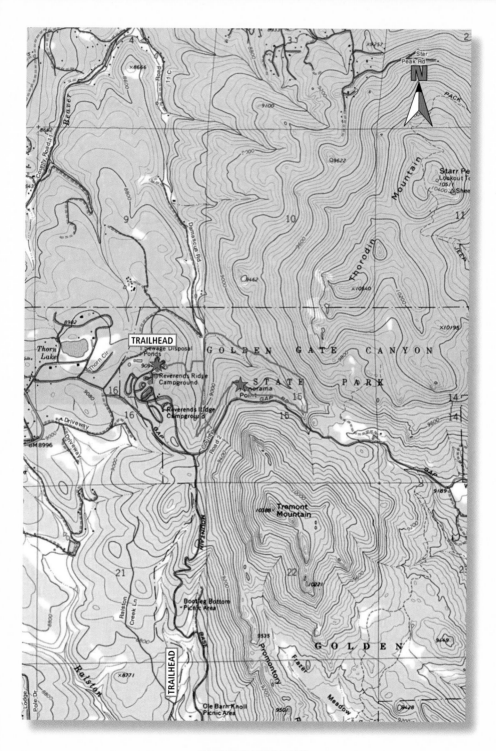

RACCOON LOOP TRAIL

Central Colorado

Chapter 8

MOUNT EVANS AREA

"The horizon is bounded and adorned by a spiry wall of pines, every tree harmoniously related to every other; definite symbols, divine hieroglyphics written with sunbeams. Would I could understand them!"

—John Muir, *My First Summer in the Sierra* (1911)

Geer Pond, in Mueller State Park.

Snowshoers out for a fun outing.

Mount Evans is one of highest mountains in the state and one of two that has a road to the top, which was built in 1930. Ironically, it is also the home of the Mount Evans Wilderness Area, an excellent place to recreate in the winter. It is an expansive and grand high-mountain environment that inspires easily accessible and safe winter recreation.

There are a variety of trails, but this book focuses on three of the most popular and easily usable options. Mount Evans is almost the twin of 14,000-foot Mount Bierstadt. They are connected by an impressive Sawtooth Ridge and their combined massif is significant. The Sawtooth is not an easy winter route. Both peaks are discussed in this book. Snowshoeing to the summit of Bierstadt is a suggested route because it is a bit safer than attempting the summit of Mount Evans, since people have been killed by avalanches on the road near Mount Goliath. Mount Evans was first successfully climbed on snowshoes by Albert Ellingwood in March of 1916; Mount Bierstadt was first ski-climbed in 1934.

Mount Evans is approached from the north on Interstate 70 out of Denver.

46. Echo Lake and Chicago Lakes Trails

ROUND TRIP	2 miles to Echo Lake; 3 miles to Chicago Lakes
DIFFICULTY	Easy to Moderate
SKILL LEVEL	Beginner snowshoers and novice skiers to Echo Lake; advanced skiers to Chicago Lakes
HIGH POINT	10,598 feet
ELEVATION GAIN	50 feet
AVALANCHE DANGER	None for Echo Lake; moderate to considerable for Chicago Lakes Trail
MAP	Trails Illustrated #103, Winter Park, Central City, Rollins Pass
CONTACT	Clear Creek Ranger District, Arapaho National Forest

COMMENT: Echo Lake is an easy, almost flat family route around a sparkling frozen lake surrounded by sweeping views of soaring Front Range peaks. You can add a short, more challenging, jaunt for a spectacular view on the first part of the Chicago Lakes Trail before avalanche danger turns you around. The short excursion on the Chicago Lakes Trail will deliver a superb view of the Mount Evans massif and its lofty neighbors. Unless the snowpack is completely stable you don't want to wander too far on the seductive Chicago Lakes Trail because of the slide potential of the slopes above it. The Echo Lake Trail is a bit short for skiing unless you take your chances and ski the Chicago Lakes Trail or Mount Evans Byway too. Almost any ski style will work. The descent to the Chicago Lakes Trail requires advanced skills, the rest of the trail does not.

GETTING THERE: Take Interstate 70 to Idaho Springs and then Exit 40 south for Mount Evans. Take Highway 103 south for 14 miles to the shoreline of Echo Lake. There is parking at the Echo Lake Picnic Area, or go 1 mile farther south to the entrance of the closed Echo Lake Campground, seasonal restaurant, and Mount Evans Byway road.

THE ROUTE: Follow the road up to the old mining area. There is not much to look If you park at the picnic area, the trail goes counter-clockwise around the lake to the right from the picnic area and restrooms. These are the only available facilities open in the winter months. The best lake views of Mount Evans are from the southeast edge of the lake since you will be entering thick trees. That side of the

The view north across Echo Lake.

lake is usually not navigable on snowshoes, so snap a photo and head west. After 0.25 mile you will see a sign for the Chicago Lakes Trail going straight, while the Echo Lake Trail turns to the left. If you want an additional spectacular view of the Evans massif, continue straight for a short side trip. In another 0.25 mile you will round the bend, break from the trees, and see the impressive cirques and peaks of Mounts Roger, Warren, Spalding, and Evans on the horizon. This is a good time to snap a photo and turn around before you expose yourself to avalanche terrain. As the Chicago Lakes Trail continues it is bordered on both sides by avalanche terrain so don't attempt it and tempt fate. Instead reverse course to the Echo Lake Trail and turn right when you intersect it. You can continue along the flat trail under a pretty tree canopy that will protect you from the cold breeze. Venture close to the lake, though the trail travels away from the lakeshore. You will see a fork in the trail; going left will take you to Mount Evans Byway. That part of the trail ends when you reach the Mount Evans Byway and the closed restaurant. You can continue up the Byway (see the next route) if you want to extend your adventure. If you go right at the fork you will go uphill, at first gradually, and then steeply, as the trail also makes its way to a very steep access to the Mount Evans Byway at the 1-mile mark. You can also wander up to the rocky ridge and enjoy better views through the trees.

If avalanche danger is low, and you want to extend your snowshoe or ski, continue down to the Chicago Lakes Trail where you can first descend and then climb gradually up the valley for as long as you wish. If you are an experienced skier you can use any style of ski. Only the descent to the valley requires advanced skills.

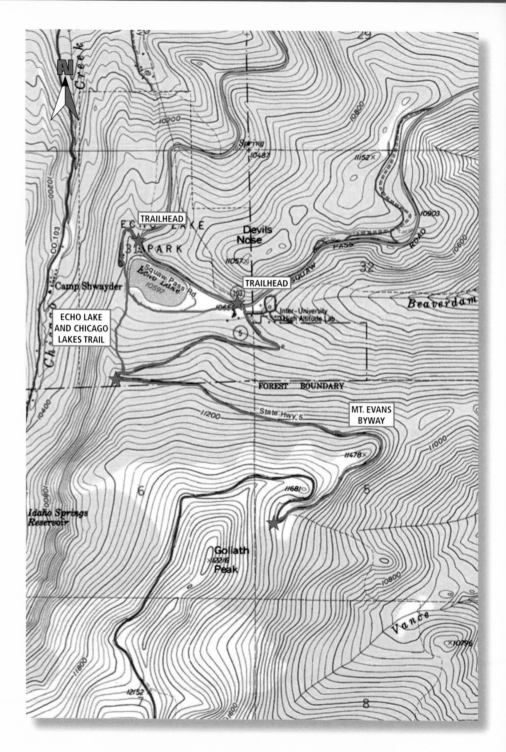

ECHO LAKE and CHICAGO LAKES TRAILS | MOUNT EVANS BYWAY

47. Mount Evans Byway

ROUND TRIP	5 miles to Goliath
DIFFICULTY	Easy to Moderate, Challenging to the summit
SKILL LEVEL	Beginner for partial route; intermediate/advanced for summit
HIGH POINT	11,598 feet
ELEVATION GAIN	50 feet
AVALANCHE DANGER	Low to Goliath Peak; considerable to high near Goliath Peak Natural Area

COMMENT: This heavily traveled scenic highway is closed in the winter to motorized travel, making it a fun snowshoe or Nordic ski. It is a steady, though not steep, climb with ever-expanding views of Mount Evans and Mount Goliath. Parts of the road are sun-exposed and wind-swept and can be completely snow-free early or late season. If the snow is not good try the tree-sheltered Echo Lake route. You can use any style of ski to ski up the wide road.

GETTING THERE: Take Interstate 70 to Idaho Springs and take Exit 40 for Mount Evans. Take Highway 103 south for 15 miles to the south end of Echo Lake. There is parking at the entrance to the closed Mount Evans Byway, Echo Lake Campground, and seasonal restaurant.

THE ROUTE: Assuming either an out-and-back or a full trail from the north, the This wide paved road makes a nice roomy winter trail. Just go around the gate and as far as you desire. The first 2.5 miles are low-angle terrain with no avalanche exposure. The road starts off traveling in the trees southeast 0.25 mile to a hairpin turn where it begins to climb west a bit more steeply. You will gain around 400 feet over the first mile. When you reach the next turn you will see the 1-mile marker on the right side of the road. You will have some nice views of the peaks of Independence (11,450 ft.) and Alpine (11,552 ft.) to the west and Griffith (11,568 ft.) and Alps (10,552 ft.) to the north. If you want a good view of Grey Wolf Mountain (13,602 ft.), Mount Spalding (13,842 ft.), and part of the Mount Evans massif, round the turn and go right, off road, uphill, through the trees. Once you clear the trees you will see the massif if it is not too cloudy. If the snow is mediocre, you can descend near the mile marker down to the extension of the Echo Lake/Chicago Lakes Trail. The snow can improve with elevation. It is a very steep descent, a bit less so in the trees on the left, so be careful if you go that way.

The Mount Evans Byway.

The road continues northeast surrounded by trees for another mile to the 2-mile marker, gaining another 300 feet. In around 0.5 mile you will reach the next turn where the road tracks southwest and you can see Goliath Peak (12,216 ft.). It is a good place to turn around since you will be treading into potential avalanche terrain. If you are sure the snowpack is stable you can continue on another 0.25 mile or so to the summertime nature center and Goliath Natural Area trailhead. This is a good place to get out of the wind, have a snack, and enjoy the twisted krummholz trees. Don't go to the nature center, or up Goliath Peak's slope unless you have had an avalanche class and can dig a snow pit to evaluate the risk. There was a recent avalanche fatality near the Mount Goliath Nature Center. You can stop short of the steep slopes of Goliath and have a fun, scenic jaunt. If you have winter mountaineering skills, you can continue on the road. It goes to the upper slopes of Goliath Peak. Taking the Goliath Natural Area trail is not advisable since it treks directly below very risky avalanche terrain. Some experienced mountaineers snowshoe the road all the way to the summit in the winter. If you have had an avalanche course, and are well prepared, this is a possible option on a clear day.

If you have a stable snow day and favorable weather you can ski or snowshoe all the way to the summit. Some members of the Colorado Mountain Club do it safely every winter. The longer days of spring would make it easier. Avoid Goliath on high hazard avalanche days.

SEE MAP ON PAGE 186.

48. Saint Mary's Glacier and James Peak

ROUNDTRIP	4 miles to top of Saint Mary's Glacier
DIFFICULTY	Moderate
SKILL LEVEL	Beginner for glacier; advanced for James Peak
HIGH POINT	11,200 feet
ELEVATION GAIN	600 feet
ROUNDTRIP	7.5 miles to James Peak
DIFFICULTY	Challenging
SKILL LEVEL	Intermediate to expert
HIGH POINT	13,250 feet
ELEVATION GAIN	2,700 feet
AVALANCHE DANGER	Moderate to considerable
MAP	Trails Illustrated #103, Winter Park, Central City, Rollins Pass
CONTACT	Clear Creek Ranger District, Arapaho National Forest

COMMENT: This is a very climbable glacier in a spectacular setting that is an easy drive from Denver. It is a permanent snowfield that most call a glacier, and, though it shrinks in the summer, there is usually enough snow for year-round use. You have a lot of recreational options when visiting Saint Mary's Glacier, especially if you have avalanche training. Many people enjoy the climb from the lake to the top of the glacier, take in the nonstop round-trip views of the Front Range, and call it a day. If you have an ice axe, know how to self-arrest, and want to do some glissading, this route is an option. You can also do some laps on skis. When you reach the area above the summit of the glacier you can see an impressive panorama of James Peak and its Front Range neighbor, Mount Bancroft. Some find this sight to be an irresistible invitation and extend their adventure to the summit of James Peak. Avalanche danger on the slopes of the glacier and peak could be high, so check on conditions with the Colorado Avalanche Information Center or US Forest Service before attempting the route. Heavy usage by other snowshoers and skiers doesn't necessarily mean it is safe. This area is not recommended for families with children, as it requires sound mountaineering skills to scale the glacier in the winter. You will

Near the summit of James Peak.

need AT or tele skis and skins to ski this route. If you are climbing James Peak, take an avalanche beacon and shovel and don't do it alone.

GETTING THERE: From the intersection of Business Interstate 25 (Main Street) From Denver take Interstate 70 west about 30 miles to the Fall River Road/Saint Mary's/Alice exit. Follow the signs approximately 8 miles north to the Saint Mary's Glacier Area paid parking lot. Bring small bills for the parking pass machine.

THE ROUTE: Set out from the trailhead and reach treeline after 2.9 miles and 800 Go south from the parking lot, then turn north and follow the drainage toward Saint Mary's Lake. On this approximately 0.5-mile trek you might have to carry your snowshoes. You will gain about 200 feet to reach the edge of the lake. Go to the right along its eastern shore for total mileage of around 1 mile to the foot of the glacier. This is as far as families or the inexperienced should go unless you just want to get your toes wet on the bottom of the glacier. If you have steep snow experience, climb steeply up the slope another 0.3 mile, gradually turning north-west, and you will reach the mid-point of the glacier. After gaining another 250 feet you will enjoy views of the rock outcrops. The ascent is not as steep for the next 0.5 mile but you will climb up to approximately 11,200 feet to reach the top of the glacier and even better views. At 1.5 miles and 11,600 feet you will reach a relatively flat saddle where you can enjoy James Peak views on a clear day.
To get to James Peak from the saddle, continue west and then northwest on a very obvious well-traveled route that is relatively flat and easy for about 1.5 miles. If it is socked in and/or snowing and you cannot see James Peak or there are no tracks to follow, reconsider unless you are an experienced mountaineer and have a topo map and compass or GPS unit and are a good route finder. Don't track too far to the northeast or you will climb a false summit and be on steep slopes. Reach the foot of the peak at about 3 miles from the trailhead. From here the route steepens considerably and you'll have to employ some route-finding skills. Once you reach the base of the peak, continue to follow the right-hand/northeast slope. Stay just below the ridge and you can angle your way to the summit in another 0.75 mile.

SAINT MARY'S GLACIER and JAMES PEAK

49. Beaver Brook Watershed

ROUND TRIP	6 miles, out-and-back
DIFFICULTY	Easy to Moderate
SKILL LEVEL	Beginner
HIGH POINT	9,250 feet
ELEVATION GAIN	650 feet, starting at 8,600 east gate, and 9,250 west gate
AVALANCHE DANGER	Low to Goliath Peak; considerable to high near Goliath Peak Natural Area
MAP	Trails Illustrated, Boulder-Golden
CONTACT	Clear Creek Ranger District, Arapaho National Forest

COMMENT: This pretty area near Evergreen features easy rolling hills interspersed with beautiful high mountain meadow, and a pleasing mixed forest of conifer and aspen. The trail is good for snowshoeing or cross-country skinny skis and beautiful foothills views. The elevation is relatively low at 8,500 feet, so you will want to wait for a good Front Range foothills snowfall or two before exploring it. (If you arrive and the snow is lacking, continue up hill to the Chief Mountain or Echo Lake Trail.) It isn't well known so you won't see a lot of people. The main trail is a closed road so it is wide enough for ski turns. You can go west or north from Lewis Gulch or the Beaver Brook Reservoir. There are many trails to choose from so look for tracks or break trail. The trail is not well marked but the closed roads are easier to follow. The route can be extended toward Blue Valley or North Beaver Brook.

GETTING THERE: From South Sante Fe Avenue, head south on Sante Fe, US 85, 4 From Denver, take I-70 west and then go south on the Evergreen Parkway (CO 74) to Squaw Pass Road (CO 103). Go west/right on 103 to Old Squaw Pass Road (170) and turn right/north; the gate and trailhead is on the left/west side immediately after you turn. From Idaho Springs, drive 10 miles on CO 103, look for the parking area on a curve on the north side of the road. The trailhead is unnamed at the west end. The west end is across from Witter Gulch Road (#475).

THE ROUTE: The well-marked trail is easy to follow. Begin from the visitor center From the east end of the trail: You will descend gradually and then a bit more steeply the farther you get from the gate. When you reach a fork in 0.5 mile, bear left. The tree cover thickens and that usually provides better snow cover. The trail

Beaverbrook Trailhead.

then curves into a southwest direction and rolls over a small ridge with views of Beaver Brook Reservoir. It descends as it passes meadows that adjoin the reservoir. It climbs another small ridge and travels west and south away from the reservoir, then descends into Lewis Gulch. When you intersect the road in Lewis Gulch you have gone around 1.2 miles. Bear left. (If you want to extend your snowshoe or ski beyond 6 miles, take a soft right and climb north out of the gulch toward North Beaver Brook Road. Go as far as you wish through the open meadows and return.) Bear left for the main route toward Squaw Pass Road (103). Going straight/west/left, the road will edge meadows on your right and trees on your left. Turn left/south at the next intersection to go back to Squaw Pass Road. (If you want to extend your outing from this intersection, go straight toward Blue Valley through the thick forest and climb out of the gulch.) When the main trail/former road crosses a large meadow, bear left. You will go back into trees and in 0.25 mile cross another meadow. After another 0.3 mile you will reach the last large meadow that will take you to the west end trailhead at Highway 103.

BEAVER BROOK WATERSHED

50. Chief Mountain

ROUND TRIP	4.5 miles
DIFFICULTY	Moderate
SKILL LEVEL	Intermediate for snowshoers and skiers
HIGH POINT	11,700 feet
ELEVATION GAIN	900 feet
AVALANCHE DANGER	Low
MAP	40 Colorado Front Range Trails
CONTACT	Clear Creek Ranger District, Arapaho National Forest

COMMENT: This pleasant trek offers striking views of Mount Evans as well as Roslin, Rogers, and Goliath Peaks to the west, and Griffith, Saxon, and Alps Mountains to the north. This panoramic view is one of the best close to the Denver area. The starting elevation also means more reliable snow. The final climb of 200 yards to the summit is often too windblown and rocky for either snowshoes or skis. You will want AT or tele skis for this outing if you aren't snowshoeing.

GETTING THERE: You can take I-60 to Idaho Springs Exit 240 toward Mount Evans and go to mile marker 18 on CO 103. Or, take I-70 to Exit 252 and go south on CO 74, the Evergreen Parkway, to Bergen Park. Then turn west on CO 103 toward Mount Evans. Drive 11 miles just past the Echo ski area and park on the north side of the road. The trail is on the south side of the road.

THE ROUTE: The trail climbs steeply southeast away from the road and then intersects the Old Squaw Pass Road. After crossing the wider road, you will see the continuing trail turning west and a sign that says Chief Mountain 2 miles. The trail goes directly northwest after 0.25 mile, breaking out of the thick tree cover. The spectacular panorama to the northwest opens up as you climb on switchbacks near rock formations. The trail switchbacks southwest and then sharply north-northwest as it approaches the summit from the south. The trail levels just below the summit, and a rocky scramble will take you to the very top. It is usually wise to shed your skis or snowshoes for the final scramble. Enjoy the view of the Mount Evans Byway and massif, and Squaw Mountain to the east. On the way back, some

Chief Mountain.

people like to ski repeats through the trees back and forth to the Squaw Pass Road or CO 103. It can be fun if the powder is deep since there are well-spaced routes through the trees.

SIDEBAR: Moose

Magnificent moose have now become a common sight in much of the Front Range. They were only transient visitors to Colorado until the Colorado Division of Wildlife introduced 24 in 1978 and 1979 from the Uintah Mountains of Utah and Grand Tetons of Wyoming to the Never Summer Range near Rand and Gould, Colorado, north of Rocky Mountain National Park. They are now roaming from the San Juan Mountains to Steamboat Springs and through most of the Front Range. It is best to admire these large animals from a distance, as moose kill more people than bears. They are around 7 feet tall, can weigh up to 1,600 pounds, and can run up to 35 miles per hour. They are not dog friendly.

CHIEF MOUNTAIN

51. Jones Pass Trail-Butler Gulch Trail

ROUND TRIP	3.5 miles (short of summit)
DIFFICULTY	Easy to challenging
SKILL LEVEL	Novice snowshoers for Jones Pass; intermediate skiers for Butler Gulch
HIGH POINT	11,000 feet
ELEVATION GAIN	720 feet
AVALANCHE DANGER	Low to high; can be avoided. Check with USFS, CAIC
MAP	Trails Illustrated #103, Winter Park, Central City, Rollins Pass
CONTACT	Clear Creek Ranger District, Arapaho National Forest

COMMENT: This beautiful mountain valley close to Denver does not require a drive over Berthoud Pass. There are several trails you can explore at this popular location near the Henderson Mine and Red Mountain. You can just snowshoe or ski a section of this trail and be very happy. You could also venture up the Butler Gulch Trail, which is closed to snowmobiles. You will have to share the Jones Pass Trail with some snowmobiles. If you want a quiet experience, and much less traffic on Interstate 70, visit during the week. Go up Butler Gulch or continue up to the top of Berthoud Pass for snowmobile-free trails. Off-trail slopes in this area can be very hazardous high avalanche zones; stay on the main trail and away from the slopes of Red Mountain where people have been buried by avalanches in the past. Experienced skiers will want to use AT or tele skis and skins for these routes.

GETTING THERE: From Denver take Interstate 70 west about 40 miles and exit at Empire/US 40 for Berthoud Pass/Winter Park. Drive west on US 40 through Empire toward Berthoud Pass for about 12 miles until you come to the first sharp hairpin turn to the right. Before the hairpin turn, exit to the left onto CR 144 for Henderson Mine. Continue west on the mine road until you come to the designated parking area. The road is closed at the trailhead that serves both the Jones Pass Trail and Butler Gulch Trail.

THE ROUTE: Follow a quarter-mile-long approach trail and join the reservoir service Travel west through the trees on the joint trail until the junction at approximately 0.3 mile (left is the somewhat less difficult and quieter Butler Gulch Trail); bear right for the Jones Pass Trail. The Butler Gulch Trail is less open and is a bit more of a tree tun-

Avalanche class trekking to fatality site on Jones Pass Trail.

nel initially but is a nice option on a windy day. On the Jones Pass Trail you will have some glimpses of the ridgeline as you travel northwest through the trees. At a little less than 0.5 mile you break out of the trees and enjoy the panorama of the valley and soaring ridgeline. Avalanche run-out zones are observable across the valley on the steep slopes of Red Mountain to the west. Gradually bear northwest and then north, following West Fork Clear Creek. At 1.25 miles cross the creek.

On the other side of the creek where the trail/road veers sharply southwest, stay about 120 feet lower than the trail in the flat meadow area rather than traversing the ridge. The trail travels west through a varied landscape of high mountain meadows and trees, gradually curving southwest. At about 1.75 miles when you reach another creek, turn around because the avalanche danger can be high beyond this point. You can go all the way to the summit of the pass, but this is only advisable in late spring after the snow has consolidated; check snow conditions with the Colorado Avalanche Information Center or US Forest Service before doing so.

SIDEBAR: Gaiters

The goal when putting on your gaiters is to get the buckles to the outside so that they don't catch on each other as you are snowshoeing. I don't know how many times I have put my gaiters on the wrong feet, said a few choice words, taken them off and started all over again. It doesn't help that my now ex-hiking partner looks at me and says, "So, got your gaiters on the wrong feet again? HAWHAWHAW?" When you look at your gaiters before putting them on it is fairly hard to figure out right from left unless, in a stroke of brilliance and foresight, you have written RIGHT and LEFT on the appropriate gaiter.

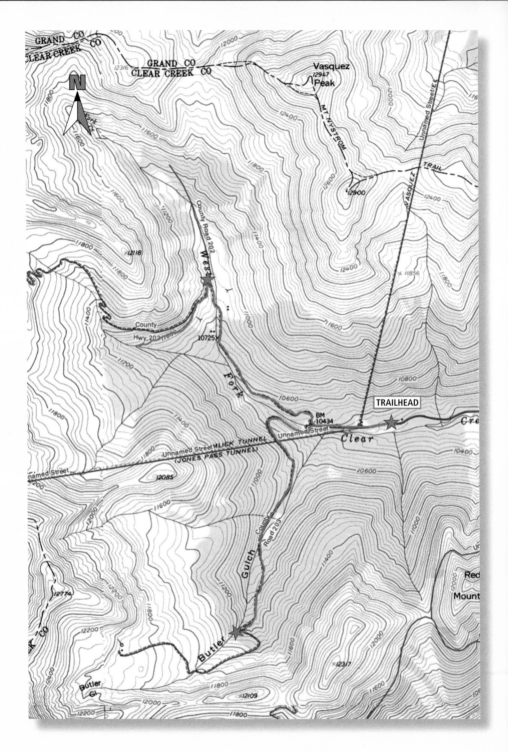

JONES PASS TRAIL-BUTLER GULCH TRAIL

Central Colorado

Chapter 9

BERTHOUD PASS-WINTER PARK AREA

"It is a pity we have let the gift of lyric improvisation die out. Sitting islanded on some gray peak above the encompassing wood, the soul is lifted up to sing the *Iliad* of the pines."

—Mary Austin, *The Land of Little Rain* (1903)

Looking toward the top of Grayback Peak.   PHOTO BY DAVE COOPER

The trails atop Berthoud Pass offer spectacular, serene views. The easy access from Highway 40, however, means they don't necessarily offer complete serenity but the 360-degree panorama is ample compensation. The top of the pass is a former downhill ski area that operated from 1937 to 2001 when it went bust. It has now become a de facto backcountry, earn-your-turns ski and snowshoeing area. The base area elevation of over 11,000 feet means the snow is good early, late, and throughout the snow season. It is a very popular area, so snowshoers will have to avoid the old downhill slopes and fast-moving riders on snowboards and skis. It is a large area and there is more than adequate space for different winter sports enthusiasts.

Avalanche control is an on-going effort by the Colorado Department of Transportation to protect the highway. This does not mean the entire area is always safe. Wear an avalanche beacon, take a shovel, and know how to dig and evaluate a snow pit to be safer. Check the CAIC website so you know the general danger level before venturing onto the slopes. There are thousands of users and there have been some avalanche fatalities in the general area because of foolhardy users. You can recreate at the pass safely.

Berthoud Pass can be reached from Denver via Interstate 70 to US 40.

View of the Continental Divide from a west side Berthoud Pass Trail.

52. Eastside Trail-Continental Divide Trail-Colorado Mines Peak

ROUND TRIP	4 miles
DIFFICULTY	Moderate
SKILL LEVEL	Novice snowshoers; intermediate skiers
HIGH POINT	12,200 feet
ELEVATION GAIN	1,000 feet
AVALANCHE DANGER	Low to moderate. Check the CAIC website
MAP	Trails Illustrated #103, Winter Park, Central City, Rollins Pass
CONTACT	Clear Creek Ranger District, Arapaho National Forest

COMMENT: This trail offers a wide, easily followed route and a gradual climb to non-stop magnificent views. It originates next to the plowed parking area and heated restrooms on the east side of the Berthoud Pass Summit. Most of this route is low angle and less likely to avalanche, especially on the Continental Divide Trail. Experienced skiers can use any style of ski but AT or tele skis with skins would be best because of the descent, especially if you ski all the way to the top of the peak. The snow is rarely good much above tree line because of exposure to sun and wind.

GETTING THERE: From Denver, take Interstate 70 west and exit at Empire/US 40 for Berthoud Pass/Winter Park. Travel 14 miles to the summit of Berthoud Pass. Park in the large lot on the east side of the summit.

THE ROUTE: Follow the well-groomed trail through numerous rock formations The Continental Divide Trail is on the south side of the parking area. If you are facing the steep hill, with the restrooms on the left/north, the trail is on the right. From the south side of the parking lot go southeast into the trees. It is a wide trail that was probably a service road or catwalk for the ski area. You will see a sign on the right side of the trail. The trail travels east gradually uphill for about 0.25 mile before turning sharply to the north and continuing uphill. After 0.5 mile it intersects other northbound trails and a former ski run. A Nordic trail continues on the other side of the ski run. Instead, turn sharply to the southeast and continue to follow the very long switch-backing trail uphill and out of the trees. As you clear the trees the panorama begins to unfold to the west. You will see the south side of Berthoud Pass and the Greys-Torrey massif to the southwest. Continue to follow the trail/road as far

Looking toward the top of Grayback Peak.

as you wish before turning around as it widely switchbacks and slowly climbs. It is sometimes obliterated by deep snow. If it is, make your own switchbacks up toward the cell towers and former ski area facilities on top. With every traverse and turn you will have amazing views in every direction. The former ski area facilities are at 12,200 feet. The summit offers an even more commanding view of the Continental Divide to the north and Mount Evans to the south. You don't have to reach the summit of Colorado Mines Peak for a thoroughly enjoyable outing. You will have lots of company from backcountry skiers and snowboarders. If you do want to go all the way to the summit, continue to follow the switchbacks. Eventually you will see the facilities on top of the peak. A great panorama awaits you on top. The snow can be very wind blown and crusty because of wind and sun. You will also have a good view of the trails on the west side of the pass and can decide if you want to go for a second adventure.

SIDEBAR: Alpine Tundra

Alpine tundra is the magic land above tree line (11,500 feet) where trees generally cannot grow because of the severe wind and snow. Krummholz (German for crooked) fir and spruce trees twisted and shaped by the wind often mark this transition zone. Some of the krummholz firs are thousands of years old. Winds at this elevation can exceed 170 miles per hour and windchills and temperatures can plummet to 40 degrees Fahrenheit below zero. Damage to tundra can take centuries to repair, so take off your snowshoes when you reach snow-free areas. Average annual precipitation up high is often only 25 inches, so snow-free areas high on mountainsides are not unusual. Few animals can survive on tundra year round: pikas stash plants for winter, marmots hibernate, and ptarmigans, the only birds in the alpine zone that remain there during winter instead of migrating, grow feathers on their feet and toenail "teeth" for their own snowshoes.

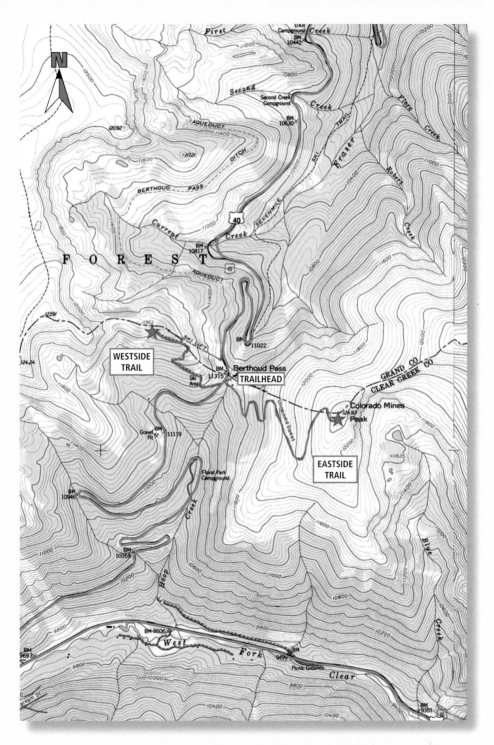

EASTSIDE and CONTINENTAL DIVIDE TRAILS | WESTSIDE TRAIL

53. Westside Trail

ROUND TRIP	3 miles
DIFFICULTY	Moderate
SKILL LEVEL	Novice snowshoers; intermediate skiers
HIGH POINT	12,000 feet
ELEVATION GAIN	800 feet
AVALANCHE DANGER	Low to moderate; check with CAIC or USFS
MAP	Trails Illustrated #103, Winter Park, Central City, Rollins Pass
CONTACT	Clear Creek Ranger District, Arapaho National Forest

COMMENT: This trail originates across from the plowed parking area with heated restrooms on the east side of the Berthoud Pass summit. It offers a wide, easy to follow trail and gradual climb to magnificent views. You will encounter more skiers and snowboarders on the west side of the pass but you can avoid collisions by staying in the trees on the south side of the open terrain. Use AT or tele skis to ski this terrain.

GETTING THERE: From Denver, take Interstate 70 west and exit at Empire/US 40 for Berthoud Pass/Winter Park. Travel 14 miles west to the summit of Berthoud Pass. Park in the large lot on the east side of the summit.

THE ROUTE: Go straight from the trailhead for 0.3 miles along the Eagle Pass Trail. Cross the highway to the west, put on your snowshoes or skis, and bear left/south uphill, rather than going up the steep terrain to the right/north. You can edge your way through the intermittent trees on the south side of the hill. There is an additional trail that goes southeast but it tracks under some steep slopes so it's less safe. Go straight uphill to the west instead. You will generally find the snow to be more powdery in or near the trees. *Watch out for tree wells hidden by drifted snow: don't get too close to tree trunks because sometimes a well of air or loose snow can form, and if you fall in, it is almost impossible to get out without assistance. They can collapse suddenly, and throw people into the tree causing injury and suffocation.* You will find this steady but gradual climb does offer some less-steep sections, so creating your own switchbacks to take advantage of flat spots is a good idea. The higher you climb, the better the view of the east side of Berthoud Pass and the terrain to the west. Go as high as you want to, enjoy the vista, and then switchback your way back down to the parking lot. If you reach the top of the ridge, you can safely wander around to

The Westside Trail on Berthoud Pass.

the west and north. There is another trail that travels northwest. Stay away from the steepest terrain to the west. Don't snowshoe or ski on it or under it unless you are an avalanche and ski expert.

SIDEBAR: Dogs

My dogs have loved showshoeing and skiing and I have loved having them with me, but there are some written and unwritten rules that your need to pay attention to. In this book you will see a restriction comment that usually talks about leash laws for dogs. There are good reasons for leash laws that often have to do with preventing injury to wildlife, ranch stock, or your dog. In these areas, keep your dog on a leash. In busy areas where there are a lot of skiers it can be dangerous for the dog and the skier when the skier is coming downhill and the dog is on the trail. I have seen dogs injured when a skier is trapped between a dog and a tree—they will have to choose running into the dog for self-preservation.

In most areas your dog must be under voice command. If she doesn't respond to voice command, don't bring her. Most of us love dogs, but there are people who are really afraid of dogs. Make sure your dog stays with you and doesn't approach other snowshoers or skiers without an invitation.

Let's talk a bit about dog poop. Pick it up and put it in a bag. Pack it out with you. Period. Please don't bag it up and leave it next to the trail—in winter or summer. There is no poop patrol ranger that collects these packages. Take it along with you and dispose of it properly.

Be careful with your dog's footpads. Often hard snowballs form in the creases of the footpad and are painful. Limping or stopping and licking his feet is a sure sign of snowballs. I recommend strap-on booties but some dogs may not wear them comfortably.

SEE MAP ON PAGE 205.

Central Colorado

Chapter 10

DEVIL'S THUMB RANCH (DTR) AND RESORT

The ranch is one of the best cross-country ski areas in the state, if not the nation, that also features scenic snowshoe trails. DTR is located near Winter Park-Tabernash. It isn't free but well worth the price of admission. DTR has a full service Nordic center with rentals and lessons, and there are snacks and a place to warm up nearby. DTR is especially good for beginner skiers because of the large amount of fairly level terrain. It also includes challenging expert terrain and everything in between.

Some of the stunning scenery at Devi's Thumb Ranch.

54. Lactic Grande

ROUND TRIP	5 to 8.4 miles
DIFFICULTY	Challenging
SKILL LEVEL	Expert Skiers
HIGH POINT	9,550 feet
ELEVATION GAIN	1,050 feet
AVALANCHE DANGER	Low to none
MAP	Devil's Thumb Ranch Trail Map
CONTACT	Devils Thumb Ranch and Resort

COMMENT: This is one of the best expert skis in the state. You will climb over 1,000 feet from the base of the resort and enjoy spectacular views of Byers Peak and the Winter Park Ski Area while winding your way through stately stands of aspens and conifers. If you catch it on a powder day, try to ascend very early before it's groomed for an amazing powder run, but watch out for the groomers. Climbing is easier after it is groomed. The trail features steep climbs and steep descents.

GETTING THERE: From Denver, head west on I-70. Take Exit 232 onto Highway 40. Follow Highway 40 for approximately 30 miles through Empire, over Berthoud Pass, and past Winter Park and Fraser. About 2 miles past Fraser, take a right on County Road 83. Take the right-hand fork and follow it 3 miles to the ranch.

THE ROUTE: From the Nordic center go straight out to the south toward the Ranch Walk Trail and downhill to the first intersection. Go left/east on Blue Extra to the first right onto the Radcliff Trail. Take Radcliff uphill to Blue Extra and turn right/ south toward the Sawmill Loop Trail. Bear left uphill onto Sawmill and then take the first right uphill toward the Waxwing Trail, and then left onto the Waxwing Trail. You will see sweeping views of the valley as you climb steeply northeast up to the entrance to Lactic Grande on the right. If it is early in the season the entire route might not be open all the way to the south-facing part of the trail. If that is the case go out and back as far as you can and return to the Waxwing Trail, and you will still have a great outing. If you take the Waxwing Trail down to the northeast you will enjoy a steep, hair-pinned turned descent to the Little Cabin Trail. Take Little Cabin

View of Byers Peak from the Lactic Grande Trail.

to the north side of the Sawmill Loop and take it to Blue Extra. Return to the Nordic area on Blue Extra.

If the entire Lactic route is open, continue to the south, climb to the top and take in the view of Byers Peak to the west. Then enjoy an exciting descent to Disco. Take a sharp right on the Disco Trail. If you want to minimize additional climbing, turn left on Blue Extra and take it down to the Meadow Trail. Take Meadow north/right and turn left when it dead-ends to go back to the Nordic center.

LACTIC GRANDE

55. Ranch Walk and Basin Trails

ROUND TRIP	4 miles
DIFFICULTY	Easy
SKILL LEVEL	Beginner snowshoers; experienced skiers
HIGH POINT	8,600 feet
ELEVATION GAIN	100 feet
AVALANCHE DANGER	Low to none
MAP	Devil's Thumb Ranch Trail Map
CONTACT	Devils Thumb Ranch and Resort

COMMENT: This is a great beginners route on almost flat terrain, or a relaxing kick and glide warm up for experienced skiers. You will also get to enjoy nice views to the east of the Continental Divide and a view of some of the highest peaks in Rocky Mountain National Park and the Indian Peaks Wilderness from the west.

GETTING THERE: From Denver, head west on I-70. Take Exit 232 onto Highway 40. Follow Highway 40 for approximately 30 miles through Empire, over Berthoud Pass, and past Winter Park and Fraser. About 2 miles past Fraser, take a right on County Road 83. Take the right-hand fork and follow it 3 miles to the ranch.

THE ROUTE: Go south from the Nordic center and bear left. Go downhill and then bear slightly right and ascend onto the Ranch Walk Trail. You will climb uphill gradually for almost a mile before the trail levels. You will pass the Broken Barn Trail on the left. Bear right/west to the Basin Trail as it climbs gently uphill and turns west. The trail then goes south downhill to a sharp left turn toward Ranch Walk. Turn left on Ranch Walk and return to the Nordic center.

Kick and glide Ranchwalk Trail.

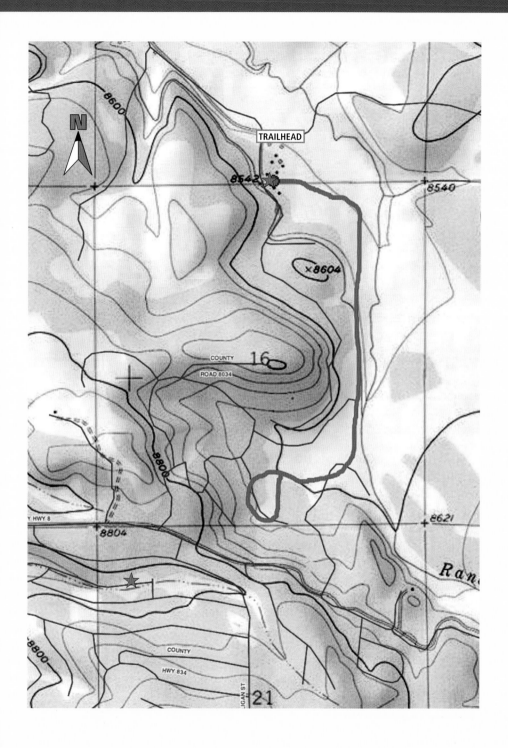

RANCH WALK and BASIN TRAILS

56. Moosestomp Snowshoe Trail

ROUND TRIP	5 miles
DIFFICULTY	Moderate
SKILL LEVEL	Beginner snowshoers
HIGH POINT	8,950 feet
ELEVATION GAIN	450 feet
AVALANCHE DANGER	None
MAP	Devil's Thumb Ranch Trail Map
CONTACT	Devils Thumb Ranch and Resort

COMMENT: This is a 5-mile snowshoe trail that climbs to a highly scenic overlook on Marker Hill, one of the highest spots at Devil's Thumb Ranch.

GETTING THERE: From Denver, head west on I-70. Take Exit 232 onto Highway 40. Follow Highway 40 for approximately 30 miles through Empire, over Berthoud Pass, and past Winter Park and Fraser. About 2 miles past Fraser, take a right on County Road 83. Take the right-hand fork and follow it 3 miles to the ranch.

THE ROUTE: From the Nordic center walk south to the Blue Extra intersection and go left downhill next to it in the snowshoe track. Turn left again more sharply at the bottom of the hill and go 0.5 mile to cross the road. Turn right and follow the snowshoe signs as the trail crosses the Blue Extra ski trail and climbs to the east next to Blue Extra. The snowshoe trail gets farther from the ski trail as the hill rolls up and then crosses Blue Extra for the final time. The trail gets much steeper as you climb Marker Hill to its flat summit. Enjoy the panoramic view.

Aspens frame the Moosestomp trail.

MOOSESTOMP SNOWSHOE TRAIL

Central Colorado
Chapter 11

GUANELLA PASS AREA

This popular area south of Georgetown offers many recreational options that are close to Denver and do not require a trip through the Eisenhower Tunnel. A bonus is Georgetown, a turn-of-the-nineteenth-century mining village that features restored Victorian architecture and a wide variety of great coffee shops, dining, and lodging options. Allowing for a snack or meal in picturesque Georgetown will add to your appreciation of this once bustling region that was mined heavily for silver and gold.

Guanella Pass Road was built as a wagon road during the mining boom in the 1860s. Most of the road has a gravel surface and parts of it are narrow with no shoulders. The pass reaches an elevation of 11,666 feet, so snow is reliable all winter, although the road can be challenging after a major storm. It is safest to use a four-wheel-drive vehicle since the road is narrow and the sides can be piled high with plowed snow or not have shoulders.

The pass is very scenic with excellent views of Fourteeners Mount Evans and Mount Bierstadt and the intimidating jagged Sawtooth Ridge that connects them. You can also see the tops of two other nearby fourteeners, Greys and Torreys, as well as numerous 12,000- and 13,000-foot summits. Best of all, you can venture out into the winter wonderland on safe trails, and even snowshoe up Bierstadt if you have winter mountaineering skills. If you don't, just venture out onto the trail and turn around after a mile when the terrain gets steep. You will still enjoy the spectacular scenery.

The standard shortest route to Guanella Pass from Denver: take Interstate 70 west about 40 miles and take the Georgetown exit (Exit 228). Drive toward town and then turn right toward Georgetown at the first four-way stop. Look for signs to Guanella Pass. Climb west and then south out of town on Guanella Pass Road/Highway 381 to the pass—10 miles. The pass can be a challenging road in the winter, but it is plowed and generally negotiable in a car with snow tires.

If the standard shorter route is closed for any reason, an alternate route is to take Highway 285 for 56 miles to Grant and turn north on Forest Road 118, which also goes to Guanella Pass.

The soaring Mount Evans massif above the Chicago Lakes Trail.

57. Silver Dollar Lake

ROUND TRIP	4 miles
DIFFICULTY	Easy to moderate
SKILL LEVEL	Novice snowshoers; intermediate skiers
HIGH POINT	12,000 feet
ELEVATION GAIN	1,150 feet
AVALANCHE DANGER	None to low
MAP	Trails Illustrated #104, Idaho Springs, Georgetown, Loveland Pass, USGS Mt. Evans, Montezuma
CONTACT	Clear Creek Ranger District, Arapaho National Forest

COMMENT: This is a short, fairly easy trail to a pristine mountain lake surrounded by soaring cliffs and high peaks. It is one of the best trails on Guanella Pass within easy driving distance of Denver. The only disadvantage is the possibility of snowmobiles or SUVs on the road to the trailhead, though they are sometimes helpful for packing down the deep snow. This is an intermediate ski trail or easy snowshoe. Mid-width, AT, or tele skis would be more fun on the descent.

GETTING THERE: From Denver, take Interstate 70 west about 40 miles to the Georgetown exit (Exit 228). Drive toward town and turn right toward Georgetown at the first four-way stop; look for signs to Guanella Pass. Climb west and then south out of town on Guanella Pass Road/Highway 381 to the pass—10 miles. The pass can be a challenging road in the winter but it is plowed and generally negotiable in a car with snow tires.

Drive on Highway 381 to Guanella Pass Campground (about 8.5 miles south of Georgetown). At the first road past the campground turn right. Park on the west side of the road.

THE ROUTE: From the Nordic center walk south to the Blue Extra intersection and Take the Silver Dollar Lake Road southwest. It is steep at first but don't be discouraged as it mellows. In fact, at about 0.5 mile, the route levels somewhat and you follow a small frozen creek for a short distance. At approximately 0.6 mile you will reach the Silver Dollar Lake trailhead on the left; it is well marked. From the trailhead, cross the frozen creek. The trail then leaves the drainage with some switchbacks, climbing to the right/west and winding through the pretty trees.

The Falls Trail in the inner canyon.

It then climbs out of an interesting hollow at about 1.25 miles and traverses along a narrow section with a small drop off on one side, which makes it more difficult to get off track. Stay away from the drop-off. You are almost there. After another 0.5 mile of climbing and winding through the trees you will emerge from the trees to a spectacular view of Silver Dollar Lake and the surrounding rock wall cirque that towers above it. You will have a unique view of Mount Wilcox, 13,738-foot Argentine Peak, and Decatur and Squaretop Mountains. From the lake you can climb the peaks in the summer, but in winter the avalanche danger could be significant above the lake, so check conditions with the Colorado Avalanche Information Center or Forest Service, or by digging a snow pit, before climbing higher. If conditions are safe, you can wander around and up higher, avoiding the steepest terrain, before returning to the trailhead.

SIDEBAR: Parking

On a number of routes in this book the parking is limited so consider your fellow snowshoers and private landowners when you park. Don't block another car when you park, or park so close that it will make it hard to access the trunk of the car in front. Do not share your music with the world by blaring your stereo while you gear up. The rest of us are not that much into Electro-Norwegian-Reggae-Punk. When you are gearing up, don't hold up traffic because you are standing in the middle of the parking lot buckling on your snowshoes, or loading your pack, or herding kids. Some of these routes abut private property. While you have a perfect right to park your car on unposted city, county, or state easements along the road, you do not have a right to trespass on private property. Letting dogs run free or pee on private property is bad form, and it is even worse when you do.

The East Preservation Trail.   PHOTO BY DWIGHT SUNWALL

SILVER DOLLAR LAKE

58. Mount Bierstadt

ROUND TRIP	1.6 miles to Scott Gomer Creek; 5.8 miles to Mount Bierstadt
DIFFICULTY	Easy to challenging
SKILL LEVEL	Novice snowshoers to base; expert snowshoers and skiers for summit
HIGH POINT	11,669 feet at trailhead; 14,060 feet at Mount Bierstadt
ELEVATION GAIN	269-foot loss to creek; 2,600-foot gain from creek to peak
AVALANCHE DANGER	None to high
MAP	Trails Illustrated #104, Idaho Springs, Georgetown, Loveland Pass
CONTACT	Clear Creek Ranger District, Arapaho National Forest

COMMENT: Mount Bierstadt, one of Colorado's highest peaks (topping out at 14,060 feet), is also one of Colorado's most accessible 14,000-foot peaks, as it is close to Denver. It is climbable in winter because much of the western side of the mountain gets blown free of heavy snow and there is a ridge on the northern edge of the western side that is relatively safe. If you plan to summit, start at dawn. Its upper slopes are not without avalanche danger but you can also enjoy safe, shorter excursions in the grand high-mountain terrain at the base of the Evans-Bierstadt massif. The first 0.75 mile can be hiked before encountering any danger and the setting is magnificent. Simply start at the Guanella Pass trailhead and go as far as you like before turning around. Use your own judgment based on snow reports and the area you are crossing. To ski to the top you should be an expert skier and excellent at evaluating avalanche danger. You will want excellent snow to cover the footbridges or the wetlands. AT or tele skis are necessary.

GETTING THERE: From Denver, take Interstate 70 west about 40 miles to the Georgetown exit (Exit 228). Drive toward town and turn right toward Georgetown at the first four-way stop; look for signs to Guanella Pass. Climb west and then south out of town on Guanella Pass Road/Highway 381 to the pass—10 miles. The pass can be a challenging road in the winter, but it is plowed and generally negotiable in a car with snow tires.

On Highway 381, when you break out into the open and see the striking view of the Bierstadt-Evans massif to the east, look for the Guanella Pass trailhead for Bierstadt on the left/east side of the road 10 miles from Georgetown.

Snowy Mount Bierstadt summit.

THE ROUTE: The first part of the trail is virtually without avalanche danger, and it actually goes downhill to the east for 0.8 mile. Using this first section as an out-and-back trek is worth the trip, in combination with another nearby jaunt just for the view. At 0.8 mile you are near Scott Gomer Creek at around 11,400 feet. In crossing the creek you will encounter the infamous willows that befuddles many climbers. The newly designed trail includes several footbridges that make avoiding the willows easy. Unless there is recent snow, you might have to take off your snowshoes to deal with the wooden bridges, or risk damaging your snowshoes.

After you make it through the flat swamp, the trail climbs very gradually to the southeast for another 0.5 mile before you encounter steeper slopes and avalanche danger. But remember, the danger is relative to the conditions on the day you are climbing and can vary greatly. Make your way south around a pyramid-shaped rock and then climb southeast. After 0.5 mile of steep climbing almost due south, the trail settles down at about 1.5 miles to a steady incline heading southeast for a mile up the wide west ridge. The last 2 miles are often windswept, so snowshoes or skis might be optional because of exposed rocks. At about 2.5 miles the trail curves northeast for the steep final climb to the summit. The final pitch is very challenging on skis. This final stretch is often snow-free and icy so be cautious about your footing.

OTHER TRAILS TO EXPLORE

A trail on the west side of the highway from the Bierstadt Trail, the South Park Trail, is another short out-and-back with great views. It starts out on a short hill, travels about 100 yards or so on a flat area, and then descends to a creek before climbing again. After another 100 yards it starts to meander and climb under avalanche zones and becomes unsafe to travel unless the snow is very thin or very stable.

MOUNT BIERSTAD

Northern Colorado

Chapter 12

POUDRE CANYON

"I frequently tramped eight or ten miles through the deepest snow to keep an appointment with a beech-tree, or a yellow birch, or an old acquaintance among the pines."

—Henry David Thoreau, *Winter Visitors* (1856)

Poudre Canyon is one of the Front Range's real treasures. One of the longest and most spectacular canyons in the state, it offers some of the state's best snowshoeing. Its upper reaches around Cameron Pass are among the most reliable for early and late-season snow.

Pingree Park, a branch summer campus of Colorado State University, is in the lower reaches of Poudre Canyon. It is surrounded by Roosevelt National Forest and features the majestic mountain backdrops of the Cache la Poudre Wilderness, Comanche Wilderness, and Rocky Mountain National Park. It is generally less heavily used than the Cameron Pass area and some of the closer trails are a real treat. But some start at low elevations (8,000 feet) and usually are not reliable until midseason unless it is an early snow year. While most of the trails are closed to snowmobiles, the closed roads are not, and snowmobile traffic on the closed roads is variable.

Cameron Pass is the summit of Highway 14, at 10,200 feet, and one of the most popular destinations for snowshoers and cross-country skiers. You might also encounter some overlap with snowmobilers approaching from the Lake Agnes area. Most of the trails in this area start at an elevation of at least 9,000 feet. This generally means snow conditions are great but windchills are potentially dangerous, so bring lots of warm clothing layers. Fortunately these trails are generally well protected by stately pine trees that act as windbreaks and there are a lot of relatively warm, sunny, calm days. The pass is bordered on the south by Rocky Mountain National Park's aptly named Never Summer Mountains, crowned by the jagged Nokhu Crags, and on the north by the Medicine Bow Range. To the west is the Colorado State Forest and the stark beauty of North Park, offering additional access to the Rawah Wilderness.

From Fort Collins go about 10 miles north on US 287 and exit west onto Highway 14 at Ted's Place.

Nokhu Crags from the Colorado State Forest

59. Crown Point Road

ROUND TRIP	3 miles to spur road; 7 miles to FR 142; 12 miles to Browns Lake trailhead
DIFFICULTY	Easy to moderate
SKILL LEVEL	Novice
HIGH POINT	10,500 feet (Browns Lake trailhead)
ELEVATION GAIN	Up to 1,100 feet
AVALANCHE DANGER	None
MAP	Trails Illustrated #112, Poudre River, Cameron Pass
CONTACT	Canyon Lakes Ranger District, Roosevelt National Forest

COMMENT: This is an easy, scenic route along a wide, unplowed road with a gradual incline. You can take worthwhile shorter trips to a spur road, FR 142, or a longer trek to the Browns Lake trailhead. In any case, you will have nice views of Poudre Canyon country and the plains from the higher reaches, even in the first couple of miles. Crown Point Road is not plowed, so how far you can drive depends on the depth of the snow and the clearance of your four-wheel-drive vehicle. If you are not driving a four-wheel-drive vehicle, you can still have a fun trip, starting at about 1 mile from Pingree Park Road. It will be more scenic if you can snowshoe around 3-4 miles up the road where some of the very best high mountain scenery starts. You can, of course, turn around at any point, and choose the distance and trekking time that best suit you given your starting point. Experienced skiers can use any style of ski for this route.

GETTING THERE: To reach Poudre Canyon, take US 287 north from Fort Collins about 10 miles and exit west onto Highway 14 at Ted's Place. This Scenic Byway winds through the Poudre Canyon alongside the largely unfettered Poudre River. The Pingree Park Road/CR 63E turnoff is on the left/south side of Highway 14 approximately 27.5 miles west of the entrance to the canyon at Ted's Place. Pingree Park Road is a well-maintained dirt road that is plowed all winter, but it might not be plowed immediately after a snowstorm. From Highway 14, take Pingree Park Road south for 4 miles. At a sign for Crown Point Road, turn right/west. After heavy snowfall, Crown Point Road is closed approximately 5.5 miles or less from Pingree Park Road and offers snowshoeing or skiing from that point.

Crown Point Road is a skiers- and snowshoers-only route in winter.

THE ROUTE: Starting 5.5 miles from the intersection with Pingree Park Road there are good views in the first mile. There are some sunny lunch or snack spots in the trees on the right in the first mile or so. Just beyond the initial road switchbacks you can see a good view area from the main road before you enter a tunnel of trees. Once you exit the switchbacks there are a couple of side trails on the left. The first one, a spur road at 1.5 miles, is a short dead-end route for firewood gathering that offers nice panoramic views into the Comanche Peak Wilderness. It is an out-and-back side excursion if you are not planning to try the entire route to the Browns Lake trailhead.

After that, the main route becomes a tall lodgepole-pine tree tunnel for a couple of miles. You are on the north side of the mountain, and if it is mid-winter, your exposure to the sun will be limited until you break from the trees at 3 miles. In approximately 3.5 miles you reach FR 142 on the right. This intersection is a good place for a break and snack.

From there, Crown Point Road swings more westerly, catches a lot of late-afternoon sun, and affords more views. If you are not too tired and have plenty of time to make the return downhill trek, continue 2.5 miles to the Browns Lake trailhead. It is the best scenery on the route. (If you are really ambitious and exceptionally fit, you could go partway or all the way down to Browns Lake, but this is only advisable under ideal conditions. If you take along some skis for your return, it would be considerably faster.)

On the return, you have striking views of the top of Poudre Canyon and the plains far below. You should be able to make much better time because you are descending 1,000 feet back to your car.

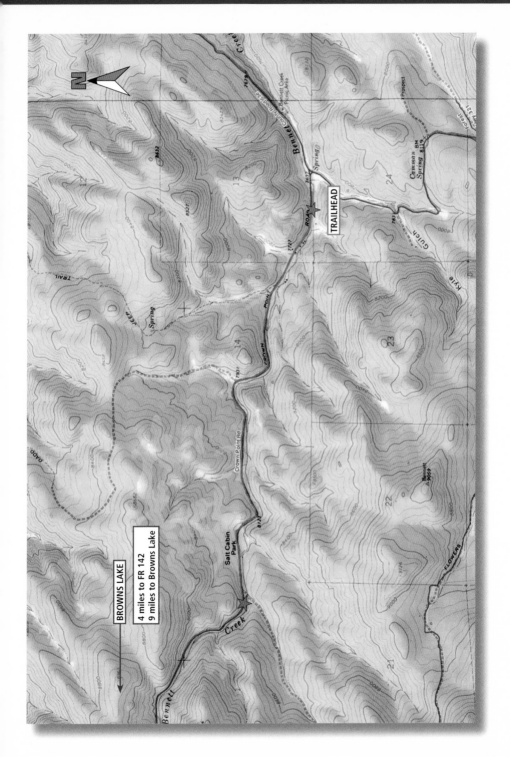

CROWN POINT ROAD

60. Signal Mountain Trail

ROUND TRIP	5 miles to beaver ponds; 10.5 miles to Signal Mountain
DIFFICULTY	Easy to challenging
SKILL LEVEL	Novice snowshoers; intermediate skiers
HIGH POINT	9,000 feet at beaver ponds; 11,200 feet near Signal Mountain
ELEVATION GAIN	450 feet to beaver ponds; 2,700 feet to Signal Mountain
AVALANCHE DANGER	None to low, except on final slope to summit
MAP	Trails Illustrated #112, Poudre River, Cameron Pass
CONTACT	Canyon Lakes Ranger District, Roosevelt National Forest

COMMENT: This little-used trail offers protection from winter winds and a tour of a magical river arroyo. The trail is down at stream level along Pennock Creek and is fairly level for the first few miles with nice views across the stream. The trail climbs gently before it steepens and pushes you to a final challenging assault of Signal Mountain. It offers a walk through a beautiful riparian area that features a mixed old-growth forest of aspen, pine, fir, and spruce and striking rock outcrops. It makes a nice out-and-back trip of any length, although climbing Signal Mountain is a serious all-day adventure. There is also a south access to this trail near Glen Haven that is immediately a steep climb.

From Pingree Park the trail climbs gradually for the first mile or two then becomes a steep ascent. If you are going for the summit use AT or tele skis. The first two miles you can use Nordic skis.

GETTING THERE: To reach Poudre Canyon, take US 287 north from Fort Collins about 10 miles and exit west onto Highway 14 at Ted's Place. This Scenic Byway winds through Poudre Canyon alongside the largely unfettered Poudre River. The Pingree Park Road/CR 63E turnoff is on the left/south side of Highway 14 approximately 27.5 miles west of the entrance to the canyon at Ted's Place. Pingree Park Road is a well-maintained dirt road that is plowed all winter, but it might not be plowed immediately after a snowstorm. From Highway 14, take Pingree Park Road south approximately 10 miles, about 0.5 mile beyond the turnoff for Pennock Pass. The trailhead is on the left/east side of the road 2 miles before the Pingree Park Campus. Park alongside the road.

Looking toward the top of Grayback Peak.   PHOTO BY GREG LONG

THE ROUTE: The first part of the trail is virtually without avalanche danger, and The trail drops down from the road to a stream and then climbs up the other side of the drainage, winding its way through the thick forest. It drops again to reach Pennock Creek at 0.5 mile. When the trail meets an old road, bear right. At approximately 1 mile cross Pennock Creek on a footbridge that goes left/east across the creek and might require removing your snowshoes. If it has been very cold and the stream is solidly frozen, you might be able to just walk across the stream, but don't take any chances.

The trail then begins to climb, gaining about 300 feet up and over a small ridge at 8,800 feet at around 1.5 miles. It climbs steadily and gains another 200 feet, rising to 9,000 feet in the next 0.5 mile or so as you parallel the stream on your right. The beaver ponds at about 2.5 miles mark the halfway point; here the trail leaves the main Pennock Creek drainage, crosses a smaller stream, and begins to climb more steeply as it leaves the streambed. There is a striking rock spire that can be a lunch or turn around point, depending on your ambitions. The trail continues to climb, crossing the stream again at about 3.75 miles. At about 10,400 feet and 4.5 miles it reaches a bit of a saddle that is still obscured by trees, where you might see an old road. Look to the right to pick up the faint trail.

Continue to climb toward tree line. This section is difficult to follow because of the good snow cover. At tree line you might encounter some windswept tundra. The summit of Signal Mountain is up to the right at a little less than 5.25 miles; South Signal Mountain (14 feet lower) is a 0.5-mile ridge walk farther on. The view from the summit ridge is superb, with a great panorama of the canyons, foothills, and plains below. You can also see Longs Peak in the distance.

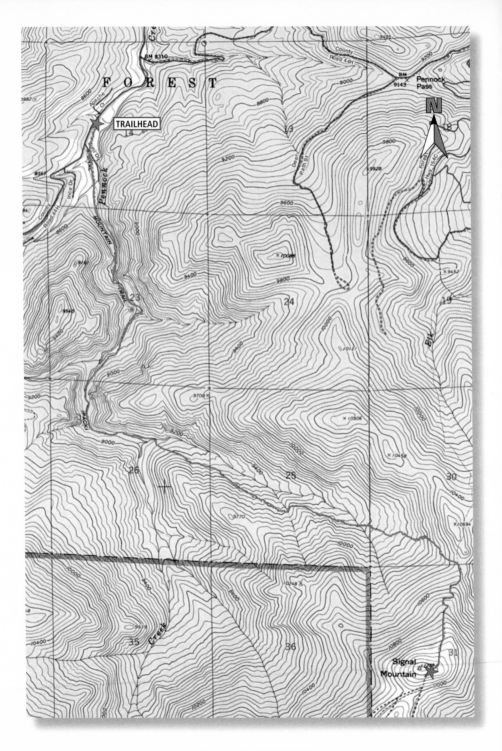

SIGNAL MOUNTAIN TRAIL

61. Stormy Peaks Trail

ROUND TRIP	3 miles to wilderness boundary; 6 miles to RMNP boundary; 10 miles to pass
DIFFICULTY	Easy to challenging
SKILL LEVEL	Novice snowshoers; intermediate skiers
HIGH POINT	9,600 feet at wilderness boundary; 10,400 at RMNP boundary; 11,700 feet at pass
ELEVATION GAIN	572 feet to wilderness boundary; 1,372 feet to RMNP boundary; 2,672 feet to pass
AVALANCHE DANGER	None to low
MAP	Trails Illustrated #112, Poudre River, Cameron Pass
CONTACT	Canyon Lakes Ranger District, Roosevelt National Forest

COMMENT: The Stormy Peaks Trail features almost nonstop views of the impressive mountain backdrop as you climb out of the valley and gradually make your way above tree line. The trail travels through the stark beauty of a burn area and eventually climbs into a forest that is primarily lodgepole pine, but also includes fir and spruce trees. The trail climbs into Comanche Peak Wilderness and then Rocky Mountain National Park. Dogs are not allowed in the park. The trail is not well marked, so a topographical map and solid route-finding skills with a compass are necessary. It climbs gradually for the first mile or two then becomes a steeper ascent. If you are going for the summit you should be at least an intermediate skier and use AT or tele skis. The first two miles you can use Nordic skis.

GETTING THERE: Take US 287 north from Fort Collins about 10 miles and exit west onto Highway 14 at Ted's Place. This Scenic Byway winds through Poudre Canyon alongside the largely unfettered Poudre River. The Pingree Park Road/CR 63E turnoff is on the left/south side of Highway 14 approximately 27.5 miles west of the entrance to the canyon at Ted's Place. Pingree Park Road is a well-maintained dirt road that is plowed all winter, but it might not be plowed immediately after a snowstorm. From Highway 14, drive Pingree Park Road south 18 miles to the end of the road at CSU's Pingree Park Campus and park.

THE ROUTE: The trail starts off through a rocky area. It might be exposed if there hasn't been a recent snowfall. Just as the trail goes into tree cover, after about 0.25 mile, it takes a sharp left turn uphill on a short set of switchbacks to the top of the

Stormy Peaks Trail view.

low ridge on the left/south side of the trail. You will see a lone, burned tree stump on the right; turn left uphill. The trail and switchbacks might be buried, and are unmarked, so this short climb is easy to miss. After you have climbed to the top of the ridge and if you prefer a shorter jaunt with an expansive view, consult your topo and turn northeast and climb the 9,360 foot high hill called Denny's Point, and call it a day. You might see a sign for it if it isn't buried. You can also visit Twin Lake Reservoir via a back door route by bushwhacking southeast for a 1-mile round-trip. Don't attempt these jaunts without a topographic map.

On the main trail you will soon enjoy a very nice view of the campus and most of the Pingree Park area. You can see the sweeping cirque that frames Emmaline Lake above the valley to the northwest. The trail isn't easy to follow, so watch for tree blazes. Stay on the west side of the ridge when in doubt. You soon reenter the area that was burned. The stark contrast of the burned trees against the white snow is dramatic. The trail parallels Pingree Park as you travel southwest with magnificent views of the Comanche Peak massif. After a mile or so you enter a tree tunnel that lasts for more than 0.5 mile until you reach the Comanche Peak Wilderness boundary at approximately 1.5 miles. As the trees thin, you have your best view yet of Comanche Peak, Emmaline Lake, and Mummy Pass off to the north. This is a good place for a snack—or a good place to turn around.

Once you enter the wilderness area, look for tree blazes: wilderness trails are not well marked. The trail gets steeper on a series of steep switchbacks; several rocky sections and stream crossings might require you to remove your snowshoes in early season. In about 0.25 mile you have a superb view of the U-shaped, glacier-carved "park" of Pingree that is in the canyon below Ramsey Peak (11,582 feet) and Sugarloaf Mountain (12,101 feet). You pay for this view by gaining another 200 feet of elevation. In the next scant mile the trail gains 600 feet, and at just under 3 miles you reach the Rocky Mountain National Park boundary. Enjoy more views of the glacier-carved box canyon below and get a good view of the Stormy Peaks above.

From here the trail veers due south—it is poorly marked. Stay parallel to the Stormy Peaks drainage. Frequently check the landscape so you can orient your direction. After 0.25 mile there is a sign for the Rocky Mountain National Park Stormy Peaks campsite. At 4 miles you emerge into a wonderland of high mountain snow, windswept meadows, and dramatic rock outcroppings at 11,000 feet. It is worth the additional effort to walk another mile and mount the pass (or even climb the Stormy Peaks, 12,148 feet).

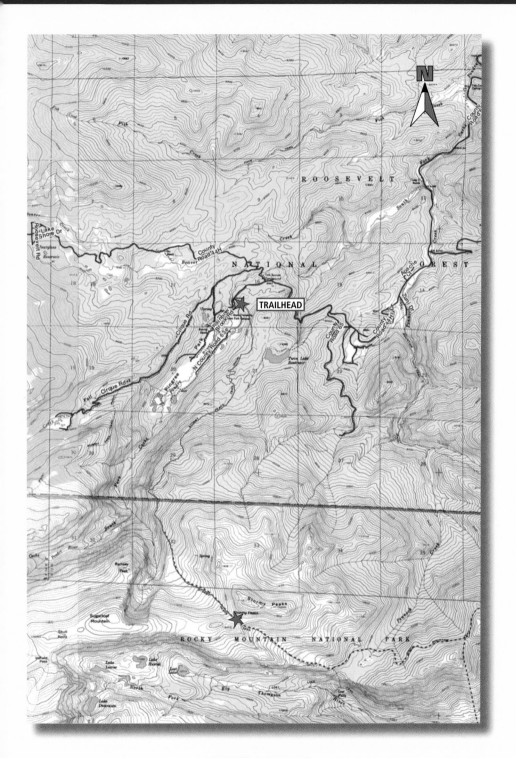

STORMY PEAKS TRAIL

62. Cirque Meadows and Emmaline Lake

ROUND TRIP	6.5 miles to meadows; 10.6 miles to lake
DIFFICULTY	Easy to challenging
SKILL LEVEL	Novice snowshoers; intermediate skiers
HIGH POINT	9,800 feet at meadows; 11,000 feet at lake
ELEVATION GAIN	900 feet to meadows; 2,100 feet to lake
AVALANCHE DANGER	None except near lake; can be avoided
MAP	Trails Illustrated #112, Poudre River, Cameron Pass
CONTACT	Canyon Lakes Ranger District, Roosevelt National Forest

COMMENT: This trail offers nice views of Pingree Park, the Stormy Peaks, and the dramatic backdrop of Fall Mountain and the Comanche Peak Wilderness framing the high mountain lake. The first mile of the trail makes a nice family out-and-back; going all the way to Emmaline Lake makes for a challenging day. Cirque Meadows is a nice intermediary stop along the way. This trail is rewarding regardless of the distance traveled. The Tom Bennett Campground road might not be plowed, adding an additional mile to the trek. You can use Nordic skis to Cirque Meadows, but AT or tele skis would better for trekking to the lake.

GETTING THERE: Take US 287 north from Fort Collins about 10 miles and exit west onto Highway 14 at Ted's Place. This Scenic Byway winds through Poudre Canyon alongside the largely unfettered Poudre River. The Pingree Park Road/CR 63E turnoff is on the left/south side of Highway 14 approximately 27.5 miles west of the entrance to the canyon at Ted's Place. Pingree Park Road is a well-maintained dirt road that is plowed all winter, but it might not be plowed immediately after a snowstorm. From Highway 14, drive Pingree Park Road south about 17.5 miles to the turnoff for Tom Bennett Campground. Continue past the campground to the first left. Park at the entrance to the unplowed road. The closure gate is around 0.3 mile from the main road.

THE ROUTE: The unnamed, unsigned trailhead is just up the road from the Tom Bennett Campground. Tom Bennett Campground might not be plowed, adding close to an additional 0.5 mile each way to your trip. Go past the campground on the main road and then look for the first road/trail on the left. The first 1.5 miles of the

Soaring cirque above Emmaline Lake.

trail are out in the open on an old unmarked logging road called Cirque Road that travels through an old burn area. It is exposed to sun and might not have sufficient snow cover for snowshoes. Don't be discouraged if you have to carry your snowshoes because you are likely to encounter excellent snow when you reach the trees. You will have a view of the Stormy Peaks and the other burn area to the south. You will also have a good view of CSU's rebuilt Pingree Park campus. It is closed in the winter, so no facilities are available. The trail climbs steadily. Enjoy the view before you reach the trees. At a little over 2 miles the trail crosses Fall Creek. At about 2.4 miles, you will reach the intersection with the Mummy Pass Trail to the left; stay to the right. If you only want to go to Cirque Meadows and back, a side excursion up the Mummy Pass Trail could be a nice add-on.

Just past the trail intersection you enter the trees and good snow conditions. The trail winds, rolls, and switchbacks through a long tree tunnel with occasional glimpses of the valley below. Past a backcountry campsite the trail climbs steeply until you break into the open to re-cross the creek at Cirque Meadows just past 3 miles. Enjoy the backdrop of the Comanche Peak glacier-carved cirque and the rust colors of the willows. This is a great photo opportunity or place for a snack break. You will find a picnic area just beyond the meadow. You have climbed around 900 feet to reach the meadows. If you want to reach the lake, you have another 1,200 feet and 4 miles of snowshoeing. Check the amount of daylight left and the energy left in your legs.

After the meadows, you reenter the trees and the real climb begins, as you gain elevation over the next mile up above the creek. At about 4.4 miles the trail climbs more steeply to once again closely follow the creek a scant mile to the wintertime magic of Emmaline Lake. The steepest climb is around 0.5 mile from the lake.

OTHER TRAILS TO EXPLORE

Mummy Pass Trail, and a cross-country route up Comanche Peak, are a couple of other moderate to challenging gems. The Mummy Pass Trail is an excellent outing for advanced skiers or snowshoers 63.

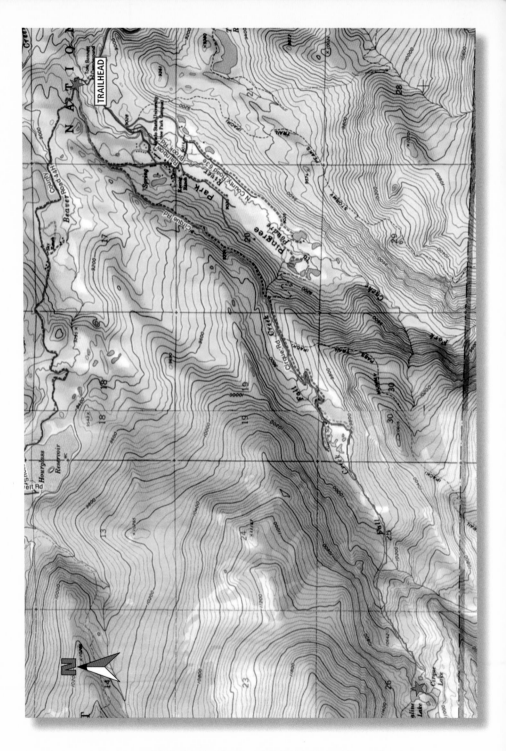

CIRQUE MEADOWS and EMMALINE LAKE

63. Big South Trail

ROUND TRIP	6 miles to viewpoint; 13.5 miles to Flowers Trail
DIFFICULTY	Moderate to challenging
SKILL LEVEL	Novice snowshoers; intermediate skiers
HIGH POINT	9,000 feet at viewpoint; 9,400 feet at Flowers Trail
ELEVATION GAIN	560 feet to viewpoint; 960 feet to Flowers Trail
AVALANCHE DANGER	None to low
MAP	Trails Illustrated #112, Poudre River, Cameron Pass
CONTACT	Canyon Lakes Ranger District, Roosevelt National Forest

COMMENT: As you near the upper reaches of Poudre Canyon and Cameron Pass, this is the first trail you encounter that has reasonably good snow cover. Big South Trail is located just past Poudre Falls, which can be dramatic in early winter as the waterfall freezes into unpredictable shapes and the sun glistens on combinations of ice and water. The Big South Trail offers similar winter ice sculptures in its first 0.5 mile. This trail is best used in midseason conditions because the elevation is lower (8,440 feet) and snow can be sketchy early in the winter. The Big South Trail follows the south fork of the Poudre River (called the Cache la Poudre River) as it descends from its origins in the high western reaches of Rocky Mountain National Park and the Comanche Peak Wilderness. With the exception of spring runoff and June rise, when the Poudre swells to a roiling river, this section is a fairly narrow stream. Most of the trail is in the Comanche Peak Wilderness, where wilderness rules apply. This is usually a challenging skinny ski route because of the side slopes.

GETTING THERE: To reach Poudre Canyon, take US 287 north from Fort Collins about 10 miles and exit west onto Highway 14 at Ted's Place. Drive west and then south on Highway 14 for approximately 48 miles. The parking lot is on the left/east side of the road 1 mile past the turnout for Poudre Falls.

THE ROUTE: The beginning of the trail is very rocky because it is a compact canyon of frozen waterfalls, beautifully contorted ice, and snow-crested trees and boulders. The first part of the trail climbs slowly through the trees and over the rocky shore. After the first 0.5 mile you enter the wilderness. The trail stays on the east side of the river, rolling, climbing, and dropping through the scenic small arroyo created by the river. It then climbs more steeply over a section of rocks that can be tricky

One of the steep slopes above the Big South Trail.

early or late in the season if the snow cover is thin. This is the point, at about 1 mile, where you find out if there is enough snow to make the trek. If you are able to surmount this section, which features a bit of climbing and a need for care if you have children in the party, you will be able to continue. The trail travels through more rocky sections and breaks out of the trees for some nice views. In a very snowy year this section of trail can be a vertical snowfield that is difficult to navigate. In this case, stay close to the streambed. If the river is frozen solid, you can venture onto to it at times. When you reach approximately 2.4 miles, you cross a bridge over May Creek. In a long 0.5 mile, you have a nice overlook of this branch canyon and the surrounding ridge lines at 3 miles. This viewpoint is a good place for a snack break and photos; turn around here for a nice shorter outing.

The trail then descends back into the arroyo and crosses another drainage, meandering through the trees and becoming much flatter. The trail climbs and descends for the next mile, with occasional vistas. Some wide sections of the river can be used for travel if it's frozen solid in mid-winter. At 5 miles the canyon opens up and offers 360-degree views of rock outcrops, meadowlands, and a stately, pristine old-growth forest. It's another 1.75 miles to the junction with the Flowers Trail and a washed-out footbridge across the river.

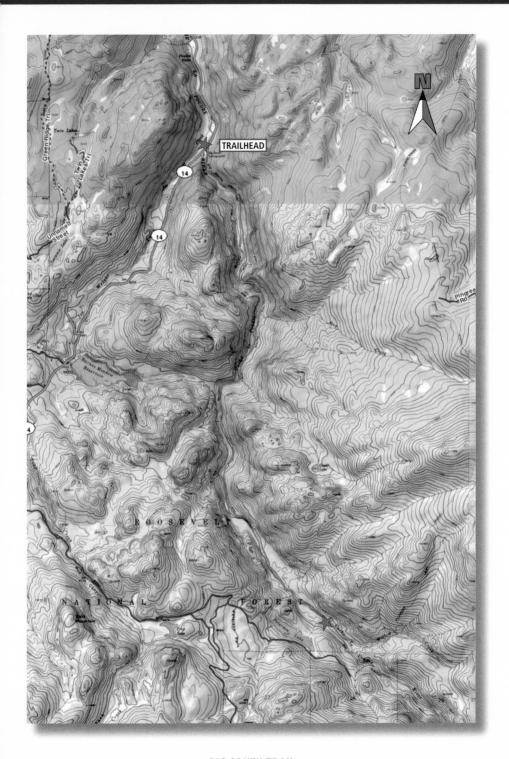

BIG SOUTH TRAIL

64. Blue Lake Trail

ROUND TRIP	4 miles to Fall Creek; 9.5 miles to Blue Lake
DIFFICULTY	Moderate to challenging
SKILL LEVEL	Novice snowshoers; intermediate skiers
HIGH POINT	9,600 feet at Fall Creek; 10,800 feet at Blue Lake
ELEVATION GAIN	100 feet to Fall Creek; 1,700 feet to Blue Lake
AVALANCHE DANGER	Low to moderate above lake; easily avoided
MAP	Trails Illustrated #112, Poudre River, Cameron Pass
CONTACT	Canyon Lakes Ranger District, Roosevelt National Forest

COMMENT: As you near the upper reaches of Poudre Canyon and Cameron Pass, One of the most popular Poudre Canyon trails offers easy, short round-trip excursions or a moderate to challenging all-day adventure, depending on snow conditions and how far you go—it's 4.75 miles one way to the pristine mountain lake surrounded by towering mountains, and a 1,700-foot rolling elevation gain for extra fun. Unfortunately the first couple of miles of this trail are the least interesting because of the thick lodgepole pine tree cover, but you will see some views along the way of the hills and reservoir. However, the lodgepole pine forest offers good protection from the wind, so this is a good trail for days with heavy windchill. Don't hike all the way to the lake if heavy snow is predicted unless you are prepared to spend the night. Blue Lake, a popular overnight destination for winter or summer backpackers, is in a magnificent setting among some of the highest peaks of the Medicine Bow Range, including its monarchs, 12,951-foot Clark Peak and 12,127-foot Cameron Peak. You can also summit Clark Peak from Blue Lake without a lot of avalanche danger if you are very ambitious or very fast and fit.

Experienced skiers can use any type of ski, but the curvy descents are easier on wider skis. The rolling trail makes it a bit difficult for skins. Attempting Clark Peak from this approach would take a very long day, expert skills, and AT or tele skis.

GETTING THERE: To reach Poudre Canyon, take US 287 north from Fort Collins about 10 miles and exit west onto Highway 14 at Ted's Place. Take Highway 14 west 60 miles to the Blue Lake trailhead parking area on the right/west side of the road. It is well marked but doesn't have any facilities. If you reach Long Draw Road or Zimmerman Lake trailhead, you missed it!

Looking to the high ridgeline from Blue Lake.

PHOTO BY ERIC ERSLEV

THE ROUTE: The trail starts at the edge of the parking lot, traveling right/north downhill for 0.5 mile, and then across Sawmill Creek and alongside Joe Wright Creek, then it veers gradually northwest. The trail gradually climbs about 300 feet in the first mile. You can see Chambers Lake in the distance through the trees, and there are even a couple of view spots if you want a photo. It levels out to a steady roll through the trees for the next mile and, as you enter the Fall Creek drainage, it opens up a little bit. The trail rolls quite a bit for most of the trip but climbs steadily farther on. These first 2 miles are under the thick cover of lodgepole pines until you cross Fall Creek and reach a nice small meadow area. This is a good spot to turn around for a shorter trip, or you can try to make it to the wilderness area boundary where the trail gets much steeper.

At about 2.75 miles you will reach the Rawah Wilderness boundary; the trail is unmarked after this, but the beauty of the scenery increases dramatically. After this you start the steady, steeper climb to almost 11,000 feet. It is heavily used so route finding likely won't be a problem unless you are first on the trail. It winds its way northwest through a relatively thick forest, but there are also some nice meadows and streams at a little under 4 miles. In another long 0.75 mile and a short downhill you reach Blue Lake. The surrounding summits are not visible from the lake because they are obscured by their steep, heavily forested shoulders embracing the frozen lake. The views as you descend to the lake are superb. If you want to summit Clark Peak too, you can head around the lake and then west and south up the steep slopes. Don't attempt it unless you have winter mountaineering experience and know avalanche danger is low.

BLUE LAKE TRAIL

65. Sawmill Creek Trail

ROUND TRIP	3 miles to trail fork; 4 miles to creek fork; 7 miles to bowls
DIFFICULTY	Moderate
SKILL LEVEL	Novice snowshoers and skiers
HIGH POINT	10,000 feet at trail fork; 10,200 feet at creek fork; 11,160 feet at bowls
ELEVATION GAIN	500 feet to trail fork; 700 feet to creek fork; 1,660 feet to bowls
AVALANCHE DANGER	None to high in bowls; can be avoided
MAP	Trails Illustrated #112, Poudre River, Cameron Pass
CONTACT	Canyon Lakes Ranger District, Roosevelt National Forest

COMMENT: This relatively lightly used trail offers access to a high mountain panorama of snow-covered peaks in the Rawah Range. It is also an access trail for above-tree line bowls used for telemark skiing. On out-and-back trips of any length you will enjoy nice views. The trail follows a steep old logging road for the first 2 miles, eventually leveling off and offering great views without additional steep climbs. The trail ends up in the Rawah Wilderness Area.

Experienced skiers can use any style of skis for this trail. Advanced skiers like to wander off trail and up hill to the left/west side of the trail, climb steeply with skins and ski down through the trees back to the trail.

GETTING THERE: To reach Poudre Canyon, take US 287 north from Fort Collins about 10 miles and exit west onto Highway 14 at Ted's Place. Take Highway 14 west approximately 60 miles to the Blue Lake trailhead parking lot on the right/ west; the Sawmill Creek trailhead is just beyond the Blue Lake parking lot. It is very easy to miss because it is marked by only a road and closed gate. From the Blue Lake parking lot walk 200 yards west on the highway shoulder to the trailhead on the right. Do not park on the road because of almost daily work by snowplows. You could be ticketed, towed, or buried by a snowplow.

THE ROUTE: The trail starts at the edge of the parking lot, traveling right/north The Sawmill Creek Trail starts off in the trees on a gradual and then steep uphill following the old logging road. You can sometimes see blue diamond markers up fairly high on the trees, directing you away from dead-ends and incorrect old logging roads, if they haven't blown down. After 0.5 mile or so traveling northwest, the

Rawah Range from the Sawmill Creek Trail.

trail turns sharply to the left/southwest and goes up a steep switchback. This is a very sunny section of trail and you will warm up considerably. There are nice views back to the southeast of the mountains and cliffs above Zimmerman Lake. In 0.25 mile the trail turns back toward the Sawmill Creek drainage and travels primarily west-northwest. At 1 mile the trail levels somewhat and then goes slightly downhill 0.5 mile to reach a trail intersection at about 1.5 miles. This is a nice viewpoint for photos and a good place for a snack or lunch break. At this point the nonstop views are quite spectacular, but the wind can become a factor.

To continue the journey beyond this point, you should have good route-finding skills. No matter which way you choose you will encounter steep powder sections and multiple, sometimes confusing trails. In 0.5 mile reach another trail junction at 2 miles. You can choose between the north or south route to travel another mile or so on trails. The north route over the ridge on old logging roads to Blue Lake is a serious winter mountaineering adventure requiring expert skills.

North: The trail to the right follows a tributary of Sawmill Creek northwest across avalanche terrain; at about 2.75 miles you reach a creek crossing and trail junction: straight ahead eventually reaches the Blue Lake Trail, Route 12, near the lake; to the left is a trail back to Sawmill Creek.

South: The trail to the left climbs above Sawmill Creek, connecting at a little over 3 miles with the other end of the trail that goes either north to intersect the north route, or south all the way to Montgomery Pass. If you keep traveling straight ahead and upslope to the southwest through the tall trees, in another 0.5 mile you break through the trees for a terrific sight. It is worth the extra effort to see the base of the Medicine Bows, the high bowls, and the peaks. Be sure you carefully note the way back so you don't get lost. Use a compass. Enjoy the ski through the trees.

Avalanche hazard in the cirques can be high. If you plan to use the glacier-carved bowls, proceed very cautiously. It is wise to check for potential avalanche conditions and to know how to dig a snow pit. Also call ahead for avalanche danger levels. The trail itself is generally quite safe, but going off trail always increases the risk.

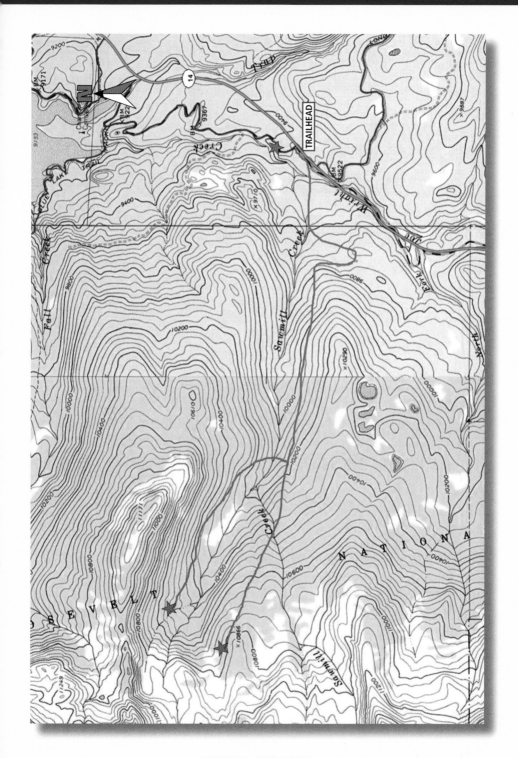

SAWMILL CREEK TRAIL

66. Trap Lake and Park, Iron Mountain

ROUND TRIP	6 miles to Trap Lake; 11.5 miles to Trap Park
DIFFICULTY	Moderate to Challenging (Iron Mountain)
SKILL LEVEL	Novice snowshoers; intermediate skiers
HIGH POINT	10,500 feet
ELEVATION GAIN	978 feet
AVALANCHE DANGER	Considerable; potential avalanche run-out zones in Trap Park near Iron Mountain; can be avoided
MAP	Trails Illustrated #112, Poudre River, Cameron Pass
CONTACT	Canyon Lakes Ranger District, Roosevelt National Forest

COMMENT: Trap Park, a draw or small canyon that is a beauty, offers varied scenery and a rolling trail. There are hills at first, followed by virtually flat terrain. It is worth the extra effort of a trip of its own, where you will have a great view of Iron Mountain and even climbing access to it, with some avalanche hazard. The trail rolls through a beautiful riparian area following the Trap Creek drainage for 2 miles or so, ending at the boundary of the Neota Wilderness. You will be at the foot of Iron Mountain. Avoid avalanche run-out zones on the mountain at times of high avalanche danger. You are likely to encounter snowmobiles on Long Draw Road, the approach to Trap Park. You can ski the slopes of Iron Mountain in the late spring after snow has consolidated and it is safe if you are an expert skier. Experienced skiers can use any style of skis for this trail.

GETTING THERE: To reach the Poudre Canyon, take US 287 north from Fort Collins about 10 miles and exit west onto Highway 14 at Ted's Place. Take Highway 14 west 60 miles to the Blue Lake parking area on the right/west side of the highway. Less than 0.25 mile before the parking lot, just beyond the bulletin board, look for the Meadows/Long Draw winter trailhead parking lot. Long Draw Road itself is on the west side of the highway opposite the Blue Lake parking lot. You can park at the Blue Lake parking area, the Meadows/Long Draw winter trailhead, or at Long Draw Road.

THE ROUTE: The first part of this route along Long Draw Road can be obnoxious if there are a lot of snowmobiles on the road. The road itself can be pleasant with some nice views as it climbs. There is a side trail next to the road that you can use part of

The ridge above Trap Lake on a snowy day.

the way to avoid the snowmobiles. They are usually only intermittent in their use of the road. They might even save you some work by packing down the road when it is covered with loose powder. They are not allowed in Trap Park. Follow Long Draw Road approximately 2.5 miles to the shortcut trail on the right to Trap Park, which is marked on a map. You can also continue on the road another 0.3 mile to the turnoff to Trap Park trailhead. If you reach Trap Lake that is on/next to Long Draw Road, you have gone too far. Trap Park begins in a small draw with very steep sides. The trail climbs over rocks and up onto a small ridge that provides a pretty overlook of the lake. The shortcut trail joins from the right at just under 3.5 miles. The main trail then descends to the creek and crosses it at 4 miles. The branch canyon opens up with spectacular views as the trail levels. At 4.75 miles a side trail climbs onto the north-facing ridge and offers another overlook. The main trail continues south another mile along the right side of the creek. If you are ambitious, you can continue toward Iron Mountain. This area is wetlands so it has to have excellent snow cover unless you can stay on the unmarked trail. You will enjoy views of Iron Mountain until the trail enters thick tree cover. Don't attempt the climb unless you have winter mountaineering skills. Recently an illegal snowmobiler was killed in an avalanche here when he got too close and high onto a lower slope.

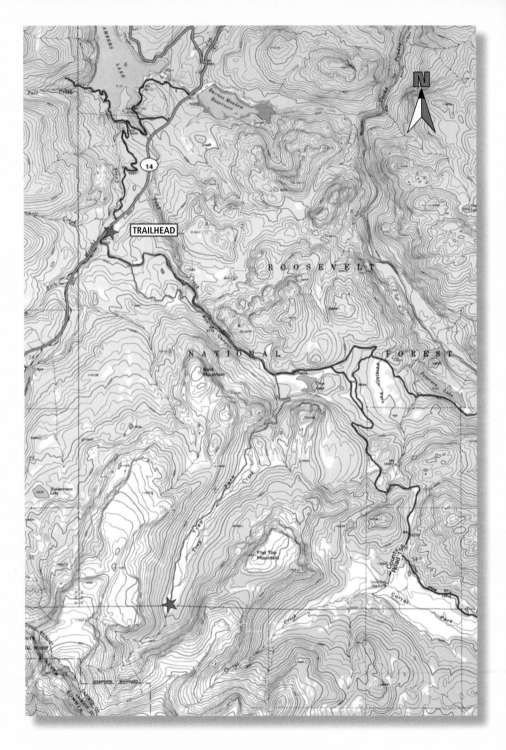

TRAP LAKE and PARK, IRON MOUNTAIN

67. Zimmerman Lake and Meadows Trail

ROUND TRIP	2.2 miles
DIFFICULTY	Moderate
SKILL LEVEL	Novice snowshoers; intermediate skiers
HIGH POINT	10,495 feet
ELEVATION GAIN	476 feet
ONE WAY	4.25 miles to Meadows/Long Draw winter trailhead
DIFFICULTY	Moderate
SKILL LEVEL	Intermediate
HIGH POINT	10,495 feete
ELEVATION GAIN	1,000 feet
AVALANCHE DANGER	None to low
MAP	Trails Illustrated #112, Poudre River, Cameron Pass
CONTACT	Canyon Lakes Ranger District, Roosevelt National Forest

COMMENT: Zimmerman Lake is one of the more popular winter destinations for snowshoers and skiers. A simple round-trip to the lake is a nice half-day (or less) activity that can easily be extended by taking the Meadows Trail north from the lake. Don't be discouraged if the parking lot is nearly full and the trail to the lake crowded. Once you get to the lake you can achieve solitude. The short, gentle trail has views of the mountains in the Rawah Wilderness and Never Summer Mountains that form the northwest border of Rocky Mountain National Park. If you want an all-day adventure add the Meadows Trail, which is best done one-way with a car shuttle at the Meadows/Long Draw winter trailhead. It is downhill starting from Zimmerman Lake. The Meadows Trail round-trip is only realistic during the short days of winter if you are fast, fit, and have route-finding skills. Just doing a portion of the Meadows Trail is also a nice out-and-back. The Meadows Trail enters the Neota Wilderness near Zimmerman Lake.

Experienced skiers can use any style of skis for this trail, because it is a rolling trail; waxable skis or pattern skis are better than skins for climbing and gliding.

Fresh powder on the Zimmerman Lake Trail.

GETTING THERE: Take US 287 north from Fort Collins about 10 miles and exit west onto Highway 14 at Ted's Place. Take Highway 14 west about 63 miles to the Zimmerman Lake trailhead/parking lot on the left/east side of the road a few miles before Cameron Pass. There are chemical toilets but no running water.
Tip: Although Highway 14 generally travels east-west when you first enter Poudre Canyon, it dips dramatically to the southwest at Kinikinik. By the time you reach the Zimmerman Lake trailhead the road is actually more north-south than east-west.

THE ROUTE: The trail to Zimmerman Lake goes to the right/southeast out of the parking lot and then immediately left/east into the tall pine trees. It climbs gently for about 200 yards and then gradually steepens and narrows into a few switchbacks. The trail climbs almost 400 feet over the next 0.75 mile before exiting the trees and leveling out slightly into a tree-rimmed meadow. The trail widens on the right edge of the meadow. There is a view of the Medicine Bow Range from the top of the meadow. The trail continues to climb, then levels out as it goes left/north back into the trees. In another 0.25 mile you reach the west edge of the lake.

At the lake you have several options. You can climb a short hill to the right up to the surface of the lake. You can snowshoe around the lake in either direction. The walk to the left/northeast is on a terra firma-supported trail; the walk to the right/southwest requires walking on the lake surface, which is not recommended unless it has been very cold. Do not attempt it in warm, early or late-season conditions. You can simply survey the scenery, have a snack, and reverse course. You can also stay on the trail to reach the northeast edge of the lake. Continue north on the trail and at 1.1 miles reach a fork. The almost-flat right/easterly fork takes you to the north end of the lake for more loop trails; the Meadows Trail is straight and left/north. Once you reach the northeast corner of the lake you can bushwhack your way onto the hills above the lake.

At the trail fork at 1.1 miles is the start of the Meadows Trail, which goes straight and left/north. Look for a brown wood sign at the beginning of the trail. There are other brown markers after the start of the Meadows Trail. The delightful Meadows Trail travels through part of the Neota Wilderness in open meadows. It goes over ridgelines that offer great views of the Medicine Bows and winds through old-growth forest of stately fir and spruce trees. It is a rolling trail with some small climbs and descents, but is generally downhill from Zimmerman Lake. It traverses and descends gently along the ridgeline for 1.5 miles affording nice views of the Medicine Bow Range across the valley. Your best photo opportunity and a good place for a lunch break is at about 2.5 miles before you descend the ridge. At about 3 miles the trail descends more steeply through the forest that eventually gives way to an old clear-cut area. You enter a small meadow. At approximately 3.75 miles turn left and travel on Long Draw Road until you see the trail resume on the right. In another 0.5 mile you reach the Meadows/Long Draw winter trailhead.

Diamond Peaks Ski Patrol at Zimmerman Lake.

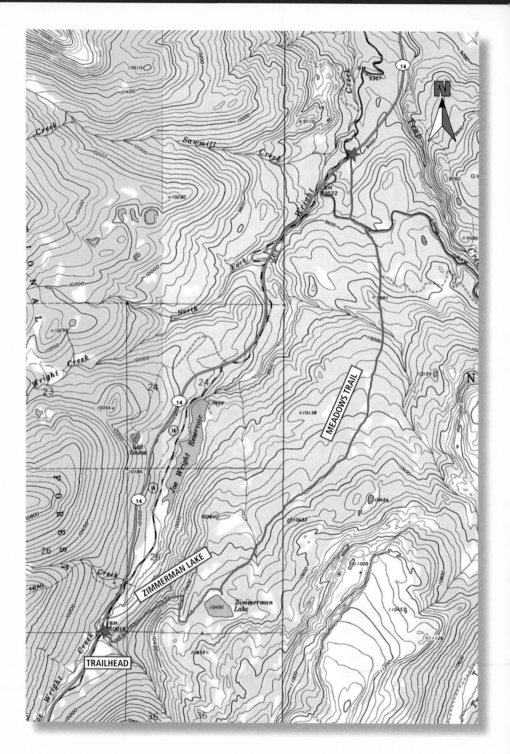

ZIMMERMAN LAKE and MEADOWS TRAILS

68. Montgomery Pass Trail

ROUND TRIP	3.5 miles
DIFFICULTY	Challenging
SKILL LEVEL	Advanced snowshoers and skiers
HIGH POINT	11,000 feet
ELEVATION GAIN	1,000 feet
AVALANCHE DANGER	Moderate to high near pass; can be avoided
MAP	Trails Illustrated #112, Poudre River, Cameron Pass
CONTACT	Canyon Lakes Ranger District, Roosevelt National Forest

COMMENT: This is one of the most rewarding and spectacular but demanding destinations in the Cameron Pass area that takes you high above tree line. It is a very popular area for telemark skiing and snowboarding because of the nice powder bowls northwest of the pass. The view from the pass is a panorama that includes the Nokhu Crags, Diamond Peaks, and the northern reaches of Rocky Mountain National Park. Going above the ski bowls is not recommended in times of high avalanche danger though the trails to tree line below the bowls and the pass are fairly safe. This route to Montgomery Pass is much safer than the Diamond Peaks route that comes from Cameron Pass. There have been several avalanche deaths on Diamond Peaks.

You will need advanced ski skills and AT or tele skis with skins to ski this trail. Skiing the bowls and the trail can be an exceptional powder day.

GETTING THERE: To reach the Poudre Canyon, take US 287 north from Fort Collins for about 10 miles and exit west onto Highway 14 at Ted's Place. Take Highway 14 approximately 63 miles to the Zimmerman Lake trailhead/parking lot on the left side of the road before you reach Cameron Pass. The Montgomery Pass trailhead is across Highway 14 and slightly to the right/north of the Zimmerman Lake trailhead. It is well marked but not easily visible from the road and can be spotted in the trees down the road from the Zimmerman Lake parking lot.

THE ROUTE: From the road the trail climbs north gradually for the first 0.5 mile and then steepens following the Montgomery Creek drainage through trees. After about 0.5 mile it veers to the left (slightly southwest). After 0.25 mile it flattens out

Ski bowls near Montgomery Pass.

somewhat for another 0.25 mile so you can catch your breath. It then steepens again. Overall it climbs west steadily at the rate of about 200 feet per 0.25 mile with alternating relatively flat and steep stretches. It is not extreme, but is not for the faint-hearted or poorly conditioned considering the elevation.

At about 10,800 feet at 1.25 miles the trail starts to switchback steeply and opens up so you can see a small meadow ahead. There is a sign that shows that going straight uphill will take you to the ski bowl, while bearing right will take you toward the pass itself. The trail to the pass descends briefly before resuming its climb. The trail toward the bowl climbs very steeply for another 0.25 mile before mellowing somewhat. The next 0.5 mile to the top of the pass takes you out of the trees to spectacular other-worldly views in all directions. Zimmerman Lake and Joe Wright Reservoir are to the east and north. The Medicine Bow Mountains and Clark Peak lie to the northwest, and the Nokhu Crags of Routt National Forest and Rocky Mountain National Park's Never Summer Mountains are to the southwest. It is often fairly breezy on top, and 10 degrees colder, but at least you don't have to worry about the afternoon thunderstorms of the summer climbing season. The worst you can face is a horizontal hurricane-force snow squall or whiteout; fortunately the latter is not a frequent occurrence. Depending on the weather, have a snack and then return down the trail or climb to the ridge top if avalanche danger is low.

You can hike south from the pass and traverse through the trees to the ski bowl area if there are not potentially dangerous cornices above. Stay low and don't make the traverse if the cornices above are large due to avalanche hazard or if the avalanche ratings are above moderate. Be capable of digging a snow pit and evaluating it to be sure.

TIP: It's fun to enjoy running and floating through the deep powder in the nearby bowls above the pass, or off trail on the way down in the trees if you aren't on skis. An alternate route down is in the Montgomery Creek drainage. You can switchback on skis or snowshoes through the powder and float on top. This isn't advisable early in the season or if fallen timber and tree stumps are not covered by snow. Don't attempt this if you are alone or there are any avalanche warnings. Fortunately, there are many periods of stable snow so you can enjoy this area.

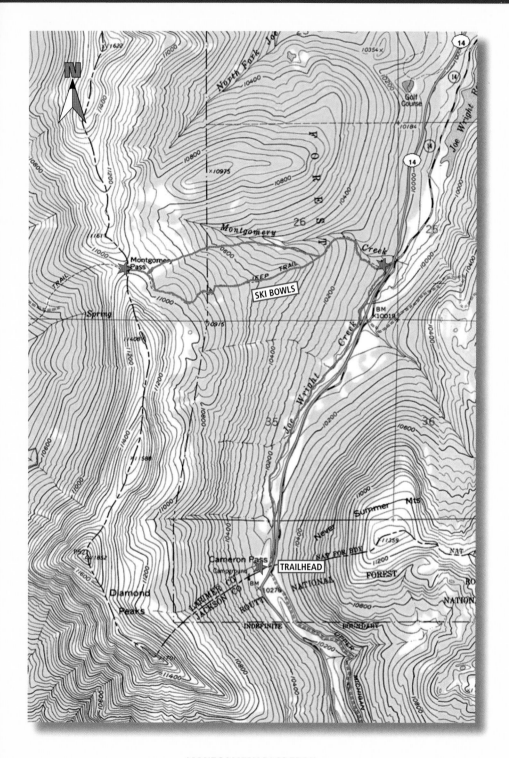

MONTGOMERY PASS TRAIL

69. Cameron Connection

ROUND TRIP	3.4 miles
DIFFICULTY	Easy
SKILL LEVEL	Novice
HIGH POINT	10,200 feet
ELEVATION GAIN	200 feet
AVALANCHE DANGER	None to low (one run-out zone)
MAP	Trails Illustrated #112, Poudre River, Cameron Pass
CONTACT	Canyon Lakes Ranger District, Roosevelt National Forest

COMMENT: This is a short, very scenic trail through an old-growth forest of spruce and fir that shares its trailhead with the Montgomery Pass Trail. It is often overlooked. It is one of the easiest and most lightly used trails at Cameron Pass. It rolls gently through the tree cover with occasional views. It offers excellent shelter from prevailing winter windchill and, though it parallels the highway, is far enough from it to be completely buffered from its sound or sight. You can also start from the Cameron Pass summit parking lot or use two vehicles to make this a one-way trip. This trail is usable only in the winter because it crosses many streams and wetlands so it is best to wait until mid-winter when the wetlands are frozen and covered. Experienced skiers can use any style of skis for this trail, skinny skis are usable because the trail is not steep.

GETTING THERE: To reach Poudre Canyon, take US 287 north from Fort Collins about 10 miles and exit west onto Highway 14 at Ted's Place. Take Highway 14 approximately 63 miles to the Zimmerman Lake parking lot, on the left side of the road, before you reach Cameron Pass. The Montgomery Pass trailhead is across Highway 14, and slightly to the right/north of the Zimmerman Lake trailhead. It is well marked, but not easily visible from the road, and can be spotted in the trees down the road from the Zimmerman Lake parking lot. The Cameron Pass parking area is 1.5 miles west on the right/northwest side of the road. Blue diamonds mark the trail on the northeast side of the Cameron Pass parking area.

THE ROUTE: After parking in the Zimmerman Lake parking lot, go to the east end of the lot and cross Highway 14. The trailhead is hidden in the trees on the other side of the road next to the Montgomery Pass trail. Though the wind might be howling

Cameron Connection trailhead at Cameron Pass.

in the parking lot you will be protected by trees on the trail. Sometimes the most difficult climb is getting up and over the drifted and plowed snow to the trailhead. From the Montgomery Pass trailhead, turn left/southwest. You will see the sign for the Cameron Connection Trail. You will initially be paralleling Highway 14. The Cameron Connection climbs slowly and rolls gently southwest gaining 200 feet in about a mile, making it a good beginner's trail. The trail above Joe Wright Creek features beautiful spruce and fir trees that will shelter you from much of the wind most of the way on windy days. At a little over 1 mile the trail nears the creek, following it more closely through three nice meadows with views of the Neota Wilderness near the pass. The meadow areas are the best places for photos. Reach the summit of Cameron Pass at about 1.7 miles. If you start at the Cameron Pass parking lot, the trail goes downhill at the start, and uphill for the finish, assuming you go out and back. If you want to extend your outing go part way up the Montgomery Pass Trail and back. The first 0.5 mile is not that steep. If you want a significant aerobic workout, continue up to the steeper portions of the Montgomery Pass Trail before turning around, or go at a higher rate of speed on your way back. Since you will be at 10,000 feet, you will elevate your heart rate.

SEE MAP ON PAGE 257.

Northern Colorado
Chapter 13
COLORADO STATE FOREST

The sky opens above us, as clouds scud across the Divide
in the setting sun.
The mountain ridgeline explodes with soaring spindrifts
wind and snow descend to envelop us.
The trees sway, circle the trail,
speak to us through the snow; on our finite planet, in our infinite universe.

The Colorado State Forest is made up of state trust lands that are, in this case, part of the Colorado State Park system. North of Highway 14, the state forest lies between the Routt and Roosevelt National Forests with the majestic backdrops of the Medicine Bow Mountains on its northern and eastern borders and the Never Summer Mountains of Rocky Mountain National Park on its southeastern border. Within the state forest are non-motorized and motorized trails. The Never Summer Yurt system and Michigan Reservoir cabins are available for rustic overnight luxury.

Just driving west over Cameron Pass into Colorado State Forest is a treat because you get to enjoy several peaks on the northern border of Rocky Mountain National Park. First you are greeted by the rugged splendor of the Nokhu Crags, with their rooster-top rocks and sparkling avalanche chutes. You can see Mount Richthofen peering over the Crags' shoulder, daring you to come back another day. Then you see the tail end of the Never Summer Mountains: Static Peak, Teepee Mountain, and, finally, Seven Utes. You also get to glimpse the edge of North Park and sample a piece of one of the least-developed recreational areas in the state, the Colorado State Forest.

Thunder Pass View from Montgomery Pass bowls.

70. Michigan Ditch, American Lakes, and Thunder Pass Trails

DISTANCE OF MICHIGAN DITCH TRAIL	Up to 5 miles
DIFFICULTY	Easy
SKILL LEVEL	Novice snowshoers or skiers
HIGH POINT	10,249 feet
ELEVATION GAIN	200 feet
AVALANCHE DANGER	Low
ROUNDTRIP TO AMERICAN LAKES	9.8 miles (5 miles to trail junction)
DIFFICULTY	Easy to challenging
SKILL LEVEL	Novice to intermediate snowshoers or skiers
HIGH POINT	11,240 feet
ELEVATION GAIN	960 feet
AVALANCHE DANGER	Low
ROUNDTRIP TO THUNDER PASS	10.3 miles (5 miles to trail junction)
DIFFICULTY	Challenging
SKILL LEVEL	Intermediate to expert snowshoers or skiers
HIGH POINT	11,330 feet
ELEVATION GAIN	1,050 feet
AVALANCHE DANGER	Moderate to considerable
MAP	Trails Illustrated #200, Rocky Mountain National Park
CONTACT	Colorado State Forest

COMMENT: This is one of the most popular trails in the Cameron Pass area because it has something for everyone. The almost-level trail is an excellent entrance to

Thunder Pass and the Never Summer Mountains of Rocky Mountain National Park. It offers spectacular views of the Never Summer Mountains and Nokhu Crags across the Michigan River drainage, Diamond Peaks to the northwest, and North Park off in the distance to the southwest. It also features a gentle incline and very reliable snow. It can be savored both by beginners or backcountry adventurers who want to spend the night or surmount the pass. The trail is actually a jeep road that is used to maintain the Michigan Ditch, which is part of the trans-mountain water storage system that funnels water from the western slope to the thirsty cities of the eastern slope. The ditch trail can be skied by beginners on Nordic skis. It is more fun to use AT or tele skis for Thunder Pass. The Pass requires advanced ski skills.

Snowshoer on her way to Michigan Lakes.

GETTING THERE: To reach Poudre Canyon, take US 287 north from Fort Collins about 10 miles and exit west onto Highway 14 at Ted's Place. Take Highway 14 west 65 miles to the top of Cameron Pass. Parking and toilet facilities are on the right/west side of the highway. The well-marked, gated trail is on the left/east side of Highway 14.

THE ROUTE: The almost flat Michigan Ditch Trail follows the road and Joe Wright Creek at first. If you are on a novice or family expedition, you can turn around in about 1 mile at some cabins. If you want more adventure and scenery continue on the winding road. At about 1.25 miles the highway turns west while the trail continues southeast. In another 0.75 mile at a trail junction, continue straight. Reach the intersection with the trail to American Lakes and Thunder Pass in another 0.5 mile, at 2.5 miles.

From this junction you can go to the right to continue following the Michigan Ditch Trail west around the bottom of the ridgeline of Nokhu Crags. This is an easy and short trek on a flat trail. You will cross to the south side of the drainage, stopping in less than a mile before reaching the avalanche chutes north of Nokhu Crags.

Or, at the junction you can go to the left on the American Lakes Trail, which climbs steadily toward the rocky panorama above tree line at 11,000 feet. This is a longer, more challenging route on a constantly climbing, rolling trail. There are some very steep stretches but also some moderate to easy sections. You can essentially go as far and as high as you desire. Keep an eye on the time and allow enough daylight for your return. From the junction it is a little less than 2 miles to American Lakes. You reach the first lake at just under 5 miles, and a short distance later is the trail on the left to Thunder Pass. The trail straight ahead continues about 0.25 mile to the middle and upper lakes. The upper reaches of this trail offer very impressive views of the northern edge of the Never Summer Mountains including the summit of Mount Richthofen.

The trail to Thunder Pass reaches its summit in another long 0.5 mile, at about 5 miles, unless you have included the lakes in your tour. If you make it to the top of Thunder Pass you can see all the way down into the Colorado River drainage of Rocky Mountain National Park. Reaching the summit of Thunder Pass should only be attempted as an all-day adventure for the very fit and well prepared. You should have winter mountaineering gear with you. It is by no means dangerous, but is definitely a long, challenging day in high-altitude snow and cold, with some avalanche danger, especially if you venture far off trail onto steep slopes.

Colorado Mountain Club group at Michigan Lakes.   PHOTO BY WARD WHICKER

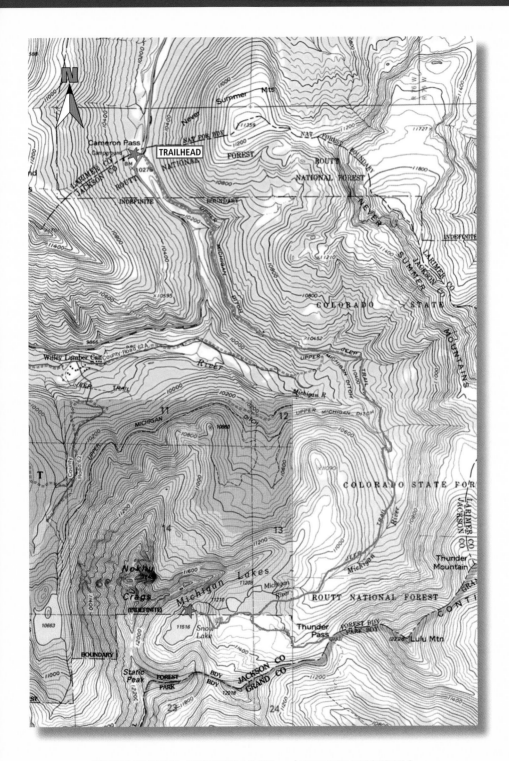

MICHIGAN DITCH, AMERICAN LAKES, and THUNDER PASS TRAILS

71. Lake Agnes

ROUND TRIP	5 miles
DIFFICULTY	Moderate to challenging
SKILL LEVEL	Novice snowshoers; intermediate skiers
HIGH POINT	10,800 feet
ELEVATION GAIN	1,000 feet
AVALANCHE DANGER	Low to considerable
MAP	Trails Illustrated #200, Rocky Mountain National Park
CONTACT	Colorado State Forest

COMMENT: This is a steep, popular, and spectacular trail. The first mile is shared with snowmobiles, but the last 1.5 miles are for snowshoers and skiers only. Experienced skiers can use any style of skis for this trail, but some of the steep descents on the return are more fun on wider skis. Restrictions: A daily Colorado State Forest Pass is required for each vehicle. Carpool, since parking is limited.

GETTING THERE: To reach Poudre Canyon, take US 287 north from Fort Collins about 10 miles and exit west onto Highway 14 at Ted's Place. Take Highway 14 west 65 miles to Cameron Pass and continue 2.5 miles west of the pass. The trailhead is on the left/south side of Highway 14. You are likely to see several vehicles parked in the driveway and along the road.

THE ROUTE: After The trail follows the campground road downhill into an open area where you have nice panoramic views of the Nokhu Crags and Iron Mountain. At the bottom of the road, in about 0.75 mile the trail/road splits. Go right/ south, uphill, crossing a footbridge. Going straight takes you up to the Michigan Ditch Trail and American Lakes on a route used by snowmobiles. Take the trail/ road uphill into the trees where snowmobiles are not permitted. The trail is very steep in this section. Once you crest the hill at about 1 mile, the trail flattens out and comes out of the trees so you can enjoy the stunning, panoramic view of the Never Summer Mountains. You will see the trail for the Agnes Creek Cabin/Nokhu Hut go downhill to the west; go straight unless you want to see it.

    At about 1.25 miles, and 500 feet of gain, you will reach the summer trailhead and parking area. The view from this point is superb. If you have run out of gas,

Never Summer Mountains above Agnes Lake.

snap some photos and retrace your steps because the next section is very steep, gaining another 500 feet, and the trail can be buried in deep drifts, depending on your timing. In a good snow year, the trailhead outhouse will be almost covered by snowdrifts, so it is not open in the winter. The trail is marked with blue diamonds and travels to the left/southeast toward the Nokhu Crags. This area is the only section with avalanche hazard, unless you go to the south side of the Lake Agnes. The route climbs steeply through the trees and it is sometimes difficult to follow the blue diamonds. If you lose the formal trail, head south toward the lake. Avoid getting too close to the Crags, especially if they are snow-covered. You will have to climb steeply over a hump that is higher than the lake and then descend 100 feet to the lake. You will reach Lake Agnes in a little under 2.5 miles. The lake is in a beautiful setting with a stunning ridgeline of the Never Summer Mountains as a backdrop. Stay away from the south side of the lake because of the avalanche hazard. There is no danger on the north side of the lake unless you wander over toward the Crags. Some skiers like to ski the bowls above the lake to the southwest. Do so if you have excellent avalanche skills.

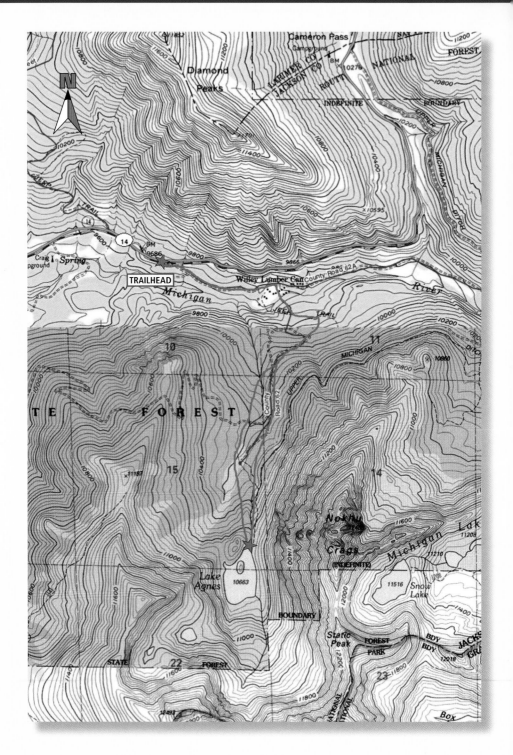

LAKE AGNES

72. Seven Utes Mountain and Mount Mahler

ROUND TRIP	6.5 miles (2.75 miles to viewpoint)
DIFFICULTY	Moderate to challenging
SKILL LEVEL	Advanced expert snowshoers and skiers
HIGH POINT	11,453 feet
ELEVATION GAIN	2,000 feet
ROUNDTRIP TO MOUNT MAHLER	8 miles (2.75 miles to viewpoint)
DIFFICULTY	Moderate to challenging
SKILL LEVEL	Advanced to expert snowshoers and skiers
HIGH POINT	12,480 feet
ELEVATION GAIN	3,000 feet
AVALANCHE DANGER	Moderate to high at the upper portion; can be avoided
MAP	Trails Illustrated #200, Rocky Mountain National Park
CONTACT	Colorado State Forest

COMMENT: These little-known mountains are nestled in Colorado State Forest at the edge of the Never Summer Range of Rocky Mountain National Park. They offer challenging trails with panoramic views of Mount Richthofen and the Diamond Peaks from the top of Seven Utes, and views of the Never Summer, Medicine Bow/ Rawah, and Zirkel Ranges from the top of Mahler. Climbing these mountains in the winter is an adventure—with avalanche risks—that should be attempted only by very experienced snowshoers or skiers who are prepared. Knowing how to dig a snow pit and evaluate avalanche conditions is a recommended skill. Neither of these peaks should be attempted during times of high avalanche danger. Even beginners can have a very nice, satisfying shorter out-and-back trip that affords great views of the Diamond Peaks. If you can venture just a mile or two uphill on this gradually steepening trail, you will enjoy superb views of the Medicine Bow Range. And the closer you get to Seven Utes the more impressive it is. The trailhead begins at the former site of a failed cross-country ski lodge that has since been torn down. There are no signs or markers for it.

The mountains are left to right : Noku Crags, Richthofen, and Mahler Mountains

This route is only for experienced skiers with AT or tele skis and advanced ski skills unless you go out and back short of the summits.

GETTING THERE: Take US 287 north from Fort Collins about 10 miles and exit west onto Highway 14 at Ted's Place. Take Highway 14 west 65 miles to Cameron Pass and continue west approximately 3.8 miles past the pass. Almost at the bottom of the hill, on the left/south side of the road, is a partially plowed drive angling to the southeast with a green gate. This is the former Seven Utes Lodge entrance. (If you reach the Ranger Lakes Campground, you have gone about 2 miles too far west.) Park in the driveway, or go down about another 0.25 mile to a turnout on the same side (south) and park there, then snowshoe back on the road on the other side of the fence. The snow is likely to be deep enough for you to be able to step over the fence. **TIP:** If you have trouble finding the trailhead, you can get directions at the State Forest Moose Visitors Center 2 miles west of the trailhead on Highway 14. It doesn't open until 9:00 A.M., however, so if you are planning an early start they won't be able to help you.

THE ROUTE: Take a look at your topo map and the drainage you want to be in before starting; route finding can be a bit tricky once you are in the trees and encountering lots of logging roads. The trail is just beyond the green gate, which is usually open. Go through the gate and take either of the next two trails you see on the right. They intersect after 200 yards. At first you go downhill for a short stretch, and gradually and then steeply uphill east and southeast on an old logging road. Ignore a trail going left/east near the crossing of the Michigan River, before the road steepens. There are no markers such as blue diamonds, but the trail is distinct even if you are the first one to use it.

Right after the trail gets significantly steeper, at about 0.75 mile, you intersect another wide, old logging road that is used by snowmobiles. Go to the left/east uphill on the road; you will see the continuing trail on the left as you round the very first hard right turn. It might not be well marked, so look carefully for it. Remember which drainage you want to be in—the one just east of Seven Utes Mountain—and the route will be more obvious. When you turn off the road, you will be on a narrow trail rather than an old road, with a 30- to 40-foot drop-off on your left. This con-

Colorado Mountain Club group on Mount Mahler.   PHOTO BY WARD WHICKER

tinues for about 0.25 mile. There is a spectacular view of the Diamond Peaks behind you to the northeast. This 1-mile point is a good spot for a photo and snack break. This is also a good turn around point for the inexperienced.

After approximately 200 yards the trail crosses to the other side of the drainage, crossing the stream that is out of sight under the snow unless your trip is too early in the season. The trail then goes east and south uphill and back into the trees, steepening considerably at a couple of big hairpins that straighten out at about 2 miles. It wanders around trees as you steadily make your way to tree line next to the drainage. You will see another ridge and peak to the right/west, which is Seven Utes. At intersecting trails bear to the right. When you emerge from the trees at about 2.75 miles you can see Seven Utes to the right/southwest and Mount Mahler to the left/southeast. From this point you can choose to climb either.

The shorter, easier, and somewhat safer choice is Seven Utes. There is a trail going to the right/west across the top of the drainage cirque; that is your route over to Seven Utes. Once you cross the top of the drainage, pick the least steep route up to the saddle at about 3 miles and avoid areas that look like starting zones or runouts for avalanches. There are definitely avalanche hazards on this route, but you can avoid them. From the summit at 3.25 miles enjoy the Never Summer Mountains or Rocky Mountain National Park and the Medicine Bow Mountains.

Mahler is a much higher summit that can be climbed from the same drainage as Seven Utes. There are many avalanche hazards on Mahler but it can be safely climbed if you stay on the southern shoulder of the mountain, pick your route carefully, and confirm reasonable snow stability with a snow pit. When you emerge from the trees at about 2.75 miles, where you can see Seven Utes to the right/west and Mount Mahler to the left/east, bear left/southeast. Continue uphill bearing straight for a little more than 3 miles south and then go left, making your way away from the obvious avalanche zones and toward the right/south side of the mountain.

Avoid the dangerous potential avalanche zones dead ahead on the west-facing slopes. The south ridge is not without some avalanche danger. From the south flank carefully pick your way up to the top of the ridge saddle in a little more than a mile and then right (south and east) to the summit at 4 miles.

Enjoy the Nokhu Crags to the northeast, Richthofen a bit farther southeast, and the Never Summer Mountains and Zirkel Range visible to the south and west.

SEVEN UTES MOUNTAIN and MOUNT MAHLER

73. Ranger Lakes and Silver Creek

ROUND TRIP	3 miles to saddle; 10 miles to upper creek
DIFFICULTY	Easy to Moderate
SKILL LEVEL	Novice snowshoers and skiers
HIGH POINT	9,600 feet at saddle; 10,200 feet at upper creek
ELEVATION GAIN	300 feet to saddle; 900 feet to upper creek
AVALANCHE DANGER	None
MAP	Trails Illustrated #200, Rocky Mountain National Park
CONTACT	Colorado State Forest

COMMENT: This easy-to-find trail starts at the Ranger Lakes Campground (closed in winter) on Highway 14 west of Cameron Pass. You can have an enjoyable and easy 3-mile round-trip jaunt to see the views, or continue on for more of a workout, although the rest of the trail is primarily a tree tunnel on what is a road in the summer until you climb over the ridge into the next drainage, where it opens up onto a spectacular valley surrounded by peaks. You might encounter snowmobiles on part of the trail/road.

Experienced skiers can use any style of skis for this trail and can be skied by beginners on skinny Nordic skis.

GETTING THERE: To reach Poudre Canyon, take US 287 north from Fort Collins about 10 miles and exit west onto Highway 14 at Ted's Place. Take Highway 14 west 65 miles to Cameron Pass and continue approximately 5.8 to 6 miles west of Cameron Pass to the Ranger Lakes Campground on the left/south side of the road. It is not heavily used, so you should be able to park in the entrance driveway. There is a recreational area parking lot another 0.8 mile west of the campground.

THE ROUTE: After To find the trailhead go downhill and keep the restroom on your right. Pass the campground loop road. You want the next trail on the right, which takes you west through the trees, and then next to a somewhat open area that is tree-lined. It is almost flat at the outset and swings around the Ranger Lakes, hidden in the trees, at about 0.5 mile. There are some trails on the left that go to the Ranger Lakes if you want a short side trip to see the frozen lakes. The main trail then goes slightly downhill and emerges from the trees to give you a gorgeous view of the ridgeline of the Never Summer Mountains, Seven Utes Mountain, and

Michigan Creek near Ranger Lakes.

Mount Mahler to the east. Cross the Michigan River on a small bridge at a little past 0.5 mile and enjoy the meadow and mountain views. This is a very good place for photos. The trail then reenters the trees and climbs uphill steeply for more than a mile, weaving through the thick trees with some meadow views. There is an intersection a little before 1.5 miles with confusing signs. Don't go left as the sign suggests for Silver Creek; bear right toward Illinois Pass. A little past the 1.5-mile mark, the trail crests a saddle with a few glimpses of the hills. Turn around here if you don't want to descend toward the Silver Creek drainage; it is another 2 miles to meadows.

Though the trail is in a beautiful and peaceful forest, you might encounter an occasional snowmobile. At the intersection at 1.75 miles, turn left and follow the open rolling trail into the Silver Creek drainage. Once you reach Silver Creek at 2.25 miles, follow it upstream and cross at about 2.75 miles. Wander through a beautiful meadow area to around 3.5 miles, where you can have a snack and reverse course, or continue to climb another 1.5 miles higher along the creek into the foothills of the Never Summer Mountains. You can continue for additional mileage or even set up a winter camp for the night.

SIDEBAR: Hat

When you are out in the cold without a hat, you lose from 40 to 75 percent of your body heat. The figures vary, but the heat loss is significant. The rule is simple—always wear a hat. I wear a ratty old wool ski cap and have an ultra-lite stocking cap as a backup in my pack.

RANGER LAKES and SILVER CREEK

74. **Grass Creek Yurt Trails**

LOOP	6 miles
ROUND TRIP TO END OF TRAIL	9 miles
DIFFICULTY	Easy to Moderate
SKILL LEVEL	Novice snowshoers and skiers
HIGH POINT	9,200 feet on loop; 9,600 feet at end of trail
ELEVATION GAIN	200 feet on loop; 600 feet to end of trail
AVALANCHE DANGER	Low
MAP	Never Summer Nordic Yurt System/Colorado State Forest
CONTACT	Colorado State Forest; Never Summer Nordic, Inc.

COMMENT: This is one of the closest huts to visit and it is near two nice trails; one a very easy loop trail, and the other an end-of-trail out and back that goes up a nice hill that can be used for repeated turns on skis. The setting is exceptional because of the backdrop of the Medicine Bow Mountains and Clark Peak towering above. You can also see the craggy Nokhu Crags along the way gleaming in the distance in their own mountain world. Experienced skiers can use any style of skis for this trail and can be skied by beginners on Nordic skis.

GETTING THERE: To reach Poudre Canyon, take US 287 north from Fort Collins about 10 miles and exit west onto Highway 14 at Ted's Place. Take Highway 14 west 65 miles to Cameron Pass and continue west and then south over the pass 10 miles to Gould. Watch for signs on the right side of the highway for the State Forest campground and KOA. Turn right onto CR 41. Get a map from the unstaffed entrance station. Information is also available at the Moose Visitor Center south of Gould. Follow CR 41, a dirt and snow-packed road, approximately 4 miles east past the North Michigan Reservoir and cabins to the parking area for the Grass Creek Yurt trailhead on the left side of the road.

THE ROUTE: Cross the road to the trailhead. From the trailhead, travel east toward the yurt. At a trail junction in over 0.25 mile, continue straight/southeast. At about 0.75 mile you will come to another trail junction.

If you want to trek on the loop trail, bear right and go directly past the yurt. (You can, of course, do the loop in either direction.) The trail will roll pleasantly and

The Grass Creek Yurt.

easily through the trees and in about 1.25 miles, after you have gone past the yurt, you will climb more steeply up on top of a small ridge at 2.5 miles. Traverse the ridge and then turn left to meet the upper end of the loop at just past 3.5 miles. Go left to return to the trailhead, traveling the trail that parallels Grass Creek. This is a road in the summer that affords a nice view of the yurt without passing too closely. At about 5.25 miles complete the loop, and go straight 0.75 mile back to the trailhead.

If you prefer an out-and-back trek: Take the trail straight ahead from the road where you parked rather than traveling across the meadow and uphill to the yurt. The trail is a summertime road so it is wide. You will roll pleasantly past pretty meadows and through a mixed forest. At a junction at 0.75 mile, take the left branch. If you want to practice jogging up and down hill on a gentle slope, this is a good place to do it. The trail continues to gradually climb up the draw/drainage for another 1.5 miles. At another junction a little past 2.25 miles the other leg of the loop is to the right; go straight. As you continue straight ahead, you will reach Saw Mill Pile Hill, a steeper place to try hill activities if there is good powder. The trail continues uphill into thick trees. The end of the trail is about 4 miles out, giving you an 8-mile round-trip.

You can also combine the loop and the out-and-back, traveling up one leg of the loop and down the other on the way back for 9 miles total.

OTHER TRAILS TO EXPLORE

All of the other yurt trails are enjoyable outings: Ruby Jewel Trail and Jewel Lake below Clark Peak, Montgomery Pass Yurt Trail, and Dancing Moose Trail. You can ski all the way to Montgomery Pass with minimal avalanche danger.

GRASS CREEK YURT TRAILS

Southern Colorado
Chapter 14
COMO AREA

"I wish to preach not the doctrine of ignoble ease, but the doctrine of the strenuous life."
—President Theodore Roosevelt, speech before the Hamilton Club (1899)

One of the hidden treasures of the state, the unincorporated town of Como has a magnificent backdrop; it is the recreational gateway to Boreas Pass and the Gold Dust Trails, both of which are delightful ways to enjoy the scenic Tarryall Mountains, Tenmile Range, and Mosquito Range. Como is 9 miles north of Fairplay, on the northern end of scenic South Park. It was founded during the gold and silver mining boom that started in 1859. The scars of mining in the area are more readily visible when the snow melts. The town was named by Italian miners from Como, Italy, who worked locally looking for gold. There are presently no services in Como, other than a private Christian Camp and post office, though it is rumored that there is a general store. You can be sure of supplies in Fairplay. The road to Como is plowed, and generally passable to passenger cars with good snow tires, but a four-wheel-drive vehicle is a good idea after major snowstorms. Be aware that the road may be passable in the morning, and not passable by afternoon because of drifting snow. Boreas Pass road and the South Gold Dust Trails are the closest to Como.

If you are driving from Denver, you will reach Kenosha Pass before reaching Como; it is 10 miles north of Como. Kenosha Pass, at 10,000 feet, offers easy access to the popular Colorado Trail. It also offers a magnificent view of South Park and the 14,000-foot peaks of the Mosquito and Tenmile Ranges. This group of mountains is much more impressive when snowcapped and viewed from a distance than they are dotted by droves of people climbing them in the summer.

SIDEBAR: The Denver, South Park, And Pacific Railroad
The Denver, South Park and Pacific Railroad operated in the Kenosha Pass and Como area traveling south from Denver in the late 1800s to support miners during the gold and silver boom. It was a narrow-gauge railroad that generally followed the route of current US Highway 285. It reached Kenosha Pass in 1879 and eventually connected to Buena Vista and Gunnison. An engine from the railroad is on exhibit in the South Park Museum in Fairplay.

Kenosha Pass West looking at the Fourteeners of the Mosquito Range.

75. Kenosha Pass — Colorado Trail West

ROUND TRIP	10 miles with a 0.8-mile side trip
DIFFICULTY	Easy to Moderate
SKILL LEVEL	Novice snowshoers; intermediate skiers
HIGH POINT	10,300 feet
ELEVATION GAIN	300 feet to viewpoint; elevation loss: up to 800 feet
AVALANCHE DANGER	None to low
MAP	Trails Illustrated #105, Tarryall Mountains, Kenosha Pass
CONTACT	South Park Ranger District, Pike National Forest

COMMENT: This very popular summer trail is also frequently used in the winter, but relatively lightly compared to many trails closer to Denver. This segment of the Colorado Trail on the west side of Kenosha Pass makes for short, easy out-and-back family excursions or more ambitious adventures. The first 2 miles of the trail is a very gradual climb, emerging out of the trees to a panoramic view of South Park, and the massive backdrop of the 14,000-foot wall of the Mosquito Range. On the way up the trail, you get some scenic glimpses of the Tarryall Mountains to the north, too. Avalanches are unlikely unless it has been a very heavy snow year and the south slope has been undermined by spring melt. The steep descent on the return makes wider skis a better option.

GETTING THERE: From Denver go southwest on US 285. At about 65 miles you reach Kenosha Pass. Park on the west side of US 285 outside of the Kenosha Pass Campground, which closes for the winter. The Colorado Trail is on the south/right side of the closed road as soon as you enter the campground.

THE ROUTE: Go through the main gated entrance that is straight ahead for the Colorado Trail (1776), and USFS Trail 849. If you go up the campground road you will also see a sign for the Colorado Trail and the 849 trail that dead ends on the ridge top to the south. Bear left, and follow the Colorado Trail 1776—it is well marked. The Colorado Trail heads northwest. At first you are in a very thick tree tunnel as you climb 150 feet steadily but gradually to about 0.5 mile, where you will cross a power line.

Mosquito Range Fourteeners from Kenosha Pass West-Colorado Trail.

TIP: If you want to see views of South Park and the Mosquito Range more quickly, you can take the 849 trail that goes south and west from the main trailhead, or connect with trail 849 when you reach the power line by turning south/left uphill. You can enjoy some deep unpacked powder on this side trip, but this might also mean breaking trail and sinking down into the powder. The 849 trail is not well marked, and its route can be very confusing with multiple social trails. Just bear south and then west up the ridge. This side trip is approximately a 1-mile roundtrip, with some steep climbing to mount the ridge, where it dead-ends. After you top out in the view area at about 0.6 mile from the Colorado Trail, turn around and go back down 849 to the Colorado Trail. When you come back to the power line, you can use this open area as a connector between the trails to get back to the Colorado Trail and continue your trek to the west. From the 849 trail area, descend the power line to the north and then turn left/west on the Colorado Trail.

If you stay on the Colorado Trail and skip the 849 side-trip excursion, you will climb gradually in the trees and gain another 150 feet over the next mile before it levels off and then starts to go downhill to emerge from the trees. There is a stunning view of South Park and the Mosquito Range and a bench for a snack break. This part of the trail slants to the south so the snow can be very thin to nonexistent early or late in the season. After about 200 yards of downhill travel it reenters more trees so the snow should improve.

Once you descend, the trail gently rolls. At just short of 1.5 miles the trail overlooks Baker Lake (which is on private land); if you turn around near here you will have about a 3-mile round trip and about 400 feet in total elevation gain. In another 0.25 mile the trail starts dropping down to Baker Lake's outlet stream, the low point of this route.

Continuing on from the Baker Lake overlook you lose around 250 feet as you drop down 0.75 mile to the outlet stream, crossing it and then Guernsey Creek at 2.5 miles. Then you climb steadily but gradually, regaining those 250 feet and gaining another 250 feet in the next mile as you meander into and out of the trees. At about 3.75 miles you drop to cross another stream, rise again on the other side, and then at about 4.25 miles you descend 200 feet on the side of Jefferson Hill to Jefferson Creek Campground at around 5 miles (9,900 feet). As always, be cautious and turn around early if the weather is changing and a storm is blowing in.

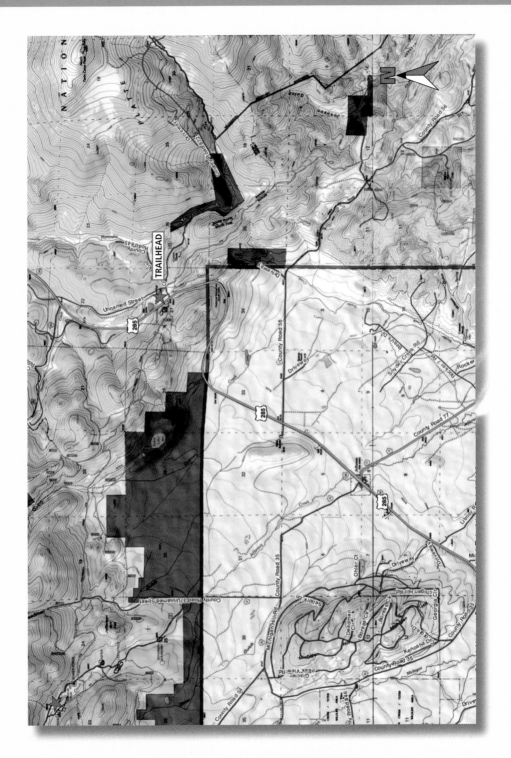

KENOSHA PASS — COLORADO TRAIL WEST

76. **Kenosha Pass — Colorado Trail East**

ROUND TRIP	3 miles
DIFFICULTY	Easy
SKILL LEVEL	Novice snowshoers; intermediate skiers
HIGH POINT	10,350 feet
ELEVATION GAIN	350 feet
AVALANCHE DANGER	None
MAP	Trails Illustrated #105, Tarryall Mountains, Kenosha Pass
CONTACT	South Park Ranger District, Pike National Forest

COMMENT: This section of the Colorado Trail features sweeping views of South Park, magnificent aspen groves, and meadows. It is an easier excursion than the West Kenosha Pass option because it is more of a rolling trail and not as steep of a climb. It is also easy to make this a short excursion of any length and enjoy nice views of South Park and the distant mountains. Experienced skiers can use any style of ski for this route.

GETTING THERE: From Denver go southwest on US 285. At about 65 miles you reach Kenosha Pass. Park on the west side of US 285 outside of the Kenosha Pass Campground, which closes for the winter. The Colorado Trail is on the south/right side of the closed road as soon as you enter the campground before you reach the 126 trail/road. There is a large sign and you will also see a smaller one as you look south.

THE ROUTE: The trail travels south and then southeast very gradually uphill. You will go through a livestock gate and then come to a bench and viewpoint in 0.3 mile. There are excellent views from the bench area if you want to take pictures of South Park. One hundred yards farther is a plaque about the multiple railroads that operated in South Park (it is only visible when the snow is not deep). You will enjoy an even more sweeping view of South Park with good photo opportunities below the power lines. This section of the trail is sun and wind exposed, and the snow can be thin early or late in the season, so you might have to carry your snowshoes for a while. The mountainside of aspen forest to the southeast offers the stark beauty of countless beige branches reaching for the winter sky. At less than a mile from

Snowshoers on the Kenosha Pass and Colorado Trail East.   PHOTO BY DAVE COOPER

the trailhead you will enter a forest of predominantly aspen, and enjoy its shelter from the wind. Views of the Tarryall Mountains open up in another 0.5 mile. The trail very gradually climbs up to a high point of around 10,350 feet before leveling. When you are about 1.5 miles from the trailhead, the trail begins to descend. Unless you want a long, more ambitious excursion this is a good turn around point. Or, you can go another 6 miles one-way into Johnson's Gulch. You will enjoy even more mountaintop vistas on your return trip since you will be walking toward the higher mountains of the Mosquito Range.

SIDEBAR: Bears

Black and brown bears in Colorado do hibernate. They snooze from mid-December to mid-March or April, with the males emerging first. Unlike humans, they lose fat, not muscle, while they sleep. They bed down in natural caves, snow caves, hollow trees, and logs. In colder climes some bears gather twigs and bark and just wait for Mother Nature to blanket them with snow. If you encounter a bear, back away slowly and speak softly. Do not run. Bears can run 35 miles per hour, so don't try to outrun one, and they can also climb trees. They are omnivores, but prefer nuts, berries, and plants. Just hope you don't look interesting, threatening, or tasty.

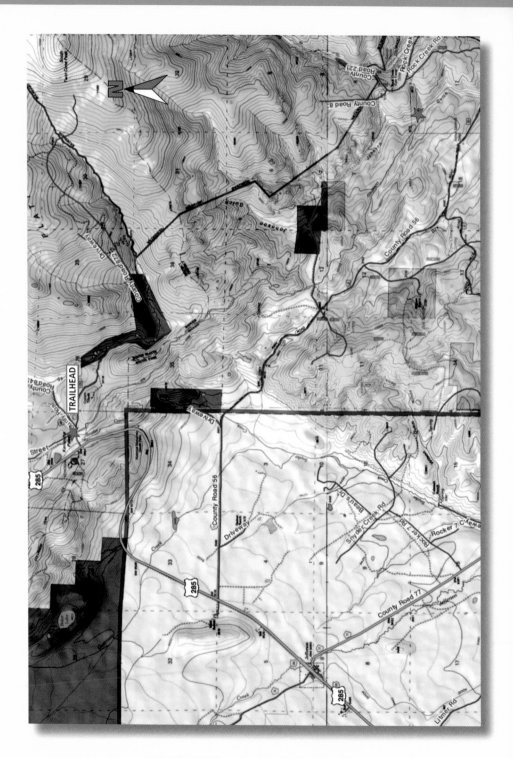

KENOSHA PASS and COLORADO TRAIL EAST

77. North Twin Cone Peak

ROUND TRIP	8.8 miles
DIFFICULTY	Moderate to challenging
SKILL LEVEL	Novice snowshoer, intermediate skier
HIGH POINT	11,300 feet
ELEVATION GAIN	1,300 feet
AVALANCHE DANGER	None to low
MAP	Trails Illustrated #105, Tarryall Mountains, Kenosha Pass
CONTACT	South Park Ranger District, Pike National Forest

COMMENT: This route follows FR 126, which is closed to cars but open to snowmobiles in winter, and meanders gradually up toward the summit of North Twin Cone Peak (12,323 feet). This little-used road is a good way to escape the crowds and enjoy a trail that is primarily tree-covered but does offer some tree breaks and views of the Tarryall Mountains. The trail is not well marked for winter use, but is a fairly obvious route because of the wide roadbed. Experienced skiers can use any style of ski on this route.

GETTING THERE: From Denver go southwest on US 285. At about 65 miles you reach Kenosha Pass. Park on the west side of US 285 outside of the Kenosha Pass Campground, which closes for the winter. The trailhead is across US 285 from the Kenosha Pass Campground, but parking is available on both sides of the road.

THE ROUTE: From the highway the route heads east across a meadow and then enters the mixed forest of aspen and evergreens. At about 0.6 mile the road/trail rounds a small hill with a radio tower offering some views of the Tarryall Mountains and gradually curving southeast to reach Kenosha Creek at 1 mile. There are breaks in the trees with nice views of the Lost Creek Wilderness Area. The road follows the creek closely for the next mile and a half, crossing it at about 1.25 miles. At about 2.5 miles the switchbacks begin in earnest from about 10,400 feet. You could turn around here for a pleasant 5 mile out-and back with only about 400 feet of elevation gain. The higher you go on the switchbacks, the better the view of South Park and the distant fourteeners of the Mosquito Range.

The intense switchbacks take you up 900 feet in 0.75 mile, then at about 3.25 miles it settles down to more moderate but steady climbing that takes you up 400

Snowshoers on the Kenosha Pass and Colorado Trail East.   PHOTO BY DAVE COOPER

feet in about a mile. You reach a good viewpoint at 11,300 feet at about 4.4 miles; turn around after enjoying the view of the Tarryalls, Lost Creek Wilderness, and South Park. If you continue on to the summit at 12,323, you will have to climb another 1,000 feet.

SIDEBAR: Bighorn Sheep

Bighorn sheep are one of the most rare and striking animals to see in Rocky Mountain National Park. Their agility is remarkable, and they can perch on or sprint across very steep and treacherous terrain. They have hooves that are soft and flexible on the inside, allowing them to make astounding jumps and precarious climbs. They also have thick double-layered coats of hair that protect them from bitter windchills. Both males and females have permanent horns rather than seasonal antlers. They were almost hunted to extinction in the early 1900s, but now, thanks to the protection of Rocky Mountain National Park, they have recovered and there are 800 living in the park. You might see them above Wild Basin on the Continental Divide, near the Mummy Range and Horseshoe Park, or on the higher parts of Trail Ridge Road.

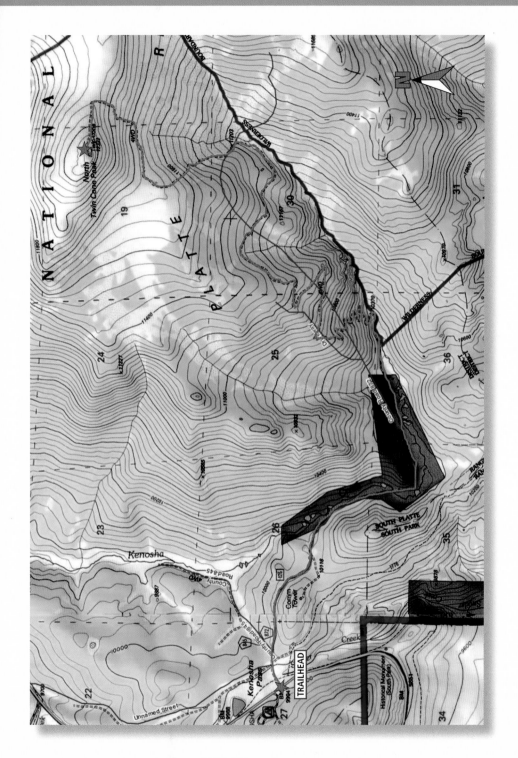

NORTH TWIN CONE PEAK

78. Boreas Pass Road and Halfway Gulch

ROUND TRIP	5 miles
DIFFICULTY	Easy to moderate
SKILL LEVEL	Novice snowshoers ande skiers
HIGH POINT	10,550 feet
ELEVATION GAIN	450 feet
AVALANCHE DANGER	Low to considerable
MAP	Trails Illustrated #109, Breckenridge, Tennessee Pass
CONTACT	South Park Ranger District, Pike National Forest

COMMENT: The road to Boreas Pass is a gradual then steep climb that offers superb views of South Park and the Tarryall Mountains. You might have to share the road/trail with snowmobiles. The road is usually well packed because of snowmobile use. With a little luck there will not be a major fleet of them starting off or returning when you are. Sections of the road are wind and sun exposed and might be snow-free after warm weather. You can do an out-and-back of any distance if the snow is stable and there is no avalanche danger. You can even go up to the top of the pass and continue all the way to Breckenridge for a winter mountaineering overnight if the snow has consolidated and there is no avalanche danger. If the snow is unstable, then an out-and-back of 4 or 5 miles is recommended because the road travels next to slopes that are steep enough to produce avalanches. Keep your eyes on the north side of the road and turn around when the slope equals or exceeds 35 degrees. Experienced skiers can use any style of ski on this route.

GETTING THERE: From Denver, take US 285 approximately 75 miles to Como; at Como, take CR 33/Boreas Pass Road northwest. In approximately 5 miles there is a fork. Boreas Pass Road is on the north/right; the road you are on continues straight ahead and becomes CR 50. Park near Boreas Pass Road, which is closed in winter and isn't plowed. Sometimes it is usable by high-clearance four-wheel-drive vehicles for a short distant from the turnoff.

THE ROUTE: The trail/road heads east with great views of South Park ahead and the Tarryall Mountains behind. You will immediately have a nice overview of the

Boreas Pass Road looking northwest.

riparian area. This part of the trail is south-facing so might be blown free of snow because of sun exposure. You might have to carry your snowshoes for a while. When the trail rounds the 10, 500-foot hill in a mile, you will have a partial view of South Park. The road then heads north, steadily gaining elevation and rounds another hill that is over 10,000 feet high in 0.5 mile. It quickly gains enough elevation to give you nonstop views of the surrounding mountain ranges and more of the South Park valley. At 1.5 miles you reach Davis Overlook at around 10,300 feet; this is a good turn around point if you are not ambitious or it is a family expedition. The road then heads northwest, gradually ascending over the next mile. As the road swings to the northwest, the views diminish for about 0.5 mile. You will see more views of Iron and Little Baldy Mountains if you trek another 0.5 mile. At 2.5 miles you reach Halfway Gulch.

Beyond Halfway Gulch the road curves north, and at around 3 miles there is considerable avalanche hazard for a mile. It is possible to cross the drainage and continue another 0.5 mile to enjoy the views, but at the 3-mile mark where avalanche danger begins, it is definitely time to turn around. A 3- to 6-mile round-trip on this road/trail can be very rewarding for anyone, including families.

Attempt the pass only when the snow is consolidated and only if you are an experienced winter mountaineer with survival gear and skills. At 4.5 miles the road reaches Selkirk Gulch then heads northwest to reach the pass in another 2.5 miles.

BOREAS PASS ROAD and HALFWAY GULCH

79. **Gold Dust Trail South**

ROUND TRIP	4 miles
DIFFICULTY	Easy
SKILL LEVEL	Novice snowshoers and skiers
HIGH POINT	10,600 feet
ELEVATION GAIN	600 feet
AVALANCHE DANGER	None
MAP	Trails Illustrated #109, Breckenridge, Tennessee Pass
CONTACT	South Park Ranger District, Pike National Forest

COMMENT: This very enjoyable trail, surrounded by a gorgeous aspen forest, is not heavily used and does not allow motorized traffic. It offers a scenic tour of the Tarryall Creek hills and valleys off the beaten path. This southern segment is good only in a snowy mid-winter; the snow is very spotty to nonexistent early and late in the season. This is a pleasant, meandering trail that rolls in and out of beautiful aspen and pine tree forest and over gentle terrain offering tree-filtered views of the Tarryall Creek valley and surrounding mountains. It winds its way around the shoulder of Little Baldy Mountain, climbing very gradually to 10,600 feet before descending into the gravelly creek beds. It is described here as an out-and-back. Experienced skiers can use any style of ski on this route.

GETTING THERE: From Denver, take US highway 285 approximately 75 miles to Como, exiting onto CR 33. In Como, when you turn off US 285 onto CR 33, follow signs to Camp Como. You will drive all of the way through Como and then turn left on Church Camp Road (the last left in Como), and travel southwest a little less than a mile. Park on the north side of the road near the entrance gate to the camp.

THE ROUTE: The trailhead is on the left/south side of the road; look for a brown forest service trail marker on the left very close to the fence for the camp. The trail is well marked once you find the trailhead. Follow the blue diamonds through thick aspen forest and wander through the stately trees, stark against the blue or snowy sky. You will be going gradually uphill, just south of the Church Camp boundary that is marked by the fence. As you go uphill you will be skirting above the camp and can see some of the buildings below through the trees. It doesn't take long to get out of sight of the rustic camp. The trail then steepens considerably,

Thick aspens on the Gold Dust Trail South.

climbing 300 feet over the next 0.5 mile before mellowing. It then takes 0.75 mile to climb the next 200 feet to the high point of 10,600 feet, with nice intermittent views through the trees. At this point you will have traveled around the shoulder of Little Baldy Mountain at about 1.75 miles. This is a good place to reverse course unless you want to go down to the creek and then have to regain around 300 feet on the way back. If you are ambitious, continue on if there is sufficient snow and the creek is frozen, and enjoy the great views as you roll over a small hill and then drop about 300 feet to cross scenic South Tarryall Creek at 3 miles. This is a good turn around point since warm weather and exposure often make the creek impassable.

SIDEBAR: Boreas Pass

Boreas Pass is named after the ancient Greek god of the north wind. It can certainly blow here in the winter. The road was a spur line of the Denver, South Park and Pacific Railroad and went all the way to Breckenridge; a major engineering feat given the elevation and avalanches. Now it is a gravel road used by four-wheel-drive vehicles in the temperate months.

GOLD DUST TRAIL SOUTH

80. Gold Dust Trail North

ROUND TRIP	8.0 miles
DIFFICULTY	Moderate
SKILL LEVEL	Novice snowshoers to creek; intermediate skiers to Boreas Pass Road
HIGH POINT	11,482 feet
ELEVATION GAIN	500 feet to creek; 1,100 feet to Boreas Pass Road
AVALANCHE DANGER	Low to moderate near the pass
MAP	Trails Illustrated #109, Breckenridge, Tennessee Pass
CONTACT	South Park Ranger District, Pike National Forest

COMMENT: The northern segment of the Gold Dust Trail is an enjoyable, lightly used trail that does not allow motorized traffic and frequently has more snow than the southern segment. It is a bit more interesting and challenging because you have the option of making the exhilarating climb all the way up to the Boreas Pass Road, with avalanche hazard only as you get near to the road itself. It starts off as a narrow pine-tree tunnel and then opens up into a mixed forest of aspen and evergreens with very nice peek-a-boo views of Boreas Peak and North Tarryall Creek. As is almost always the case, the climb up takes considerably longer than the descent. Get an early start for the entire round-trip. Though the view from the Boreas Pass Road is well worth the effort, the round-trip is suitable for only the very fit and experienced because of the need for route finding as you near the pass. A shorter out-and-back can be accomplished by novices. Most of the trail is well marked with blue diamonds. Experienced skiers can use any style of ski on this route.

GETTING THERE: From Denver, take US 285 approximately 75 miles to Como. At Como take CR 33/Boreas Pass Road northwest. In approximately 5.5 miles there is a fork; Boreas Pass Road is on the north/right; continue straight ahead, now CR 50. In 0.8 mile reach the trailhead that is next to a large log cabin with a solar system. It is easy to miss the brown forest service sign on the south side of the road because it is set back from the road and parking is 0.3 mile west past the trailhead. The trailhead is signed, though not easy to spot from the road because of piles of snow.

THE ROUTE: The trail climbs northwest for the first 0.5 mile through a pretty mixed forest to offer some views back to the south and then climbs again through a

Thick aspens on the Gold Dust Trail South.

narrow draw before leveling out on a ridge top at around 10,660 feet. The trail then switchbacks broadly with a general north and west direction for 1.5 miles above an old water flume and so it's relatively flat. It then descends, crossing North Tarryall Creek at about 2.25 miles, and intersecting with CR 801, which is unplowed in the winter. If your ambitions have faded this is a good turn around point. You actually have two other options: Follow the 801 trail/road coming in from the right/east down into the Selkirk Campground and then reverse course. Otherwise, climb very steeply for a mile to the northwest on the Old Boreas Pass wagon road toward the Boreas Pass Road. The last 0.7 mile is a more gradual climb to reach the pass road for a total of around 4 miles. The avalanche danger increases dramatically as you near the Boreas Pass Road because of the steep slopes of Boreas Mountain on the north side of the road. If you can dig a snow pit, and know that the avalanche danger is not high, proceed, enjoy the views, and reverse course. Otherwise turn around short of the pass to be safe.

GOLD DUST TRAIL NORTH

Southern Colorado

Chapter 15

LEADVILLE AREA

"This step, that view, this breath, that landmark to get me home. On snowshoes, my body succumbs to topography. Sure, there are times I yearn to reach the top of a mountain. Sometimes I make it, sometimes I don't. Lately I have been learning when to give up, which is a kind of victory in itself. Why do I need a summit every time, when everywhere is the poetry of snow, of graupel, cornice, aspect, of champagne powder and breakfast crust, of sunrollers and punk, of crust, slab and drift?"

—Christopher Cokinos, "The Tao of Pow: Learning to love winter,"
High Country News, March 21, 2011.

A perfect day for snowshoeing among the aspens.   PHOTO BY DAVE COOPER

Leadville, the highest-altitude incorporated city in the United States, is a historic mining town surrounded by some of the most stunning scenery—and devastation—in the state. Colorado's highest mountain, 14,433-foot Mount Elbert, is to the southwest. The views of it and its neighbor, Mount Massive, would be the envy of any city. Unfortunately Leadville is just a dozen miles south of the infamous open-pit mine at Climax, with its massive tailings pond. It is also surrounded by the scars of the gold and silver mines that scoured the area during the mining boom that started in 1878 and peaked by 1890, swelling the town to its largest population of 24,000 people. In spite of tailings that decorate the south end of town, the historic downtown is well worth a visit. It has been admirably rebuilt and refurbished and now offers a variety of dining and lodging options.

Don't be fooled by the somewhat funky state of Leadville and the surrounding area where mine waste and tailings dominate some of the scenery. Though little of the surrounding terrain has not been mined or turned over, it still offers some spectacular and unique recreational opportunities. Tennessee Pass north of Leadville is replete with railroading history dating back to the narrow-gauge lines of the nineteenth century. Because of the mixed reputation created by mining, the trails around Leadville are not overrun by people. The very forgiving white carpet of snowfall does a thorough job of hiding the warts that are obvious during the warmer months.

Leadville is about 118 miles west Denver via Interstate 70 and US 24.

Snowshoers on the Mitchell Creek Loop Trail near Leadville.

81. Vance's Cabin

ROUND TRIP	5.5 miles
DIFFICULTY	Moderate
SKILL LEVEL	Novice snowshoers; intermediate skiers
HIGH POINT	11,200 feet
ELEVATION GAIN	800 feet
AVALANCHE DANGER	None to low; can be avoided
MAP	Trails Illustrated #109, Breckenridge, Tennessee Pass
CONTACT	Holy Cross Ranger District, White River National Forest

COMMENT: One of the most accessible of the 10th Mountain Division huts, Vance's Cabin is less than 3 miles from the trailhead at Tennessee Pass. It is an easy trail to follow, featuring superb views of the Holy Cross Wilderness Area, Mount Elbert, Mount Massive, and Ski Cooper. There are some nice routes nearby for repeatable ski routes with skins. AT or tele skis make the return descent more fun.

GETTING THERE: From Leadville is on US 24, 38 miles south of Interstate 70 at the Minturn/Vail area. From Denver, drive west on Interstate 70 about 80 miles to Copper Mountain and take Exit 195, before Vail Pass, to Highway 91. Drive southwest about 38 miles to reach Leadville. From Leadville drive north on US 24 approximately 8 miles to Tennessee Pass. The Ski Cooper ski area is on the right/east side of the road. Pull into the parking lot. As you near the main lodge look for a small one-story building on the right/south side of the road and the west side of the parking lot. It is the Nordic ski and snowshoe rental hut where you can get information about trail conditions and permission to park overnight.

THE ROUTE: The trailhead is a cat-tracked road across the road from the Nordic building, 100 yards from the main lodge on the left/north edge of the ski area. Follow the road, Piney Gulch/Cooper Loop Nordic trail, downhill into the drainage toward Chicago Ridge, crossing Burton Ditch at about 0.3 mile, and reach the intersection with the turnoff for Vance's Cabin at about 0.6 mile. The 10th Mountain Trail is marked with some blue diamonds, but is not signed to the hut. To the right, the trail climbs higher, going south around Cooper Hill; take the trail to the left/north alongside the irrigation canal.

Looking west from Vance's Cabin Trail.

The trail then climbs gradually northeast along the edge of the trees and Burton Ditch into an open wetlands and meadow area where there is a trail junction at about 1.25 miles. The other leg of the Cooper Loop goes to the right/east. Go left (due north)—don't take the trail hard to the left (due west), which goes back down Piney Gulch to the highway. Shortly you reenter thick tree cover and cross the confluence of the ditch and Piney Gulch. Follow the gulch upstream in a narrow drainage for 0.5 mile to another intersection at 1.5 miles. Here the trail to Taylor Hill continues straight/right to the northeast up the drainage. Take the hut trail to the left/northwest.

Begin the steep slog 600 feet up toward the shoulder of the ridge. The 10th Mountain Trail climbs sharply uphill to the northwest/north and then switchbacks. There are times when you have to look sharply to see the trail markers. There are widely spaced blue diamonds but because of the switchbacks they are easy to miss, especially if it is snowing. Once you reach the shoulder of the ridge in a little over 2 miles, the trail levels considerably and you have views of the mountains that surround the area. If it is early or late in the season you will have to detour around fallen trees.

In another 0.5 mile the trail rounds the ridge and you come to a beautiful open meadow with spectacular views of the Holy Cross Wilderness Area to the west, Turquoise Lake to the south, and Mount Elbert and Mount Massive down valley. If you aren't staying at the hut, this is a good place to turn around because the trail goes steeply downhill to the left/west, edging the left side of the meadow and dropping in 0.3 mile to the hut. It is hidden below the lower left quarter of the meadow in the trees. The cabin has a nice deck with a superb view of Ski Cooper and the Holy Cross Wilderness.

VANCE'S CABIN | TAYLOR HILL

82. Taylor Hill

ROUND TRIP	6 miles
DIFFICULTY	Challenging
SKILL LEVEL	Intermediate to expert snowshoers and skiers
HIGH POINT	11,725 feet
ELEVATION GAIN	1,325 feet
AVALANCHE DANGER	Moderate to considerable; can be avoided
MAP	Trails Illustrated #109, Breckenridge, Tennessee Pass
CONTACT	Holy Cross Ranger District, White River National Forest

COMMENT: Climbing Taylor Hill gives a panorama of the Tennessee Pass area, with 360 degrees of great views. You get a close up look at Chicago Ridge to the east, the spectacle of the Holy Cross Wilderness to the west, and the Sawatch Range to the south. It is not a good route to attempt at times of high avalanche danger. Most of the route is low-angle, but there is avalanche potential toward the top. Winter mountaineering skills are preferred for this route. Backcountry skiers also love this hill for earning turns through the trees, so you are likely to have company. There are lots of options for skiing through well-spaced trees. This route is more fun with AT or tele ski.

GETTING THERE: Leadville is on US 24, 38 miles south of Interstate 70 at the Minturn/Vail area. From Denver, drive west on Interstate 70 about 80 miles to Copper Mountain and take Exit 195, before Vail Pass, to Highway 91. Drive southwest about 38 miles to reach Leadville. From Leadville drive north on US 24 approximately 8 miles to Tennessee Pass. The Ski Cooper ski area is on the right/east side of the road. Pull into the parking lot and as you near the main lodge, look for a small one-story building on the right/south side of the road and the west side of the parking lot. It is the Nordic ski and snowshoe rental hut where you can get information about trail conditions and permission to park overnight.

THE ROUTE: The trailhead is a cat-tracked road across the road from the Nordic building, 100 yards from the main lodge, on the left/north edge of the ski area. The route leaves the road in less than 0.5 mile, when you will go downhill to cross the irrigation ditch and the road continues uphill. There is a trail sign near the ditch to watch for.

Looking toward the top of Grayback Peak.

Follow the road, Piney Gulch/Cooper Loop Nordic trail, downhill into the drainage toward Chicago Ridge, crossing Burton Ditch at about 0.3 mile. Bear right after crossing the ditch as the trail climbs higher, going along the edge of a meadow and then entering trees. The trail reaches the intersection with the turnoff for Vance's Cabin at about 0.6 mile. The 10th Mountain Trail is marked with some blue diamonds, but is not signed for the hut. At the junction where the trails separate (the trail to Vance's Cabin tracks to the left, northwest), stay to the right/northeast for Taylor Hill, and continue toward the Piney Gulch drainage heading northeast. The trail for Taylor Hill is not well marked and is often hard to identify. Watch for tree blazes. If you miss it, consult your topo map and compass and head for a saddle that is northeast from the Vance's Cabin trail. When you reach a secondary drainage coming in from the left/north at about 2 miles, turn north, and shoot for the saddle on the northeast side of Taylor Hill. Avoid open slopes that are more than 30 degrees, which are farther northeast than you want to go; make your own switchbacks to the saddle. This is the steepest section of the trek, and requires patience, given the elevation. You will be gaining 600 feet in this short stretch and ending up on a saddle that is around 10,900 feet. From the top of the saddle at about 2.75 miles follow the ridgeline north/northeast to the summit of Taylor Hill for a real treat. You will have a much more gradual trek on the saddle as you slowly climb another 800 feet to reach the summit. You will have nice views before actually reaching the summit, so you can reverse course at any point and feel satisfied. Snow conditions can vary widely. Decide how far to go based on the difficulty level of the snowpack. Enjoy the panorama and have a nice snack and water break before retracing your steps through the powder to the trailhead. There are lots of opportunities for romping through the powder on the return, but stay off the steepest slopes and weave your way through the trees to the west where possible in order to avoid avalanche danger.

SEE MAP ON PAGE 303.

83. Mitchell Creek Loop

ROUND TRIP	6.5 miles
DIFFICULTY	Easy to Moderate
SKILL LEVEL	Novice snowshoers or skiers
HIGH POINT	10,600 feet
ELEVATION GAIN	200 feet
AVALANCHE DANGER	Low
MAP	Trails Illustrated #109, Breckenridge, Tennessee Pass
CONTACT	Leadville Ranger District, San Isabel National Forest

COMMENT: The Mitchell Creek Loop follows the Tennessee Pass portion of the Colorado Trail, part of which is a former railroad bed, which rolls gently across the interesting terrain. This trailhead is across the road from the Cooper Ski area. There are facilities and a coffee shop with tasty snacks in the Nordic area. The loop offers great views of the Holy Cross Wilderness and Homestake Peak to the west. It is a good trail for beginners but interesting enough in location and terrain to be fun for snowshoers and skiers of all skill levels. Even though it is on Tennessee Pass, there is no avalanche terrain though you are starting off at 10,000 feet. Keep the elevation in mind for visitors from flatlands. You will generally have excellent snow because of the elevation. Experienced skiers can use any style of ski on this route.

GETTING THERE: Leadville is on US 24, 38 miles south of Interstate 70 at the Minturn/Vail area. From Denver, drive west on Interstate 70 about 80 miles to Copper Mountain and take Exit 195, before Vail Pass, to Highway 91. Drive southwest about 38 miles to reach Leadville. From Leadville drive north on US 24 approximately 8 miles to Tennessee Pass. The Ski Cooper ski area is on the right/east side of the road. The loop trailhead is on the west side of Tennessee Pass across the road from Ski Cooper at the end of a large parking lot.

THE ROUTE: The loop starts on the Colorado Trail, an old railroad grade that descends gradually, traveling to the northwest. After you climb back up a bit, at approximately 0.25 mile, you pass old picturesque charcoal kilns and then the trail gradually descends about 200 feet over the next mile. For the first 0.6 mile you enjoy great views of Homestake Peak, a good place for photos. When you come to the Powderhound Trail junction at about 0.7 mile (it goes uphill to the left), stay to

An old kiln on the Mitchell Creek Loop.

the right. The trail then turns right, to the north. At about 1.5 miles it levels out at 10,200 feet, then turns left to round the toe of the ridge, heading west.

At a junction just before 2 miles, the Colorado Trail turns off to the right and goes west, then north; stay left on the Mitchell Creek Loop Trail as it travels southwest into the Mitchell drainage, where it bottoms out at around 10,110 feet at 2.5 miles. You can of course add in a quick out-and-back on the Colorado Trail if you wish. A trail on the right goes down Mitchell Creek to the highway; stay to the left. The railroad grade ends and the terrain becomes more difficult as the trail begins to climb again for about 1.5 miles. The trail climbs steadily up to 10,600 feet and intersects the Wurts Ditch Road at a saddle at about 4 miles.

Shortly after, the trail crosses over the drainage and enters the trees, traveling downhill and dropping about 200 feet in 0.25 mile, following the road for approximately 0.25 mile to an intersection with the Colorado Trail again. The road continues to the right. Turn sharply left onto the Colorado Trail as it starts to go back to the east and north. You then cross the stream again and another trail goes off to the right; stay straight/left. The Colorado Trail then goes gradually up, and then downhill 2 miles to the pass. Along the way you will have excellent views of mountains to the south for photo opportunities on clear days.

SIDEBAR: 10th Mountain Division

Tennessee Pass not only has railroad history, but it was also a training sight for the famous 10th Mountain Division during World War II. These hardy troops trained here for fighting in the Alps and had very high casualty rates during the war. Some returned to Colorado to open ski areas.

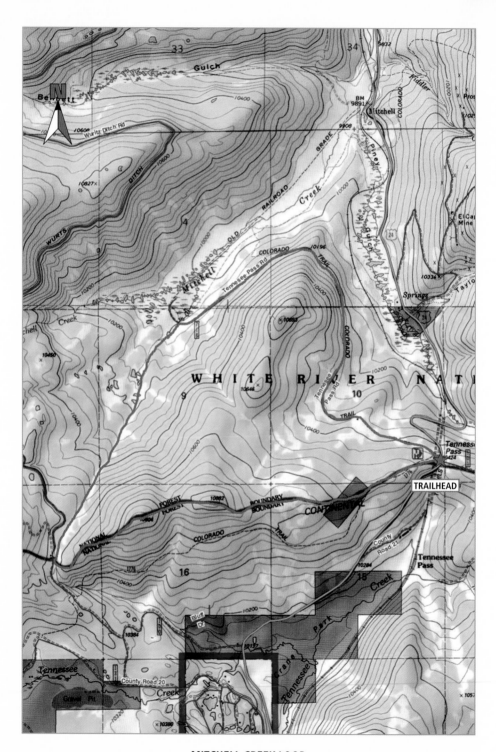

MITCHELL CREEK LOOP

84. Twin Lakes

ROUND TRIP	12 miles
DIFFICULTY	Easy
SKILL LEVEL	Novice snowshoers or skiers
HIGH POINT	9,400 feet
ELEVATION GAIN	200 feet
AVALANCHE DANGER	None
MAP	Trails Illustrated #127, Aspen, Independence Pass
CONTACT	Leadville Ranger District, San Isabel National Forest

COMMENT: This route along the road that leads to Independence Pass is surrounded by superb views of Mount Elbert, the highest peak in the state, Parry Peak, 13,000-foot Rinker and Twin Peaks, and 13,461-foot Quail Mountain. It is an easy out-and-back or a suitable one-way with a vehicle shuttle in a great setting that is ideal for families or for a quick workout. It is not a good place for snowshoeing early or late in the season because of unpredictable snow. Parking can sometimes be challenging immediately after a storm because of snow plowing. Allow time for the plows to work their magic after a storm. An out-and-back trek is probably the best option for families with young children.

Nordic skis are the best choice for this fairly flat but highly scenic route.

GETTING THERE: Leadville is on US 24, 38 miles south of Interstate 70 at the Minturn/Vail area. From Denver, drive west on Interstate 70 about 80 miles to Copper Mountain and take Exit 195, before Vail Pass, to Highway 91. Drive southwest about 38 miles to reach Leadville. From Leadville take US 24 south 14 or so miles to Highway 82 and turn right/west toward Aspen. In a few miles you reach the eastern edge of Twin Lakes Reservoir. After about 3 miles from US 24, just before a bridge over Lake Creek, watch for a gravel road to the left that goes south below the dam. Take the gravel road around a wetlands area about 0.5 mile to the Twin Lakes trailhead. You might need a four-wheel-drive vehicle to navigate this road after a major storm. For a vehicle shuttle, go back out to the highway, turn left, and drive west about 8 miles through the town of Twin Lakes to the Willis Gulch trailhead on the left/south.

THE ROUTE: From the Twin Lakes trailhead, take the Colorado Trail to the left (south, then west). The rolling trail takes you around the southern edge of Twin

Twins Lakes adventure.

Lakes Reservoir with immediate spectacular mountain views to the west. At about 1.7 miles the Main Range Trail comes in from the left; stay straight, unless you want to do some climbing to get your heart rate up even higher. In that case, do a quick out-and-back on the Main Range Trail. That is not to say that the Twin Lakes Trail doesn't offer some hilly terrain, too. The trail does roll as it travels along the lakeshore. Cross Flume Creek at about 2.3 miles; shortly after you can enjoy the ruins of the ghost town of Interlaken Historical Site between the Twin Lakes. It is a spectacular setting with views of the southern flank of the Mount Elbert massif and Mount Hope to the north; west and south are Twin Peaks and Quail Mountain. If you choose to go only as far as the ghost town, it is around a 5-mile out-and-back.

Continuing farther on the trail, you pass a wetlands area and then climb 200 feet to the 3-mile point. The trail now stays on the hillside above the second of the Twin Lakes going southwest toward the western end of the lake. At about 4.4 miles you will cross Boswell Gulch past the western end of the upper Twin Lake. There is a trail intersection at 5 miles; stay straight and then cross another stream. In another mile reach the Willis Gulch trailhead on Highway 82.

OTHER OPTIONS: Independence Pass is closed in the winter and offers snowshoeing opportunities. Drive until you reach the road closure, put on your snowshoes, and continue on the Independence Pass road

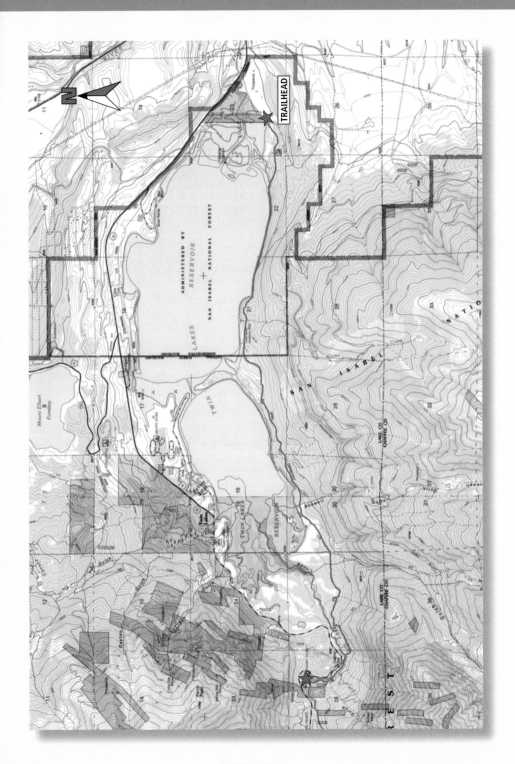

TRAILHEAD

TWIN LAKES

Southern Colorado

Chapter 16

COLORADO SPRINGS AREA

"Nature we have always with us, an inexhaustible storehouse of that which moves the heart, appeals to the mind, and fires the imagination."

—John Burroughs, *The Writings of John Burroughs, Volume XV: Leaf and Tendril* (1908)

Sunrise on Pikes Peak.　　PHOTO BY DAVE COOPER

Colorado Springs provides a jumping off point for numerous snowshoe and ski routes. Rampart Reservoir in Pike National Forest is perfect for beginners, and the Mueller State Park and Wildlife Area and the nearby Crags in the Pikes Peak foothills are real jewels.

Just 26 miles from Colorado Springs, Mueller State Park looks out on the western slopes of the Pikes Peak massif from its east-oriented trails. The snowcapped Sangre de Cristo Mountains are the majestic backdrop for its westerly trails. Views from park trails are 360 degrees because the park is essentially draped over the top of a 10,000-foot mountain, with all trails going downhill from the top. There is enough tree cover—a colorful tapestry of aspen, pine, fir, and spruce trees—to protect the snow, but most of the trails open up for good views and sunshine. A look at the map for this state park and wildlife area will show you that there are a seemingly infinite number of possibilities for combining trails. It simply depends on the conditions and your ambitions. Note that the large number of intersecting trails can make route finding a bit tricky because some of the trails are not well marked. The park's campground makes a good starting point because it is on the highest point along the access road. The campground has a limited number of RV and tent sites available throughout the winter. Though the showers and flush toilets are not open, vault toilets are available. In winter the visitor center is open only on weekends. There is a self-service entry station near the campground. A short distance across the highway is The Crags, northwest of the long Pikes Peak ridge.

85. School Pond and Preacher's Hollow Loops

SCHOOL POND LOOP	1.75 miles
PREACHERS HOLLOW LOOP	1.6 miles
DIFFICULTY	Easy
SKILL LEVEL	Novice snowshoers; intermediate skiers
HIGH POINT	9,500 feet at trailhead
ELEVATION GAIN	100 feet
AVALANCHE DANGER	None to low
MAP	Mueller State Park and Wildlife Area
CONTACT	Mueller State Park

COMMENT: These two loop trails originate near the Mueller State Park Visitors Center, located just south of the Revenuer's Ridge trailhead. The visitors center is open only on weekends during the winter. Both loops stay on the ridgeline and don't descend as steeply as some of the other trails. They drop down to ponds at their far ends. They can be done singly or together for a 3.2-mile combined loop. Skinny/Nordic skis work well for most of the route.

GETTING THERE: For Mueller State Park, take US 24 From Colorado Springs west 25 miles to the town of Divide. Go west through Divide until you reach the intersection with Highway 67 and then turn left to take it south 4 miles. The entrance to Mueller State Park is on the right/west side of the road. The signed turnoff for The Crags Campground/Rocky Mountain Camp is in another 0.5 mile, on the left/east.

From the Mueller State Park entrance, drive Wapiti Road (the park road) west/southwest about 1.25 miles. Find the trailhead on the south side of the road.

THE ROUTE: The School Pond Loop Trail heads south through heavy tree cover of aspen and pines, which preserves snow when other trails have thinned and offers protection from any wind. The trees are uniquely beautiful spectacles among the whites of winter. In 0.25 mile at a trail junction, the other leg of the loop is to the left, and Stoner Mill Trail is to the right; continue straight. At 0.5 mile when the other end of the Stoner Mill Trail comes in from the right, stay straight/left. Just before 0.75 mile, School Pond Loop itself is to the right; the trail then curves left/

north. A little before 1 mile, reach a T-intersection. To the right is the Aspen Trail; go left to continue the loop, now heading west. At about 1.3 miles the other end of the Aspen Trail comes in from the right; continue straight/left. In a short distance close the loop at 1.5 miles; turn right to return to the trailhead.

From the trailhead, the Preacher's Hollow Loop Trail is a short distance west of the School Pond Loop Trail. There is a nice overlook at the beginning of the Preacher's Hollow Loop Trail. Go to the left to do this loop clockwise, heading south. In 0.3 mile the trail forks with the Ranger Trail to the left, stay straight/right as the Preacher's Hollow Loop Trail curves west and then south again. Just before 0.5 mile the trail passes Never-Never Pond and curves west then northwest a short ways. At about 0.9 mile you intersect the Rock Pond Trail; go hard to the right to continue the loop, now heading northeast. At about 1.25 miles the trail goes north to curve a couple of times in the last 0.4 mile. The Revenuer's Ridge Trail is on the left shortly before you close the loop.

86. Peak View, Elk Meadow, Livery Loop, and Revenuer's Ridge Trails

ROUND TRIP	2.2 miles
DIFFICULTY	Easy to moderate
SKILL LEVEL	Novice snowshoers; intermediate skiers
HIGH POINT	9,600 feet at trailhead
ELEVATION GAIN	300 feet
AVALANCHE DANGER	None to low
MAP	Mueller State Park and Wildlife Area
CONTACT	Mueller State Park

COMMENT: This delightful route features peak views, aspens, meadows, and a pond. The route consists of a partial loop on the east side of the road, connected by a one-way stretch alongside the road combining four different trails. Skinny/Nordic skis work well for most of the route.

GETTING THERE: For Mueller State Park, take US 24 From Colorado Springs west 25 miles to the town of Divide. Go west through Divide until you reach the intersection with Highway 67 and then turn left to take it south 4 miles. The entrance to Mueller State Park is on the right/west side of the road. From the Mueller State Park entrance, drive Wapiti Road (the park road) west and then north 2.25 miles to the campground area. Peak View Trail is near a campground that is popular because of the great views of the western slopes of Pikes Peak. The well-marked trailhead on the right, about 0.25 mile past the campground entry station, is easy to locate.

THE ROUTE: The Peak View Trail heads southeast on a nice, open trail. Peak View Pond is on the right as you descend through the colorful mixture of aspen and pine trees. It is worth a short detour to get some close up shots of the pond. Take the ridge down the gentle slope to a T-intersection with the Elk Meadow Trail in a little past 0.25 mile. For an easy out and back, return to the trailhead.

For the loop, turn right onto the Elk Meadow Trail heading south. It rolls gently along the ridge, with good views to the east. At about 0.75 mile the trail curves west and eventually climbs back uphill toward the road, intersecting with the Livery Loop Trail at about 1 mile. Stay left on the Livery Loop Trail as it meanders across the ridge to the Livery Loop trailhead at approximately 1.4 miles.

Directly across the road from the Livery Loop trailhead is the Geer Pond trailhead; cross to this entry point to the Revenuer's Ridge Trail, and take it to the right/north. This trail parallels the road and the ridgeline, dipping down the ridge somewhat along the way. It features nice views to the west all along the way. This is one of the few trails that is not a trail that goes downhill on the way out and uphill on the way back, so it is ideal for families with small children or group members who are less ambitious. At 1.5 miles the Geer Pond Trail comes in from the left; stay straight/right. Reach the Homestead Loop trailhead in 0.4 mile, at 1.9 miles from the start. Continue north on the road about 0.3 mile back to the Peak View trailhead to close the loop.

SIDEBAR: Mueller State Park

West of Colorado Springs, on the west side of Pikes Peak, Mueller State park features 55 miles of trails, over 5,000 acres of terrain, and abundant wildlife. The average elevation is 9,500 feet, so snow conditions are good by mid-winter. The park is home to elk, deer, hawks, and black bears. The black bears hibernate in the winter, so aren't likely to be seen during snowshoe season except during early spring adventures. If you encounter a black bear, speak softly and back away slowly. Do not run. Don't get too close to bull elks, as they have been known to charge people who invade their space.

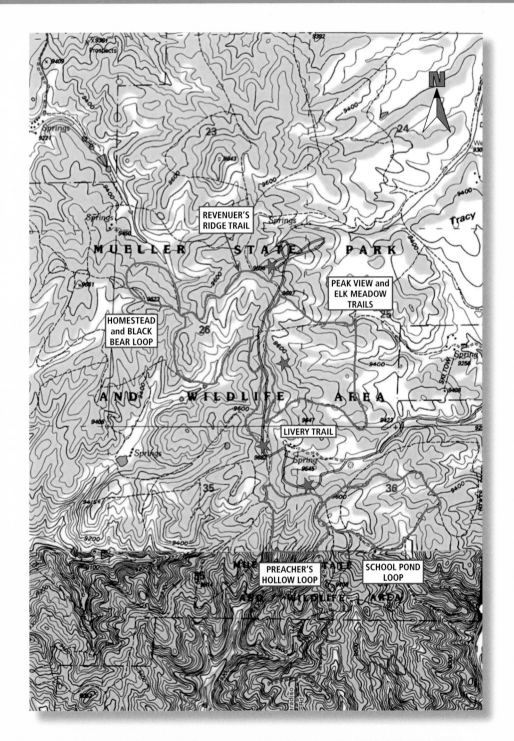

**SCHOOL POND and PREACHER'S HOLLOW LOOPS | PEAK VIEW, ELK MEADOW, LIVERY,
and REVENUER'S RIDGE TRAILS | HOMESTEAD and BLACK BEAR LOOP**

87. Homestead and Black Bear Loop

ROUND TRIP	2.2 miles
DIFFICULTY	Easy to moderate
SKILL LEVEL	Novice snowshoers; intermediate skiers
HIGH POINT	9,650 feet at trailhead
ELEVATION GAIN	300 feet
AVALANCHE DANGER	None to low
MAP	Mueller State Park and Wildlife Area
CONTACT	Mueller State Park

COMMENT: This easy route offers expansive views of the magnificent Sangre de Cristo Mountains as well as beautiful meadows and is an ideal family excursion. Skinny/Nordic skis work well for most of the route.

GETTING THERE: For Mueller State Park, take US 24 From Colorado Springs west 25 miles to the town of Divide. Go west through Divide until you reach the intersection with Highway 67 and then turn left to take it south 4 miles. The entrance to Mueller State Park is on the right/west side of the road.

From the Mueller State Park entrance, drive Wapiti Road (the park road) west and then north 2.25 miles to the campground area. Homestead Trail is near the campground entry station, on the left/west side of the road.

THE ROUTE: Begin the Homestead Trail near the campground entry station. The trailhead is well marked, with the statistics listed for more than one trail. You start off on a gradual downhill and immediately you will see the Revenuer's Ridge Trail to the left. It looks like a hiking trail, whereas the Homestead Loop Trail is as wide as a service road. After 100 yards or so you can see the Sangre de Cristo Mountains in the distance between the trees.

The trail then plunges more steeply to the wetland valley through a mixture of stately pine and aspen trees. You cross the wetlands and go downhill for a bit and then climb up to the top of a short ridge. The trail then goes downhill again, curving right/north, and intersects with the Beaver Ponds Trail on the left at just past 0.75 mile; stay right on the Homestead Trail. It travels through a delightful aspen grove and tops out on a flat spot that is a good place for a snack or lunch. You then enter another aspen-lined valley and at just past 1 mile intersect the Black Bear Trail. The

Pangborns Pinncacle separating the valley from Fourmile Creek drainage on The Crags route.

PHOTO BY EVA LIGHT

Homestead Trail continues straight ahead; instead, go right onto the Black Bear Trail.

This is a fairly hilly trail that rolls and goes uphill on the return. The last 0.5 mile or so climbs back up to Wapiti Road at about 1.6 miles. Walk south alongside the road for about 0.6 mile to connect the loop, or use a vehicle shuttle.

OTHER TRAILS TO EXPLORE

From the intersection of the Homestead and Black Bear Trails at about 1 mile, you could continue straight on the Homestead Trail to intersect the Mountain Logger Trail in a short 0.7 mile, and then follow the Homestead Trail's pine-tree tunnel to get close to Grouse Mountain in another 0.75 mile. Then it is a somewhat steep uphill to the end of the campground road and the Cheesman trailhead.

SEE MAP ON PAGE 317.

88. The Crags

ROUND TRIP	3 miles
DIFFICULTY	Easy to moderate
SKILL LEVEL	Novice to intermediate snowshoers and skiers
HIGH POINT	10,900 feet
ELEVATION GAIN	800 feet
AVALANCHE DANGER	Low to moderate
MAP	Trails Illustrated #137, Pikes Peak, Cañon City
CONTACT	Pikes Peak Ranger District, Pike National Forest

COMMENT: The rock formations of the Crags area are worth a visit any time of the year, but they are starkly and magically backlit by sun and snow in the winter months. The view from the top of The Crags pinnacles is worth the effort and the trail through the pretty valley is also worthwhile even if you don't want to summit. You can see the Sangre de Cristo Mountains in the distance as well as the backside of Pikes Peak and the interesting landscape of Mueller State Park and Wildlife Area. Winter makes climbing the actual pinnacles much trickier because of slick rock and ice. Rambling around up to their base is just as much fun and also very scenic. This is one of the summer approaches to climbing Pikes Peak for those that don't want to go up the Barr Trail. You can use this trail as an approach to the summit in the winter too, since avalanche danger is minimal. The trail eventually intersects with the road to the summit.

Skinny/Nordic skis work well for most of the route. Mid-width will be better if you plan to ski all the way to the summit since the descent will be steep.

GETTING THERE: For Mueller State Park, take US 24 From Colorado Springs west 25 miles to the town of Divide. Go west through Divide until you reach the intersection with Highway 67 and then turn left to take it south 4 miles. The entrance to Mueller State Park is on the right/west side of the road. The signed turnoff for The Crags Campground/Rocky Mountain Camp is in another 0.5 mile, on the left/east.

From the turnoff 0.5 mile south of the park entrance, follow Forest Service Road 383, a narrow, slippery dirt- or snow-packed road in winter that can be challenging because it is only plowed sporadically. Four-wheel-drive is recommended. At the minimum you need good snow tires. The road curves north and around to the south to The Crags Campground in about 3 miles. You might have to park outside of the campground and begin your trek from there. Go to the end of the campground road and you will see the trailhead.

Westernmost point (elevation 10,855 feet) of The Crags with views of North and South Catamount Reservoir and Rampart Range in the background.

PHOTO BY EVA LIGHT

THE ROUTE: Go to the end of the campground road and you will see the well-marked trailhead. The trail goes gradually uphill from the trailhead, and you will initially be in tree cover. The trail is very obvious. Follow the Four Mile creek drainage to the east, and then northeast. There is a tributary that goes southeast; ignore it. There are eventually trails on both sides of the stream and both will take you to The Crags. There is a footbridge for crossing to the other side that might not be necessary with deep snow and a frozen stream, but be cautious if and when you attempt to cross. The right fork is a bit more tree-sheltered, so it is a better choice if the snow cover is thin and it is early or late in the season. However, it does have a short stretch of boulders that might require you to remove your snowshoes. The left branch is a bit more open and not as rocky and features a pretty meadow area about 1 mile from the trailhead. From the meadow you will have an impressive view of The Crags pinnacles that might convince you that summiting in the winter is not wise. When you reach the meadow area you might also see multiple trails wandering off. You could go up on one branch and back on the other for variety if you don't ascend up to near the top of the pinnacles but stay lower. Just achieving the meadow and then the ridgeline in 1 mile is a rewarding experience because of the views. From the end of the meadow area the trail that goes to the left/north, climbs gradually, then more steeply, gaining 300 feet in less than 0.5 mile. The trail that stays in the creek bottom gains 100 feet in the same distance. There is a trail on the right/east side of Four Mile Creek that climbs very steeply, gaining 800 feet in less than a mile. Use your own judgment on the snow and ice conditions and whether to go the additional 0.5 mile to the pinnacles. You really don't have to stand on top of one of the rocks to have great view and a wonderful excursion.

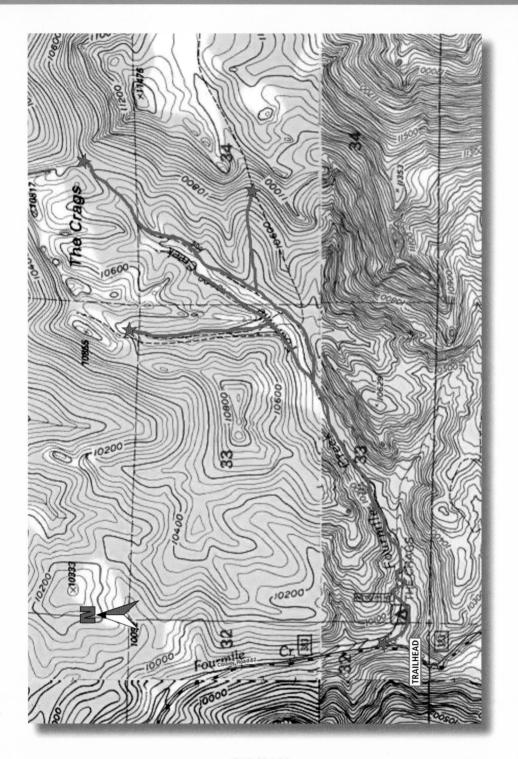

THE CRAGS